INSIGHT GUIDE

PARIS

APA PUBLICATIONS

Part of the Langenscheidt Publishing Group

L

INSIGHT GUIDE PaRIS

ABOUT THIS BOOK

Editorial
Project Editor
Caroline Radula-Scott
Editorial Director
Brian Bell

Distribution
UK & Ireland
GeoCenter International Ltd
The Viables Centre
Harrow Way
Basingstoke
Hants RG22 4BJ
Fax: (44) 1256-817988

United States
Langenscheidt Publishers, Inc.
46–35 54th Road
Maspeth, NY 11378
Fax: (718) 784-0640

Worldwide
APA Publications GmbH & Co.
Verlag KG (Singapore branch)
38 Joo Koon Road
Singapore 628990
Tel: (65) 865-1600
Fax: (65) 861-6438

Printing
Insight Print Services (Pte) Ltd
38 Joo Koon Road
Singapore 628990
Tel: (65) 865-1600
Fax: (65) 861-6438

CONTACTING THE EDITORS
Although every effort is made to provide accurate information in this publication, we live in a fast-changing world and would appreciate it if readers would call our attention to any errors or outdated information that may occur by writing to us at:
Insight Guides, P.O. Box 7910, London SE1 8ZB, England. Fax: (44 171) 620-1074. e-mail: insight@apaguide.demon.co.uk

Like all *Insight Guides*, this book is the work of many hands. Paris is a charmingly diverse city and we have gathered together a team of expert writers and photographers to pool their intimate knowledge of this compelling capital. What's more, they have worked under the direction of *Insight Guides*' chief editors, francophiles themselves, producing a special form of travel literature that gives an insight into a destination's history and culture.

From time immemorial, Paris has been known to cast a spell on visitors. Many have stayed, others keep returning, and the rest treasure the ability to savour a city that's forever changing, while maintaining a deep respect for the past. The 16th-century French essayist Montaigne wrote after a visit: "I love that citie for hir owne sake... I love hir so tenderly that hir spottes, her blemishes and hir warts are deare unto me."

Today you can still see what he meant: stand at the Arc de Triomphe – an island in a tempestuous sea of traffic – and look east down the glorious Triumphal Way to the historical edifices of the Louvre and west to the fantastic modernism of La Défense.

This may be one of the best preserved cities in Europe, but it has certainly not allowed time to stand still.

8° Arr!
AVENUE
DES
CHAMPS-ÉLYSÉES

How to use this book
Insight Guide: Paris is carefully structured both to convey an understanding of the city and its culture and to guide readers through its sights and activities:

◆ To understand Paris today, you need to know something of its past. The **History** and **Features** sections cover the city's culture in lively, authoritative essays written by specialists.

◆ The main **Places** section provides a full run-down of all the attractions worth seeing. The principal places of interest are co-ordinated by number with full-colour maps.

◆ The **Travel Tips** listings section provides a convenient point of reference for information on travel, hotels, restaurants, shops and festivals. Information may be located quickly by using the index printed on the back cover flap – and the flaps are designed to serve as bookmarks.

◆ **Photographs** are chosen not only to illustrate geography and buildings but also to convey the many moods of the city and the everyday activities of its people.

The contributors
This new edition was edited by **Caroline Radula-Scott**, who has strong connections with Paris, having studied there in her youth. With 20 years of editing consumer magazines and books behind her, she has built on the previous

edition produced by **Andrew Eames**, who went on to act as executive editor for scores of *Insight Guides*, and **Brian Bell**, now editorial director of the series.

The editors sought out writers with a firm knowledge of Paris, several having lived in or are still resident in the French capital.

Bilingual writer **Jim Keeble**, who divides his time between England and France, did most of the leg-work for the *Places* section and **Marton Radkai**, an American-educated travel writer and photographer, was responsible for the history chapters. Journalist **Susan Bell** was working in Paris for the London *Times* when she wrote the one-page features on different aspects of the capital, and former Paris resident **Lisa Gerard-Sharp**, a regular contributor to *Insight Guides*, had (costly) fun researching the chapter on shopping and markets.

With many travel books to her credit, **Naomi Peck** – whose father played in top jazz bands in Paris after the war, when the city was throbbing to the sound of music – made good use of her inside knowledge in the other *Insight On...* photo-features.

Other writers included Scottish-born artist and writer **Jonathan Brown**, who wrote the feature on art and *A Paris*

Portrait; French contributor **Philippe Artru**, who wrote on architecture; American residents in Paris, **Philip** and **Mary Hyman**, who produced the chapter on food while completing a survey of local dishes for the French government; and **Grace Coston**, project editor of the first edition of *Insight Guide: Paris*.

Musician **Skip Sempé**, an American living in Paris, eats in restaurants as a hobby, so he was the ideal person to compile a new restaurant list for the book. He also had the unenviable task of updating the *Travel Tips*, originally compiled by Glaswegian writer and Paris resident **Hilary Macpherson**. The *Travel Tips* were edited by the journalist **Sue Platt** who also did the indexing. Proof reading was by **John Leech**.

Many of the photographs were taken by **Ping Amranand**; others are by regular Insight photographers **Bill Wassman** and **Catherine Karnow**.

The allure of Paris

Countless famous writers have waxed lyrical about Paris. Ernest Hemingway described Paris as "a moveable feast" – as the city remains with you wherever you are. For centuries, artists have been drawn to it and the city has inspired the likes of Picasso to commit it to canvas. The 16th-century soothsayer Nostradamus once said, "As long as Paris does not fall, gaiety will exist in the world."

We hope this book combines gaiety and practicality.

Map Legend

Ⓜ	Metro
✈	Airport
🚌	Bus Station
Ⓟ	Parking
ⓘ	Tourist Information
✉	Post Office
✝ ☿ ♂	Church/Ruins
☿ ♀	Mosque
✡ ☥	Synagogue
★	Place of Interest

The main places of interest in the *Places* section are coordinated by number with a full-colour map (e.g. ❶) and a symbol at the top of every right-hand page tells you where to find the map.

Contributors

Radula-Scott

Eames

Keeble

Coston

CONTENTS

The Grand
Palais from
Pont
Alexandre III

CITY ON THE SEINE

The central hub of France, both physically and culturally, Paris was once described by Charles V as being not a city but a world – and this image still stands

Paris is a city of landscapes. In a natural basin, cut by the slowly meandering River Seine and edged with gentle hills, the layout of the French capital has been perfectly planned throughout the centuries, each new generation of buildings complementing, and often enhancing, the old. As a result, for just as long, Paris has been a honeypot to artists, writers, philosophers and composers. According to writer Jean Giraudoux (1882–1944), the Parisian is more than a little proud to be part of this city where "the most thinking, talking and writing in the world have been accomplished".

Situated on longitude 2° 20W and latitude 48° 50N, roughly the same latitude as Stuttgart in Germany and Vancouver in Canada, all the French channels of communication lead to Paris: highways, railways, airways and even Hertzian radio waves. It is the political, economic, historical, artistic, cultural and tourist hub of France.

The growth of Paris

The city itself covers an area close to 100 sq. km (40 sq. miles), running 13 km (8 miles) east and west, and 9 km (6 miles) north and south. On the map, 20 *arrondissements* (administrative districts) spiral out like a snail's shell, a pattern reflecting the city's historical development and successive enlargements. The site of medieval Paris corresponds roughly to the first six *arrondissements*. The Revolution of 1789 added the land that comprises the next five, while the territory covered by the last nine was acquired in the 19th century by the annexation of a dozen neighbouring villages, including La Villette, Belleville, Auteuil and Montmartre.

After leaving Burgundy 500 km (300 miles) away, the Seine enters Paris close to the Bois de Vincennes, in the southeast, and meanders

PRECEDING PAGES: the Seine and Ile de la Cité; the view from Pont Alexandre III; the Eiffel Tower from the Palais de Chaillot; a celebrated café.
LEFT: barging through the city.
ABOVE RIGHT: dancing on the Pont des Arts.

gently north and south past three small islands – Ile St-Louis, Ile de la Cité and, on its way out, Ile des Cygnes. Chains of hillocks rise up to the north of the river, including Montmartre, the city's highest point at 130 metres (425 ft), Ménilmontant, Belleville and the Buttes Chaumont, and south, with Montsouris, the Mont

Ste-Geneviève, the Buttes aux Cailles and Maison Blanche. Mont Valérien is the highest point on the outskirts at 160 metres (525 ft), providing an immense panoramic view of Paris from the west. The lowest, at 30 metres (100 ft) above sea level, is in the southeastern suburb of Passy.

The city is contained by the Boulevard Périphérique, a major ring road stretching 35 km (22 miles) around it. Constructed in 1973 in an attempt to reduce traffic jams, the Périphérique is invariably congested itself, particularly during the rush hours, when an estimated 130,000 cars storm its 35 exits.

Forming two concentric rings wrapped tightly around Paris, the suburbs (*banlieue*) are divided up into *départements* or counties. The inner ring incorporates Hauts-de-Seine, Val-de-Marne and Seine-St-Denis, and the outer ring consists of Seine-et-Marne, Essonne, Yvelines and Val-d'Oise. These counties, together with Paris and the Greater Paris conurbation around it, constitute the Ile de France and are linked by eight major highways, four RER lines and an extensive railway network branching out in all directions from six stations in Paris.

At the beginning of the 19th century, Napoleon Bonaparte imposed a special status on the city of Paris, giving it the powers of a *département* in order to maintain a firm hold on the capital's politics and populace. It wasn't until March 1977 that Paris voted a general city council into office which, in turn, elected a mayor, Jacques Chirac. Today, each *arrondissement* also has its own council and mayor to deal with local affairs. Nationally, Paris is represented by 21 delegates and 12 senators in the two houses of Parliament – the National Assembly and the Senate.

The role of the river

"She is buffeted by the waves but sinks not," reads the Latin inscription on the city's coat-of-arms, symbolising a Paris born on the flanks of the River Seine. Lutetia was indeed founded by the Romans, on the site of a Gallic Parisii settlement on the largest island in the river, as these lines suggest, but today it is the Seine that cuts a swathe through the middle of the city.

The Seine is the capital's widest avenue; it is spanned by a total of 35 bridges which provide some of the loveliest views of Paris. The river is also the city's calmest artery, barely ruffled by the daily flow of tourist and commercial boat traffic. In the 19th century, the banks were encumbered with wash-houses and watermills, and its waters heaved with ships hailing from every corner of France.

Even more difficult to imagine now are the 700 brightly painted Viking warships, which used the river to invade Paris from the north in the 9th century, or the thousands of bodies that floated past in 1572, victims of the St Bartholomew's Day Massacre. Today, barges and pleasure boats on their lazy way to Burgundy use the St-Martin and St-Denis canals to shorten their trip, cutting across the northeast of Paris.

RIGHT: how Paris looks from an orbiting satellite.

Through the heart of the city, the Seine flows for tourists, poets and lovers.

Parisian ambience

One of the most persistent images of Paris is the long avenues and boulevards graciously lined with chestnut and plane trees. Flowers and plants abound in a patchwork of 338 squares, parks and gardens, tended in the formal French tradition or following the English style so admired by Napoleon III.

Divided up by two large series of streets, one forming a long line north to south – from Boulevard de Strasbourg to Boulevard St-Michel – and the other going east to west from the Rue de Faubourg St-Antoine to as far as La Défense, Paris is a mosaic of *quartiers* (quarters) or villages, each one having a distinctive character. Publishing houses cluster around the Odéon on the Left Bank and Sentier is the place for garment wholesalers. Universities and colleges are in the Quartier Latin, fashion is in Faubourg St-Honoré, with business around the Bourse (stock exchange), Opéra and in La Défense.

Chains of boulevards encircle the centre of the city, marking where the boundary was in medieval times. Many of the streets bear witness to this in their names – those that contain the word *faubourg* indicate that there was once a village or suburb in that area.

Underground Paris is a labyrinth of Métro lines, 3,200 km (2,000 miles) of sewers, which you can visit, scores of garages and endless ancient quarries, which were converted into catacombs in the 18th century.

RIGHT: Fontaine de Stravinski on the Right Bank.

A MODERN PARIS

To keep up with the demands of modern life, whilst preserving the city's architectural heritage, changes have had to be made – often not without a fight. In 1969, the massive food market at Les Halles was relocated outside Paris at Rungis, the Boulevard Périphérique ring road was constructed in 1973 and the Sorbonne, after the 1968 riots was split into 13 autonomous universities and scattered around the outskirts.

The creation of La Défense as a financial centre outside the city perimeter started in 1958 with the first tower opening in 1964 – now there are 47 with more still planned.

LVTETIA 1600

Jacques Defreveaulx 1600 sculp. inv.

Decisive Dates

GALLO-ROMAN ERA

c. 300 BC: Parisii tribe settle on the Ile de la Cité.

58–52 BC: Julius Caesar conquers Gaul and the Romans build Lutetia on the site left by the Parisii and on the Left Bank of the Seine.

c. AD 250: St Denis establishes the first Christian community and is eventually martyred.

360: Julian the Apostate is made Emperor of Rome while in charge of Lutetia and is believed to have changed the town's name to Paris.

451: St Geneviève saves Paris from Attila the Hun.

The Dark Ages

486: Clovis pushes out the last Romans and, in 508, makes Paris the capital of his new Frankish kingdom.

751: The Carolingian dynasty begins, diverting power from Paris to Aachen and the abandoned city goes into decline. Emperor Charlemagne rules from 768 to 814.

885: Count Eudes (Odo) defends Paris against the Normans and becomes king of the Western Franks in 888.

The Middle Ages

Paris develops into a city of learning and political power and spreads north of the river.

987: Start of the Capetian dynasty when Hugh Capet is made king.

1108–54: Paris becomes an important trading centre.

1163: Building work starts on Notre Dame.

1180–1223: Philippe-Auguste builds the Louvre fortress and a wall around Paris.

1215: The University of Paris is founded.

1226–70: Louis IX (St Louis) makes judicial reforms and the Sorbonne university opens in 1253.

1328: The House of Valois inherits the monarchy in preference to its English cousin Edward III, triggering the Hundred Years' War.

1358: *Jacquerie* uprising of the peasants in Paris, led by clothmaker Etienne Marcel fighting for democracy.

1380: The Bastille prison is built.

1420: Paris surrenders to the English, who rule until 1436, despite Joan of Arc's efforts in 1429.

THE RENAISSANCE

At the end of the 15th century, wars with Italy expose the French to new ideas of art, wealth and luxury.

1469: First French printing works opens at Sorbonne.

1516: François I brings Leonardo da Vinci with his masterpiece, the *Mona Lisa*, to France.

1559: Henri II killed in jousting tournament. The new Louvre palace is completed and street lamps erected.

1572: St Bartholomew's Day Massacre of Protestants.

1594: Bourbon Henri IV converts to Catholicism.

1609: The Place des Vosges is built.

LE GRAND SIÈCLE

In an age of extravagance, Louis XIV the Sun King, moves to Versailles and starts an opulent building programme.

1629: Louis XIII's prime minister, Cardinal Richelieu, builds the Palais Royal.

1631: Paris's first newspaper, *La Gazette*, is launched.

1635: Louis XIII founds the Académie Française.

1670: Hôtel des Invalides is built.

1682: Louis XIV moves his Royal Court to Versailles.

1686: Le Procope is the first café in Paris to open.

Age of Enlightenment

The arts flourish, science develops and intellectuals, such as Voltaire and Rousseau, exchange ideas.

1722: First fire brigade in Paris is introduced.

1751: First volume of Diderot's *Encyclopédie* published.

c. 1760: Louis XV builds the Panthéon, Place de la Concorde and Ecole Militaire.

1783: First hot-air balloon ascent in Paris.

The First Empire

The Revolution leads to the creation of a Republic, which is soon turned into an Empire by the warring, but reforming and popular, Napoleon Bonaparte.

1789–95: The Revolution: after the storming of the Bastille and the Declaration of the Rights of Man, the

monarchy is abolished in 1792 and a Republic is born. The ensuing Terror kills more than 60,000 people.
1799: Napoleon Bonaparte, the First Consul of France, seizes power and is crowned emperor in 1804.
1800: Banque de France is established.
1806: Construction of the Arc de Triomphe begins.
1815: Battle of Waterloo; the monarchy is restored.

THE RESTORATION
Two more revolutions hit Paris, finally unseating the monarchy once more in 1848.
1831: Victor Hugo's *Notre Dame de Paris* is published.
1832: Around 19,000 Parisians die in cholera epidemic.
1842: First French railway links Paris with St-Germain.
1848: Louis-Philippe, the Citizen King, is deposed.

THE SECOND EMPIRE
With Napoleon III at the helm, Paris is transformed into an efficient, modern city.
1852–70: Baron Georges Haussmann undertakes a massive redesign of the city, building the Grands Boulevards, laying sewers and creating parks.
1855: First World Exhibition. The second is 12 years later.
1863: Manet's painting *Le Déjeuner sur l'Herbe* scandalises the Académie.
1870: Paris surrenders to Prussia and Napoleon flees.

THE THIRD REPUBLIC
The Métro is dug and new inventions, such as the motor car, telephone and cinema, make life more fun. Artists, writers and musicians flock to Paris and, between the wars, the city continues to attract them.
1871: Uprising by Paris Commune with 25,000 people killed and the Tuileries palace destroyed.
1888: Louis Pasteur sets up the Pasteur Institute as a hospital and research centre for infectious diseases.
1889: Eiffel Tower built for the World Exhibition.
1894–1906: The Dreyfus Affair.
1911: Diaghilev comes to Paris with the Russian ballet.
1914–18: World War I: Paris is saved from German attack by the Battle of the Marne.
1924: Poet and literary theorist André Breton publishes his *Surrealist Manifesto*.
1934: The Depression gives rise to riots and strikes.
1937: Palais de Chaillot built.
1940: World War II: Paris is bombed and occupied by the Germans.
1944: Paris is liberated by the Allies, and General Charles de Gaulle heads a Provisional Government

PRECEDING PAGES: map of Paris in 1600.
LEFT: Louis XIV, the extravagant Sun King (1643–1715).
RIGHT: a triumphant Napoleon Bonaparte (1799–1814).

until 1946, when a Fourth Republic is proclaimed.
1958: The Algerian crisis topples the Fourth Republic.

THE FIFTH REPUBLIC
General de Gaulle returns as president of the Fifth Republic, launching Paris into the Space Age, as modern buildings spring up around the city.
1958–63: The construction of La Défense begins.
1962: André Malraux, Minister of Culture, establishes a renovation and restoration programme.
1968: Strikes and student riots against the university system and the Government forces de Gaulle to call an election. He wins but resigns a year later.
1969: Les Halles food market is moved to Rungis.

1973: Périphérique ring road is built.
1977: The controversial Centre Georges-Pompidou opens. Jacques Chirac is elected mayor of Paris.
1981: Socialist François Mitterrand elected president.
1986: Right-wing Chirac becomes prime minister in a unique "cohabitation" with a socialist president, who is reaffirmed in 1988 when the socialists regain power.
1989: Bicentenary celebrations of the Revolution herald the opening of the Louvre Pyramid, Grande Arche and Opéra Bastille – Mitterrand's *Grands Projets*.
1995: Chirac is elected president in May but, later, the city is crippled by strikes against cuts in benefits.
1997: Major renovation of the Louvre completed. Socialist Lionel Jospin becomes prime minister, creating a second "cohabitation".
1998: France hosts the World Cup.

CLOVIS I.

THE EARLY YEARS

Paris has been a choice place to live for more than 2,000 years – the Parisii discovered it, the Romans usurped it and the Franks invaded it

As with many of the world's great cities, the mysterious mists of antiquity veil the origins of Paris. Around 300 BC, when the Celts were chasing each other around Europe, one tribe, the Parisii, settled on an island in the Seine river (Ile de la Cité). They were good farmers and active traders, hence the name Parisii, which is said to be derived from a Celtic word for boat. However, perhaps a more imaginative theory on the origins of the city's name claims that the tribe's founder was Paris, the emigré son of King Priam of Troy.

The ancient town of Lutetia

In 53 BC, a number of Gallic tribes failed to appear at the annual council in Ambiani (Amiens) summoned by the Romans, who were in the process of colonising Gaul. Roman Emperor Julius Caesar, sensing rebellion, quickly transferred the council into the midst of the restless Gauls, to the Parisii settlement – just an agglomeration of huts – on the Seine.

The Romans soon realised the advantage of the position for easy bridge building and developed the settlement for themselves, naming it Lutetia. A wooden bridge connected the island, where a governer's *palais* (palace) was built, to the Left Bank and a town grew up, replete with temples, baths, a theatre and other hallmarks of Roman civilisation. The ruins of one of the baths can be seen under the Hôtel de Cluny.

Dominating the Right Bank from its hilltop perch stood a temple to Mercury where, more than three centuries later, St Denis, a Christian agitator and the first bishop of Paris, was beheaded, giving the hill the name *Mons Martyrium* (Martyr's Mound) – Montmartre in French. According to legend, St Denis picked up his severed head and walked 6,000 steps before being buried by one of his apostles on the spot where the cathedral of St-Denis now stands.

Lying as it did exposed on a plain, Lutetia soon fell victim to frequent sackings by marauding barbarian tribes. In AD 358, Emperor Constantine sent his son-in-law, Julian, to Gaul to sort them out. The young man promptly fell in love with the town and some say that it was he who renamed it Paris. He became the Roman emperor, abolishing Christianity, officially tolerated since 313, and, when not in battle, he sat

in the *palais*, enjoying the wine and figs, and organising the town's accounts.

Geneviève – patron saint of Paris

About a century later, Attila the Hun appeared on the scene with his hordes. The Parisians prepared to flee but were stopped by the 19-year-old Geneviève, who assured them that the Huns would not harm the city. Lo and behold, the marauders passed southwest of the town and ran straight into the swords of a hastily raised army of legionnaires. Thereafter, Geneviève became the patron saint of Paris.

She was still around when Clovis I, king of the Salian Franks and founder of the Merovingian

LEFT: Clovis I, king of the Franks, saw off the Romans.
ABOVE RIGHT: Paris's coat-of-arms.

dynasty, invaded much of Gaul, seeing off the Romans, and swept into Paris. He promptly made it his capital (many believe it was he who gave Paris its name) and, installing himself in the *palais*, he converted the town back to Christianity. Later a basilica was built where he and St Geneviève were buried, which eventually became the Panthéon, the last resting place for France's VIPs.

Merovingian law of succession was simple: the empire was

FIRST CHRISTIANS

The first Christian bishop of Paris is martyred in AD 287. Christianity is officially tolerated from 313, until Roman Emperor Julian tries to abolish it in 350. Clovis I converts the town back to Christianity after 485.

magne divided the Frankish kingdom between himself and his brother in 768 and then made himself king of the whole empire, which included a large part of Germany, three years later. He died in 814, leaving his son Louis – the first of many – in charge.

The Norman invasions of the mid-9th century brought Paris back into the limelight. After several sackings, Count Eudes (Odo), in 885, decided to resist by building fortifications around the Ile de la Cité. The first siege

divided among the previous ruler's offspring. As a result, family members spent the better part of 250 years squeezing each other out. Paris, instead of being used as an administrative centre, served as a favourite battleground for the murderous bickering of Clovis's descendants. Nature also conspired with floods, fires, epidemics and hurricanes.

The Carolingian dynasty

The Carolingians, who ruled from 751, felt more comfortable nearer to their homelands in the lower Rhine and moved political importance away from Paris, which was left in the charge of a count and his municipal guard. Charle-

of Paris lasted an entire year and almost bore fruit: the Carolingian army came to the rescue. But King Charles the Fat, instead of attacking the siege-weary aggressors, let them sail up the Seine to pillage Burgundy.

In defiance of the king, Eudes took the crown and Carolingian unity dissolved. The French crown shifted from one dynasty to the next. The Saracens appeared in the south, Hungarians in the east, and the Vikings ran amok. All in all, it was not a happy time for France, until the ongoing power struggle led to Hugo Capet, son of Hugo the Great, a descendant of Eudes, becoming king of all France and starting a new, long-lasting dynasty – the Capetians.

The Middle Ages

Although the early members of the dynasty preferred crusading and hunting to governing, Paris prospered under the Capetians. New fountains were built to bring fresh drinking water to the citizens and *sergents de ville*, armed with clubs, walked a beat. Public punishment was common.

With new cloisters and churches and a cosmopolitan population, Paris very soon grew into an intellectual centre. At the start of the 12th century, monks, scholars, philosophers, poets and musicians flocked to the city to learn, to argue and to teach. Philosopher and theologian scholar Pierre Abélard and St Bernard hurled

merchants and craftsmen, who wisely organised themselves into guilds. The most powerful of these was the water merchants' guild, which included all river workers and gave its coat-of-arms to the city.

Philippe-Auguste built Les Halles for the guilds and improved the Seine docks. The guilds took care of levying taxes, town-crying and other municipal duties. In 1190, six guild members, so-called Grands Bourgeois (city dwellers), were chosen to act as the king's officers. The number increased to 24, meeting in regular sessions to discuss municipal business.

Later, Louis IX (1226–70), who due to his

logic at each other in the open air – although the former got into hot water and was castrated, after starting a relationship with his student Héloïse, who bore him a son.

In 1200, the first student riot took place, which led to Philippe-Auguste (1180–1223) founding the University of Paris. Hardly a European scholar failed to visit its prestigious faculties on the Left Bank.

Economic life in Paris rested in the hands of

Far Left: Roman stonework in the Musée National de Moyen Age – Thermes de Cluny.
Left: tragic lovers Abélard and Héloïse.
Above: boatmen in front of the Pont Notre-Dame.

passion for justice was made a saint, created three governing chambers. Eventually, these Bourgeois became an independent political force, often corrupt but, equally often, striving for democratic reforms, which had a long-lasting effect on political life.

The first revolution

By the mid-14th century the Capetians had given way to the Valois and the devastating Hundred Years' War began. The French knights seemed powerless before the English foot soldiers. The plague made its first deadly appearance. In 1356, the English captured King John the Good at Poitiers. The citizens of Paris, tired of incompetent leadership, rebelled. Their leader, Etienne Marcel, a clothmaker and guild chairman, was the first in a long string of genial, corrupt demagogues to emerge on Paris's political horizon. A motley crew of poor towns people and peasants under Jacques Bonhomme chose the moment to begin a revolt, later known as the *Jacquerie*.

For support, Marcel unwisely chose the King of Navarre (Charles the Bad), an English ally. When the Parisians found out about the alliance, they turned on Marcel. In July 1358, as he was about to hand over Paris to the rival Navarre camp, he was assassinated by a loyalist. Three

dian John the Fearless and his cousin Louis d'Orléans, brother of the king, who was now mentally deranged. John had Louis murdered and, in 1409, took control of Paris.

The advance of the English

While Louis's Armagnac son, Charles, raised a new army, Paris celebrated. Into the fray stepped a butcher, Caboche, demanding fiscal and administrative reforms. All hell broke loose as John's authority slipped into the hands of Caboche and his henchmen. The ensuing Reign of Terror gave Charles and his Armagnac army a chance to re-enter and "pacify" the city. See-

days later, John the Good's son, the Dauphin, entered the capital. The new regent, who was to become Charles V (1364–1380), hammered out a truce with the English, allowing France some time to put its house in order. Paris was relatively well treated, considering how fickle its loyalties had been: the Parliament still met but its powers were curtailed.

Behind a calm exterior, Paris was seething with anger. In 1382, during the reign of Charles VI (1380–1422), a group of citizens calling themselves the Maillotins rebelled against high taxes and were brutally repressed. Then, in 1407, the Maillotins became enmeshed in the violent struggle for power between the Burgun-

ing France torn apart by civil war, the English resumed hostilities. Siding with the Burgundians, they defeated the Armagnacs at the Battle of Agincourt in 1415.

Four years later, John the Fearless was murdered, whereupon Henry V of England married Catherine, daughter of mad King Charles, and occupied Paris in December 1420.

The Dauphin, the legitimate French heir, had some support in the capital, but he was feeble and couldn't keep out the English invaders. Joan of Arc, a 17-year-old girl from Lorraine, came to his rescue in 1428 by defeating the English at Orléans and, a year later, Charles VII was crowned at Rheims. However, Paris remained in English hands until 1436, when Charles recaptured his tattered capital, driving the English back to Calais.

By the early 16th century, Louis XII (1498–1515) was ensconced in the Italian Wars. Then François I (1515–47) began the struggle against the mighty Habsburgs in Europe and, in 1525, he was captured at Pavia. The Parisians paid his ransom and he promptly moved into the Louvre. In his wake came an army of Italian architects, painters,

RELIGIOUS MASSACRE

On St Bartholomew's Day, 24 August 1572, thousands of Protestants, who had come to Paris for Henri de Navarre's wedding, were slaughtered on the orders of the Catholic monarchy.

spread the new gospel of Protestantism through Catholic France.

Paris, dominated by the conservative Sorbonne theologians, was outraged and, under the reign of Henri II (1547–59), pushed for measures against the Protestants, known as Huguenots, often burning religious agitators.

Henri II's sons and heirs, François II (1559–60), Charles IX (1560–74) and Henri III (1574–89), proved inadequate in controlling France's religious factions. Nor were they helped

sculptors, goldsmiths, cabinet makers and masons, who set about the task of reshaping the city's lugubrious Gothic face.

With the rebirth of the capital under François's graceful, iron hand, French culture also returned to life. Ronsard, Du Bellay and other poets of the Pléiade carried French poetry to new heights, while Clément Jannequin put the French *chanson* on the map. The advent of the printing press increased the range of these creative activities; however, it also helped

LEFT: Henri III and Charles IX, sons of the scheming Catherine de Médicis.
ABOVE: St Bartholomew's Day Massacre in 1572.

by the intrigues of the Queen Mother, Catherine de Médicis. The country was plunged into a religious war.

War between the Henris

King Henri III's concessions to the Protestants infuriated the Catholics, led by the popular Henri de Guise and his Paris-based Holy League. In 1584, the Protestant Henri de Navarre, a Bourbon, became heir to the throne but he had to fight Henri de Guise for the right. In 1589, Henri III had Henri de Guise assassinated. Paris threw up its barricades and the Holy League's Council of Sixteen took power and deposed Henri III, who joined forces with

Navarre. His army, however, joined the Catholics. That summer, a friar, Jacques Clément, murdered Henri III and Henri de Navarre became Henri IV.

Civil war dragged on for another five years. Paris was the stage for the Council of Sixteen's gruesome repression of real and perceived plots. In 1593, Philip II of Spain, who had entered the war on the Catholic side, pressed to usurp the French throne. Henri IV opportunely chose that moment to convert to Catholicism, whereupon Paris welcomed him and overnight the war-weary nation fell in line.

Henri IV patched up France spiritually and

economically. In 1598, his Edict of Nantes set up guidelines for cohabitation between the religious groups. His (Protestant) adviser, Sully, reformed the tax laws and balanced the budget.

The glorious epoch

Despite massive deficits incurred by their violent foreign policy, the Bourbons lavished huge sums on Paris, while keeping it on a short political leash. Two deserted islets behind the Ile de la Cité became the residential Ile St-Louis. New bridges crossed the Seine. Avenues cut through the dingy labyrinth. Architects built new houses, palaces, schools and restored the old ones. Parks appeared, where society could stroll in the shade

THE ROAD TO REVOLUTION

Louis XV was only five years old when he succeeded to the throne in 1715, giving a free hand to the Regent, Philippe d'Orléans, who left government to his ministers, while he engaged in amorous pursuits in the Palais Royal. Once of age, Louis followed suit, giving his mistress, Madame de Pompadour, the power to select ministers and generals. Meanwhile, the nation's financial situation worsened. Revolution was just around the corner.

and exchange ideas, gossip or tender glances. Cardinal Richelieu, who largely governed on behalf of the young Louis XIII (1610–43) while the King was growing up, founded the Académie Française.

Under the Sun King, Louis XIV (1643–1715), the spending spree reached its peak. His minister, Colbert, sanitised entire sections of the city and set up manufacturing plants to provide the French with luxury items. Louis XIV also had hospices constructed for the poor and Les Invalides was built to house war veterans.

The influx of money and the proximity of the court attracted a huge crowd to the capital. Rich wives and courtesans opened their living rooms to conversationalists. Theatres echoed with the verse of Racine and Corneille, the booing of the *cliques* and the applause of the *claques*. Everyone laughed at the writings of Molière, Boileau and La Fontaine satirising the hustling and bustling society.

But storm clouds were gathering. In 1648, Paris revolted, demanding greater political representation. The 12 provincial parliaments joined, as did a conspiracy of nobles under Prince Condé. The Fronde, as it was called, eventually collapsed, but Louis XIV later had his lavish palace, Versailles, built outside the city limits to keep his distance from the unruly Parisian mob.

The beginning of the 18th century was a period of great inequality in Paris. French high society was having a fine time in the court of the Sun King. Theatres were busy, the new café scene was lively and the city buzzed by night. But all this activity ignored the needs and wishes of the poor, who were swept aside.

LEFT: Madame de Maintenon, governess to the Sun King's children, who secretly became his wife.
RIGHT: Louis XIV, the Sun King and a big spender.

LVDOVICVS XIV D. G. FRANC. ET NAVAR. REX CHRISTIANISS.

Ludovico Magno

REVOLUTION AND THE REPUBLIC

As the rich grew richer and the poor had nothing, discontent exploded into revolt.

Heads rolled into the first Republic. Then along came Napoleon...

French reputation no longer rested on royal glory in the latter part of the 18th century, but on the wisdom of its intellectuals – Voltaire, Rousseau, Diderot and Quesnay. Poverty increased, and when a bad harvest in 1788 caused the price of bread to soar and the people became restless, Queen Marie-Antoinette is supposed to have made her famous pronouncement that the hungry should eat cake.

By 1789, France's debts had reached a critical stage. The King took the unusual step of summoning the Estates General, a legislative body made up of three estates: the Clergy, Nobility and the rest of the populace, commonly known as the Third Estate, to vote for reforms to the French Constitution. Craftily, the King only allowed one vote per estate, meaning that the massive Third Estate could be outvoted, two to one, by the smaller Clergy and Nobility. Eventually forced out of the meeting, the Third Estate created a National Assembly in opposition to the King. On 14 July, the people of Paris stormed the Bastille prison for its weapons, proclaimed a Commune and formed a National Guard under the leadership of La Fayette, a French soldier, not long back from fighting for American independence.

The Revolutionary years

The explosion of 1789 swept the past away. Radicals of one hour became the conservatives of the next. Streets changed names, newborn babies were baptised Egalité, Liberté or République. A statue of a ballerina representing Liberty sat on the altar of Notre Dame. The First Republic was proclaimed and, in January 1793, King Louis XVI was decapitated in public on the Place de la Concorde.

Paris was the burning centre of the French Revolution. Its temperamental and bloodthirsty

"BURNING" BREECHES

As a Revolutionary symbol, the workers of Paris took to wearing trousers, instead of breeches (*culottes*), earning the nickname *Sans Culottes*.

mob was the force behind increasingly radical leaders, from Mirabeau, to Brissot, to Danton and finally the dastardly Robespierre, egged on by Marat, whose assassination by Charlotte Corday, in July 1793, threw the Reign of Terror into top gear. Anyone suspected of stepping out of line was dragged off to the guillotine as a traitor. In July 1794, it was Robespierre's turn for the chop.

It was the young General Napoleon Bonaparte who finally drew the line under the Revolution, when he quashed a royalist uprising in 1795. Four years later, he had seized power, crowning himself Emperor of a totalitarian and military state.

Romantic Paris

The glorious Napoleonic empire ended once and for all with Paris occupied by three allied armies after the Battle of Waterloo in 1815. Bourbon Louis XVIII headed a constitutional monarchy with emphasis on law and order and *laissez-faire* economics.

The Industrial Revolution might have turned Paris into an opulent and mediocre business centre were it not for the apostles of Romanticism, led by Victor Hugo (1802–85). Inspired

POWER TO THE PEOPLE

As the people of Paris turned on the monarchy, the Revolutionaries instigated a number of new ideas:

☛ The French flag – the Tricolore was invented, incorporating Paris's red and blue colours with the captive royal white standard.

☛ Worship of Reason officially took the place of Christianity and churches were destroyed or used for weapon storage.

☛ A Republican calendar was created with new months linked to nature.

☛ *La Marseillaise* (now the French national anthem) was taken up as the Revolutionaries' marching song.

PRECEDING PAGES: Delacroix's portrayal of the Revolution.
LEFT: detail from the Arc de Triomphe.

by the anti-establishment spirit of 1789, they waged a struggle against creaky academics and bourgeois respectability in garrets, cafés, journals and the "enemy's" own *salons*.

The revolutionary spirit also remained in the Republican forces, who reached for the Parisian mob whenever despotism reared its head. In July 1830, Charles X, who had succeeded to the throne six years earlier, revoked certain electoral laws, which led to three days of bloody rioting and his abdication. His cousin, Louis-Philippe, Duke of Orléans, stepped in until 1848 when another revolution forced him to quit.

The Second Empire

When Napoleon's nephew and president of the Second Republic, Louis Napoleon, crowned himself Emperor Napoleon III in 1852, he pre-emptively arrested more than 20,000 suspected political opponents, just to make sure.

The Second Empire was a gaudy and grandiose period in the city's history. Thousands of kilometres of new railway track were built to connect the city with other European capitals. Twice, in 1855 and 1867, it hosted the World Fair. Basking in financial ease, the city abandoned itself to the pleasures of masked balls, Offenbach operettas and *salon* conversation.

Aided by eager speculators and fat taxes, the Prefect Baron Georges Haussmann gave Paris a brand-new face. He gutted and rebuilt the centre. New water mains and a sewage system were installed to service the, by now, two million Parisians. Elegant boulevards, avenues and squares appeared: Champs-Elysées, St-Michel, St-Germain, Etoile, to name a few. These served

---

BONEY'S BATTLES

The rise and fall of Napoleon Bonaparte (1769–1821) can be charted by his battles as he attempted to dominate Europe and beyond.

He won the Italian Campaigns (1796–97), giving France Northern Italy. The Battle of the Pyramids (1798) gave him Egypt. He defeated Austria at Marengo (1800), Austria and Russia at Austerlitz (1805), Prussia at Iéna (1806) and the Austrians again at Wagram (1809).

He lost the battles of the Nile (1798) and Acre (1799), foiling his plans for the East, Trafalgar (1805) kept him from England. His disastrous Russian Campaign (1812) led to his defeats at Leipzig (1813) and, finally, at Waterloo (1815).

---

an aesthetic purpose, but they also facilitated troop deployment in the event of trouble and were not so easy to barricade by rioters.

Families, dispossessed by the construction, were forced to move to eastern Paris. This influx only added to that area's already notoriously seditious spirit.

The Commune

In 1870, Napoleon III went to war with Prussia. Parisians lined the streets to cheer the ill-equipped, ill-led and ill-fated army as it marched east. Two months later, he was beaten, the Second Empire had become the Third Republic, and the Prussians were besieging Paris. In Bordeaux, the government of Adolph Thiers waited for an uprising in heroic revolutionary style that never materialised.

On 28 January 1871, President Thiers, without consulting Paris, finally agreed to a cease-fire. A month later, the National Assembly ratified a peace treaty. The Prussians triumphantly marched through Paris avoiding the eastern districts, home of the starving, belligerent and vengeful National Guard, who felt betrayed by the French government. Sensing trouble, Thiers disarmed the National Guard and moved his government to Versailles. He barely escaped the ensuing explosion of rancour.

On 28 March, a Commune was proclaimed at the Hôtel de Ville after a municipal election was boycotted by the bourgeoisie. Civil war erupted.

While the Communards hoisted red flags and argued over political and military strategies, Thiers was busy raising a new army. The government forces succeeded where the Prussians had failed and some 25,000 Communards were killed in the last weeks of May, the final 147 being shot in the Père-Lachaise Cemetery. With them went the revolutionary spark that had defied tyrants and kindled republics since 1789.

La Belle Epoque

With the insurrectionist working class brutally tamed, Paris became merely the stage for the squabbles, plots, demonstrations, counter-demonstrations, and oral and written polemics of the Third Republic. The Republicans split into pro-clerical and anti-clerical factions. In the 1890s, after recovering from the Commune, the left gathered around the socialist Jean Jaurès. On the right was an array of diehard monarchists and nationalists with a strong vein of anti-

Semitism, as revealed by the Dreyfus Affair in the late 1890s. (That *cause célèbre* revolved around a Jewish army captain, Alfred Dreyfus, who was imprisoned on Devil's Island on trumped-up spying charges.)

Though crackling with tension, Paris seemed more than ever ready to accept the controversial and the provocative and decided to have some fun. The Métro was dug, the Eiffel Tower built and the first films were shown. Between 1880 and 1940,

GAI PAREE

From the 1890s, Paris hummed with life, cabarets, and dance clubs mushroomed in Montmartre, café society flourished, the first cinema opened, motor cars took to the streets and Diaghilev's dancers arrived.

through town. Diaghilev's *Ballets Russes* presented its superstar, Nijinsky, dancing to Stravinsky's latest composition, *The Rites of Spring*, that, in 1913, scandalised the packed auditoriums.

World War I dampened spirits, as the city turned to the slaughter at hand. In September 1914, the German army came within earshot. The military governor, Gallieni, rushed reinforcements to the counter-offensive on the Marne, using every means he could lay his hands

Paris housed more painters, sculptors, writers, poets, musicians and other creative artists per acre than in any other metropolis. They chattered with philosophers, theorists, critics, brawny syndicalists, gazetteers, anarchists and socialites in smoke-filled cafés.

Almost every artistic movement flourished in Paris – Realism, Impressionism, Cubism, Surrealism, Dadaism, and so on. In the pawnshops of Montmartre, paintings by Picasso, Utrillo and Modigliani were hung up by clothes pegs. Debussy, Zola, Cocteau and his apostles strolled

ABOVE: Bastille Day – the Revolutionaries storm the Bastille prison on 14 July 1789.

on, including the Paris taxi service, and the city was spared.

Normal life began to return after the armistice was declared in 1918. From the east came Russian emigrés, from the west came American writers and composers. In the 1930s, Paris became a temporary haven to the refugees of fascism.

Between the wars

With one million dead, millions of others now crippled and the agricultural north destroyed by shelling, France's part in the victory over Germany in 1914 was tarnished. Conservative Republicans and left-wing coalitions, including the Communist Party (founded in 1920), tried to come to grips with the economic and social after-effects of the Great War. The extreme right, meanwhile, made some important gains.

Fascist-type organisations had started appearing in France in the late 19th century, when novelists Charles Barras and Léon Daudet founded the Royalist paper *Action Française*. In the 1920s and 1930s, such groups proliferated, fuelled by general discontent and fear of Bolshevism, and inspired by the successes of

MERCI FOR MERCY

As the Allies advanced on Paris in August 1944, the Germans were ordered by Hitler to blow up the city. Happily, the commander, General Dietrich von Choltitz, could not bring himself to do it and, after the war, was made an honorary citizen.

against Franco. He also interrupted the labour reforms because of their negative effect on the economy. In 1937, in a wave of wildcat strikes, the shattered *Front Populaire* sank into the past. "Rather Hitler than Blum," the Conservatives muttered.

World War II

When war broke out against Nazi Germany in September 1939, France shored up the utterly useless Maginot Line, mobilised an ill-equipped

Mussolini and Hitler. They focused their efforts on Paris, parading in paramilitary garb and campaigning against the internationalists, the socialists and, above all, the Jews.

On 6 February 1934, a coalition of fascist factions attempted a *coup d'état* in Paris. It failed, but the left was finally goaded into concerted action. In 1936, a front of radicals, socialists and communists, headed by the socialist Léon Blum, won the election. The so-called *Front Populaire* promised to fight fascism and improve the workers' lot.

Initial euphoria was short-lived. The struggle against fascism split the *Front* when Blum refused to send help to the Spanish Republicans

army and waited. In Paris, statues were sandbagged and the Louvre curators carefully prepared paintings for transport to safety.

On 14 June 1940, the Nazi forces of darkness marched into the City of Light, having simply gone round the Maginot Line via Belgium. There was no siege, no National Guard, no *levée en masse*, no cabbies carrying reinforcements. Instead, 84-year-old Marshal Philippe Pétain, the withered hero of Verdun, became the titular head of a puppet regime in Vichy in unoccupied France.

Many Parisians welcomed the Nazis as racial cleansers and there were those who bravely resisted. They joined the Free French Movement led from London by the Under Secretary for War, General Charles de Gaulle, often sacrificing their lives.

On 6 June 1944, Allied forces landed in Normandy and advanced on Paris. Dietrich von Choltitz, the German commander, received orders to blow up the city, but chose to surrender instead. On 24 August 1944, Paris was liberated and, two days later, General de Gaulle paraded with his forces down the Champs-Elysées. Crowds rejoiced and collaborators scrambled into hiding or suffered the pains of summary justice. The war still had nine months to rage on but, with Paris liberated, light had returned to the European continent at last.

De Gaulle immediately formed a provisional government lasting until 1946 and, with the bane of fascism at last gone, the poets and artists continued their discussions at their favoured watering holes, the Café de Flore, the Lipp and the Coupole. Political quarrelling resumed without the extreme right. The tourists returned in droves. Bebop and rock 'n' roll arrived from across the Atlantic.

But the war and its horrors cast long shadows: the stench of the Holocaust and the indelible proof of man's capacity for evil. Post-war thought was dominated by the dark existentialism of Jean-Paul Sartre and Albert Camus. In addition, France lost two major colonial wars, the first in Indochina (1946–54) and the second in Algeria (1954–62).

May 1968 – student riots

A bloody wave of bombings swept Paris in the early 1960s, when it became clear that President de Gaulle, who had come out of retirement to head the Fifth Republic in 1958, wanted to pull out of the Algerian quagmire. De Gaulle's manner in dealing with internal matters was patriarchal and authoritarian.

His ideas, with few exceptions, were conservative. Time had eroded the legend. A generation had grown up that had not heard the comforting speeches beamed into occupied France by the BBC. It had other ideas and idols.

The 1968 agitation began uneventfully enough in March with a sit-in by students to demand changes in the antiquated university system. But instead of initiating a civil discussion with the students, the *ancien régime* promptly called in the CRS, the riot police, to restore what they saw as a breakdown of order.

Push led to shove. On the night of 10 May 1968, the police stormed 60 barricades in the Quartier Latin. Unrest spread to the factories and other cities. France was soon paralysed and Paris was left in a state of siege. Petrol was rationed and cautious housewives began to hoard food. The state-run media shuffled along with *ersatz* programming, while Parisians got the news from privateers on France's periphery or, ironically, from the BBC in London.

At the end of the month, de Gaulle announced

DE GAULLE'S ROLE IN THE WAR

General Charles de Gaulle rose to fame as the leader of the French Resistance in World War II. At the news of France's impending surrender to the Germans, he fled to England where he set up the Free French Forces, urging on BBC radio "all Frenchmen who still bear arms to continue the struggle". In 1943, he set up a Resistance Government in North Africa. After the liberation of Paris, he made his famous speech from the Hôtel de Ville: "Paris! Paris insulted! Paris broken! Paris martyred! But Paris liberated! Liberated by itself! Liberated by its people with the help of the armies of France…"

LEFT: the liberation of Paris, August 1944.
RIGHT: quelling the student riots in May 1968.

new elections and warned against impending totalitarianism. The Parisian bourgeoisie awoke. An hour later, over 500,000 de Gaulle supporters were flowing down the Champs-Elysées. May 1968 became the most important upheaval in the city since the war.

The Gaullists won the election, but not for long. Disenchantment continued and the President resigned in 1969, leaving his Republic to his ardent follower Georges Pompidou.

The Mitterrand years

The 1970s appeared tame but, when the Independent Republican President, Valéry Giscard

d'Estaing, lost to socialist leader François Mitterrand in 1981, a huge crowd marched to the Bastille in celebration.

However, in 1986, the exigent Parisian character revealed itself again, during the legislative elections. Voters on the left were dismayed by what they viewed as Mitterrand's sell-out and conservative forces, led by Paris mayor Jacques Chirac, swept in with a rightist coalition.

Chirac was well-suited to the population in his inconsistencies. In his student days, he had been a member of the Communist youth movement, then a gung-ho lieutenant, fighting with French anti-independence forces in Algeria, and, later in the early 1970s, Prime Minister for

> ### LAST RIGHTS
>
> François Mitterrand was in control of his image to the end, even organising his funeral, which had to include the presence of both his wife and mistress at the graveside.

two years under President Giscard d'Estaing.

May 1968 had reaffirmed Paris's old rebellious spirit. Parisians still demonstrated at the drop of a hat – anti-racism, pro-gays, against altering university entrance requirements, whatever. The *zeitgeist* of the 1990s has found much to admire in the legacy of the *événements de Mai* as, once again, many Parisians have been trying to find alternative ways of living.

The 1993 elections maintained the swing to the right, which was confirmed when Jacques Chirac succeeded François Mitterrand as president in 1995. Mitterrand died in January 1996. Despite all the disquiet about his personal integrity, from his war record to the true state of his health, the French mourned him as the "god" he had been nicknamed.

And, despite the decline in support for his policies, his many *grands projets* – from the Louvre Pyramid to the Grande Arche at La Défense and the new Grande Bibliothèque at Tolbiac – he had undoubtedly made an indelible mark on Paris architecture, one almost as striking as that of the Sun King himself.

An uncomfortable partnership

By 1997, Chirac's tenuous popularity had sunk to a historical low, which was borne out in the June elections when socialist Lionel Jospin was made prime minister, creating a second cohabitation with the right.

The undeniable charm of Paris lies in these exquisite tensions and juxtapositions – political, artistic, social and architectural. The old lives together with the new. Beaubourg stands an equal to Notre Dame. Brash young businessmen, punks and Dior-dressed ladies share the streets used by beslippered *ménagères*. Paris, modern and sophisticated, may claim to be the heart of Western civilisation, but in its veins still flows the blood of the rustic, untamed, refractory Gaulois.

LEFT: General Charles de Gaulle – war hero and president, who was finally brought down by the students.
RIGHT: La Défense, symbol of modern Paris.

THE PARISIANS

They may have a reputation for being rude and indifferent, but underneath the cool, Parisian exterior lies a warm and welcoming heart

For many of the inner city's 2.2 million residents and the 20 million tourists who visit each year, Paris is a grand seductress, a mistress or a lover. Hundreds of thousands of people are carrying on an illicit affair with her. Some manage a quick fling. For others, the love affair endures a lifetime.

"No other city in the world has been better loved or more celebrated," wrote American author John Steinbeck. "Scarcely has the traveller arrived than he feels himself in the grip of this city which is so much more than a city." A great part of the allure of Paris undoubtedly lies with the Parisians themselves, with their charm, their individualism, their diversity.

So who are the Parisians?

They are the prostitutes in the leather mini-skirts on the Rue St-Denis, the *clochard* sleeping off a bottle of red in the Métro, the society hostess in Chanel, the yuppie stockbroker weaving home from the Bourse on his scooter, the children of the Opéra ballet school affectionately known as "*les petits rats*", the au pairs, hiding from their mothers in the city's American bars, the Algerian greengrocer and the Portuguese concierge, the stately African chief from Sierre Leone, the law student from the Sorbonne and the old lady, in her bedroom slippers, in the park feeding the pigeons. People are what lend any city its vibrancy and Paris is no exception. Stripped of its human population, Paris would be no more than a collection of buildings and monuments, architecturally beautiful maybe, but a sad, cold place nonetheless.

There is an old joke, not familiar to many Parisians but much told in bars where foreigners congregate. It goes like this. On the eighth day, God created a city in the image of paradise and named it Paris. It was a city so beautiful, so perfect, he was afraid lest the rest of the world

PRECEDING PAGES: lady and friend in the Quartier Latin; art students busy in the Jardin du Luxembourg.
LEFT: cheerful *bonhomie* in the market.
RIGHT: traffic policeman doing a serious day's work.

became jealous. And so, to redress the balance, on the ninth day he created the Parisians.

This joke may not go down too well in the capital, but you can bet that the rest of France is joining in the laughter. A recent national survey put Parisians at the top of the list of most hated people in France (31 percent), easily topping the

traditional targets such as civil servants (21 percent), Corsicans (23 percent) and even policemen (18 percent).

Unpopular stereotypes

Visitors *and* Parisians have their favourite stereotypical Parisian whom they love to hate, from the haughty, patronising shop assistant, too busy adjusting her lipstick to give her customers the time of day, to the swearing, gesticulating taxi driver, who refuses to take you because you are not heading in "his" direction, and to the indifferent bureaucrat who keeps you waiting for three hours only to inform you that you lack a vital document (usually your electricity bill), without which he is firmly unable to help you.

In the past, articles have been published in the French press exhorting Parisians to good behaviour and deploring the unfriendly welcome they extended to tourists. This shows that at least today's Parisians are no longer under any illusions. In fact, only 38 percent consider themselves kind, while an almost unanimous 92 percent admit to being under stress. Eighty-two percent also own up, undoubtedly with more than a touch of Gallic pride, to being *individualistes*, a description which anyone who has had more than a passing acquaintance with the city may suspect of doubling as a convenient excuse for a multitude of sins of the "me first" variety.

Yet the American author Henry Miller, who spent many years in the capital in the 1930s and was better placed than most to make an objective judgement of the national character, stated that he had more respect for the French "than any other nationality on the face of the earth",

RED TAPE

Although the concept of bureaucracy was invented by the French, it's unforgiveable to call anyone a bureaucrat to his or her face. The polite reference is *fonctionnaire*.

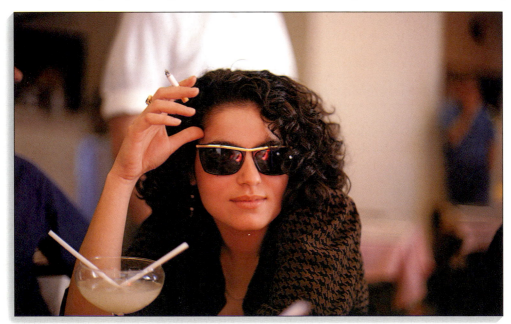

WHO LIVES IN PARIS?

More than 12 million people live in Paris and its suburbs, making it the seventh largest city in Europe. One of the most densely populated cities in the world, there are 20,000 people per sq. km in central Paris. Immigrants make up 12 percent of the population, each group forming communities in specific neighbourhoods. The Jewish population, the largest in Europe at 200,000, lives in the Marais; the White Russians in Montparnasse, North Africans by the northern Périphérique, Oriental Asians by Porte d'Italie in the southeast and Indian Asians behind the Gare du Nord. Around 8,000 live on the streets.

although they "may not be the jolliest, happiest or the easiest people to get along with".

Warm-hearted souls

Once one transcends the stereotype and becomes acquainted with the individual, the Parisian is no longer the intimidating, disdainful creature of legend, but actually quite human. Beneath that studied Parisian indifference beats a heart of intelligence, loyalty and warmth. Courtesy, charm and consideration, however, are not, perhaps, qualities which spring to mind while trying to navigate the busy intersection at Charles de Gaulle-Etoile, around the Arc de Triomphe, and yet they are abundantly evident in everyday life: in the friendly concern of Madame Defreitas, the concierge; the cheerful greeting of Monsieur Durand, the baker from his post; and the welcoming smile of Henri, behind the counter at the Café des Sports.

For, despite the reputed rudeness, Paris is a city in which the majority of the population are chivalrous to a fault and in which good manners are considered an essential part of everyday life. While a volley of verbal

AN AMERICAN IN PARIS

After living in Paris for several years during the 1930s, author Henry Miller praised his hosts by saying, "A Frenchman makes the best kind of friend. Though he may be difficult to get to know, once he lets you into his life he'll be your friend forever."

stress level can be partly put down to the fact that they live literally on top of one another, squeezed into, what are by most standards, extremely small apartments, which are packed into the city's 100 sq. km (40 sq. miles).

Virtually all Parisians live in apartments in a city where a house and garden is an almost unheard of luxury. Accommodation is not easy to come by, with families holding on to their homes for generations. There is

abuse will barely cause the average Parisian to bat an eyelid, forgetting to say *bonjour* or *merci* is considered unforgivable.

Desirable residence

In the 18th century, writer Jean-Baptiste-Louis Cresset stated: "It is only in Paris that one truly lives, elsewhere one just vegetates." Given such a universal acclaim for the city, it is hardly surprising that so many people want to live there. Paris is more densely populated than Tokyo, London or New York and the Parisians' high

intense competition for desirable living space, with an average of 150,000 people looking for a home at any one time. It is an oft-cited paradox that this battle for a place to live occurs in a city where 16 percent of apartments lie vacant.

Competition to live in the capital may be stiff but for the 2.2 million souls fortunate enough to have made it into Paris's inner sanctum, within the Périphérique, which separates the city proper from the often grim suburbs of decaying high-rises and barrack-like apartment blocks, the rewards are undoubtedly very high.

While many of the cities in other countries seem to be disintegrating from the effects of poverty and crumbling infrastructure, Paris is

---

LEFT: Parisians have perfected the art of cool.
ABOVE: stopping for a drink at a local bar.

thriving, not only as one of the world's most beautiful cities, but also as one of the best run.

Village ambience

The organisation of the capital into 20 *arrondissements* means that the city falls into easily recognised *quartiers*, or neighbourhoods, each with its own shops, markets, cafés and local eccentrics. Parisians develop lifetime attachments to their own *quartier*. Although large supermarket chains exist, residents often continue to support local merchants and to shop in specialised shops and the local markets. By always frequenting the same fishmonger or baker, taking their morning *café crème* at the local corner café, loyalties are soon built up and each *quartier* develops a village atmosphere in which everyone is known, at least by sight and often by name. Paris works, therefore, as a series of small communities co-existing under the umbrella of a big city. As a result, it is hard to imagine feeling lonely here for long.

TOO EXPENSIVE

"One reason Paris has so few problems is that the type of people who make the problems can't afford to live there."

— AN URBAN PLANNER

GOOD MANAGEMENT

Generous financing – with high taxation to match – and sound administration mean that Paris functions as a smooth-running modern metropolis:

☞ Mail can be delivered up to three times a day.
☞ During rush hour, Métro trains run every 80 seconds.
☞ Rubbish is collected seven days a week.
☞ Every one of the city's 1,300 km (800 miles) of streets is swept manually at least once a day.

Middle-class flight, which has adversely affected so many American cities, does exist in Paris but the affluent are still queuing up to live in a city which offers excellent public school education, first-class amenities, and a culture budget that could rival that of most Third World countries' overall spending for a year.

Neither is any expense spared on the parks and gardens. The Jardin du Luxembourg has 80 gardeners. In the summer months, students from the Sorbonne compare notes around the fountain, while designer-dressed toddlers sail toy boats on the pond, old men play chess or draughts, and lovers hold hands over an apéritif in the *salon de thé*. Come rain or shine, the joggers are there.

Lovers and lights

The city's image as the capital of romance has been built up by countless novels and films. It's an image that holds true for visitors, but for locals the reality fails to live up to the myth: one in three Parisians lives alone and half the city's marriages end in divorce. It is hard to be sad in Paris for long, though. The capital's reputation as a good-time girl stretches back before the bright lights came to Pigalle. In the 16th century,

BON CHIC BON GENRE

Marie-Chantals and Charles-Henris are easy to recognise. The women sport Hermès scarves, decorated with dead grouse, velvet hairbands and Chanel quilted handbags; the men, Lobb shoes, Dunhill pipes and even cravats are still in vogue.

Nova (101.5 FM), the city's most popular music station (and started by an Irishman), to hear the wonderful eclectic jumble of jazz, rap, soul, blues, reggae, African, French and international sounds. Mixed culture aside, however, there are certain recognisable types.

City stereotypes

The BCBG (*bon chic bon genre*), the French equivalent of the British Sloane Ranger or the American preppie, can be spotted easily

Nostradamus, prophet of gloom, offered the comforting thought that there was one spot on earth which could be relied on to lift the spirits: "As long as Paris does not fall, gaiety will exist in the world," he wrote.

The listening ranks

Parisians, as a whole, form such a diverse collection of races and cultures that it is almost impossible to characterise them. On the radio there are local stations broadcasting to African, Arab and Portuguese listeners. Tune in to Radio

in their main stamping grounds of Neuilly, Auteuil and Passy, the rich suburbs of the 16th and 17th *arrondissements* to the west of the city, collectively known as NAP. Also known under the acronym CPFH (*collier de perles, foulard Hermès* – pearl necklace, Hermès scarf), this type of Parisian, like their British and American counterparts, harbour a profound conservatism, adherence to classicism and traditional values and a marked dislike of anything new.

To see them in their natural habitat, try the VIP enclosure at Chantilly race course. They can also be spied sipping *chocolat africain* with pet poodle in tow at Angelina's *salon de thé* on Rue de Rivoli or, for the more *branché* (literally

LEFT: trendy is not necessarily chic.
ABOVE: a proud doorman at the Hôtel de Crillon.

"plugged in") of the species, dancing the night away at Les Bains Douches, Paris's perpetually "in" nightclub in an old swimming baths.

For a glimpse of a world at the opposite end of the spectrum, travel north on the RER commuter line B with "*les rappeurs*", the descendants of African and Caribbean immigrants. With shaved heads, baseball caps set backwards at a jaunty angle and *basquettes* (trainers) by Nike or Reebok, the names of American basketball and football heroes emblazoned across their chests, the style and philosophy of *les rappeurs* are imported directly from New York. Disenchanted with a life which offers few

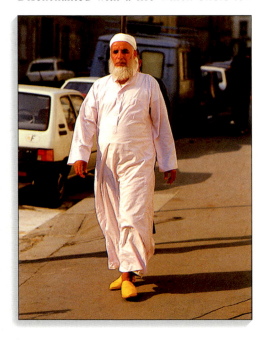

prospects in the grim housing estates which ring Paris, *les rappeurs* are nevertheless a gentle and graceful group compared to their more aggressive US counterparts.

In between these groups is the average Parisian – the *beaufs* (short for *beau-frère* or brother-in-law). A *beauf* is generally someone you are associated with by obligation rather than by choice, but good for a laugh, anyway.

To discover the city's Asian community, head for Belleville in the 20th *arrondissement* or to Chinatown in the 13th, near Porte d'Italie, which is home to the majority of the capital's 35,000 Vietnamese, Cambodians, Laotians, Chinese and Japanese. Here, green tea, 100-year-old eggs and *dim sum* compete for space with the French *baguette* and *café crème*.

For a taste of North Africa, visit the area around the Marché Dejean (Métro: Barbes-Rochechouart) in the 18th *arrondissement*. Mangoes, yams and plantain spill on to the street from tiny shops.

On the streets

The city's problems seem small compared with those of most other modern capitals. The roughest parts of Paris are probably as safe as the safest parts of most American and several British cities. Traffic congestion seems to be the Parisians' most oft-cited worry. Homelessness is also an increasingly visible problem, but the tradition of romanticising the *clochards* (tramps), who sleep rough along the Seine, keeps it from coming too high up on the list of most Parisians' main concerns.

In winter, however, with temperatures often plunging below zero, there is nothing romantic about life for the capital's homeless. The Government and various private organisations provide shelters with free room and board, medical care and job training. Attendance is voluntary, but the police will often round up those sleeping rough to protect them from the cold. Two newspapers, *Le Réverbère* and *Macadam*, Parisian equivalents of London's *The Big Issue*, endeavour to give the capital's homeless a measure of financial independence and self-respect.

But it is not all gloom and doom. One American resident recalls that, on her way home from the market one summer evening, she passed two good-natured *clochards*, who lived on a nearby grating. They were cooking up an omelette on a small spirit stove, had just opened a bottle of wine and were listening to jazz on their battered transistor. "*Bon appétit!*" they called, raising their glasses as she passed with her groceries. For her, that really said something about Paris.

A TASTE OF AFRICA

In the colourful Marché Dejean, African women in bright batik prints, babies slung papoose-style around their waists, sway gracefully among the stalls, picking out salt fish and papaya for the evening meal.

LEFT: dressed for the mosque.
RIGHT: posing in a Paris street.

THE WORLD'S GREAT FASHION HOUSES

"Haute couture" means high fashion in French, and in many other languages, too, for Paris has insisted on setting the style for what women wear

CHANEL

Poiret, Chanel, Dior... most of this century's best-known fashion houses have been French. At the end of the Second World War, discreet salons and their *vendeuses* gave way to the bright lights of the catwalk as Dior's New Look burst on to the scene with full skirts and luxurious, voluminous fabrics. During the 1950s, Chanel's commitment to freer, more carefree clothing paved the way to a more liberated style for women. But the revolution really came in the 1960s with Yves Saint-Laurent and fashion for the future, designed for the new youth generation, followed by the fun fashions, plastic and chain-link dresses of Courrèges and Paco Rabanne. With the extravagant styles and brilliant colours of Christian Lacroix in the 1980s, Paris hit the big time again. It now treads a tightrope between the traditional glamour of its image and the radical chic of many of today's designers.

Today, haute couture designs, costing thousands of dollars a garment, are worn by a handful of rich women. The designs, however, provide inspiration for new ideas and establish the all-important image for a designer which can then be applied to accessories, jewellery, perfumes and cosmetics – the real money-spinners for a fashion house.

△ **COLOURFUL LACROIX**
Christian Lacroix, who was born in Arles, introduced a flamboyant southern flavour to fashion in the 1980s, giving a much needed injection of *joie de vivre* to Paris.

▷ **CHRISTIAN DIOR**
Christian Dior claimed over half of all fashion exports by 1953. In the 1990s Dior appointed an Englishman, John Galliano, chief designer.

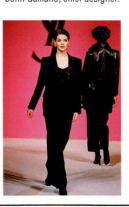

◁ **YVES SAINT-LAURENT**
Widely regarded as *the* designer of the 20th century, Yves Saint-Laurent has been celebrated for decades for his evening wear collection, including "le smoking", a tailored trouser suit which reappears, slightly reworked, on a perennial basis. YSL has an annual turnover of about $6 million, producing not only haute couture and ready-to-wear fashion, but also accessories and classic perfumes.

▷ THE GRAND FINALE

A fashion show traditionally ends with a wedding dress (such as this one designed by Yves Saint-Laurent) – an item which costs buyers several thousands of dollars.

▽ BACKSTAGE MAGIC

Europe's top make-up artists and hairdressers are enlisted to construct a distinctive "look" for each spring and autumn show.

▽ COCO CHANEL

Coco Chanel invented sunbathing and revolutionised women's fashion. Today, the Chanel line of boxy signature suits and quilted handbags with gold chains is designed by Karl Lagerfeld.

▽ WEIRD AND WONDERFUL

Some designers strike out into uncharted territory, such as this outfit by Issey Miyake, a Japanese who needs Paris to endorse his creations.

THE SHOWS MUST GO ON

Ernestine Carter, a legendary 1950s fashion writer, once tried to get a replacement ticket to a Balenciaga show because the original had been sent to the wrong hotel. Only when the original had been found, and torn up within earshot of the phone, was another ticket issued. Today, it is just as difficult to gain entrance to top Paris fashion shows – haute couture in January and July, and prêt-à-porter (ready-to-wear) in March and October.

Journalists, photographers, fashion buyers, actresses and pop stars jostle for tickets with the handful of women who will actually wear the original designs. The hierarchy is strict: front row seats of little gilt chairs are reserved for influential fashion editors, like Anna Wintour of American *Vogue* (famous for wearing her dark glasses throughout the show) and Suzy Menkes of the *International Herald Tribune*, who can make or break a collection.

Behind the scenes, designers bitch about each other's collections and vie for supermodels, who may do several shows a day, ferried by limousine between the Carrousel du Louvre, the exhibition hall where most of the shows are held, and their suites at the Ritz and George V hotels. They are pinned and tucked into an array of garments and neck-breaking heels, ready to sashay down the catwalk to the popping cameras and poised pens of the awaiting press.

THE DINING EXPERIENCE

Eating out in Paris can be a simple affair on the streets, a casual fling in a café or a more formal arrangement behind closed doors – the choice is yours

Ask a Frenchman to name a typically Parisian dish and you will usually receive a blank stare. After some coaxing, he might raise his eyebrows and hesitantly suggest *"steack frites"* (steak with French fries), before declaring that Paris is a city without any specifically regional fare. He would be wrong.

Parisian fare

One of the finest French cheeses, Brie, is produced within 50 km (30 miles) of Notre Dame, the windows of *pâtisseries* (cake shops) are crowded with Parisian specialities (*Paris Brest, L'Opéra, Saint-Honoré, Puits d'Amour, Amandines*) and the elongated French bread or *baguette,* no longer specific to the city, was perfected in Paris.

In short, Parisian foods are so frequently found throughout the country (and the world) that they are not considered "local" at all, and a list of typically Parisian bistro dishes reads like a *Who's Who* of French favourites, with such delights as *hareng pommes à l'huile* (smoked herring marinated in oil and served with warm potatoes), *tête de veau Gribiche (*calf's head with a mustardy-eggy sauce*)* or *entrecôte marchand de vin* (steak with red wine sauce), followed by *mousse au chocolat* or *île flottante* (floating island).

Such a listing, however, provides only a partial picture of what awaits the gastronomically curious in the French capital. Indeed, pavement vendors, café terraces, bistros, brasseries and elegant restaurants all offer different, but equally specific, "Parisian fare".

Street food

For centuries, the streets of Paris echoed with the cries of vendors carrying baskets that contained food ranging from fresh fish to *pâtisserie.* Today, that tradition still survives in the heart of

the Quartier Latin, along the Boulevard St-Michel, and in the Grands Boulevards around the department stores behind the Opéra. There, street vendors improvise stands during the winter and tempt passers-by with the irresistible smell of chestnuts roasting over a bed of coals. Others sell kebabs and anything with *frites* or

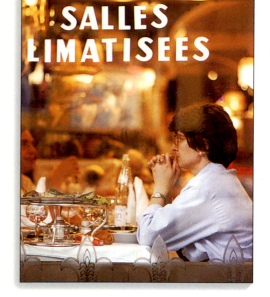

cook paper-thin crêpes on hot griddles, stuffing them with your choice of either a sweet or savoury filling. But for anything more substantial and varied you must go indoors, although not necessarily to a restaurant.

In a Parisian *charcuterie* you can buy ready-cooked or prepared dishes such as quiches, cheese- or mushroom-filled pastries (*rouleaux* or *feuilletés*), salads and specials like *poulet basquaise* (chicken with tomatoes and red peppers) or *brandade* (salt cod purée). A slice of pâté or ham can transform a crisp *baguette* from the *boulangerie* into a sandwich, making a delicious meal when finished off with cheese from the *fromagerie*, or a cake from the *pâtisserie*.

PRECEDING PAGES: ready and waiting at a fashionable watering hole.
LEFT: fresh fish on the menu.
ABOVE RIGHT: Paris takes its time over dinner..

Café lunches

When feet are sore and the queues in the shops are long, the marble-topped tables of pavement cafés look inviting at lunchtime. All cafés offer a variety of sandwiches (ham, cheese, pâté) which are notoriously short on filling and long on bread. This said, for a modest supplement, butter or *cornichons* (gherkins) can be included and Dijon mustard will be supplied free. Since the bread is generally freshly baked and the butter excellent, you can begin to overlook the paper-thin slices of ham or cheese.

Crôque Monsieur and *Crôque Madame* are two other popular on-the-run café lunches. The former, grilled ham and cheese on toast, becomes the latter with the addition of a fried egg on top, making a filling, if not particularly memorable, *casse-croûte* (snack).

Cafés also serve omelettes and *oeufs en cocotte* (baked eggs). An *omelette nature* (plain omelette), slightly runny inside and browned on the outside, with a *salade verte* (green salad) and a basket of sliced *baguette* is a typical Parisian lunch, good value and brimming with flavour.

Brasseries and bistros

One step up from the café is the brasserie. Literally translating as "brewery", brasseries serve

---

PARISIAN SPECIALITIES

"*La cuisine française* is not one cuisine but a score, regional in origin, shading off into one another at their borders and all pulled together at Paris," wrote A.J. Liebling in his book *Between Meals*. Here is a selection of traditional dishes:

- ☛ *Hareng pommes à l'huile* – marinated herring with warm potatoes.
- ☛ *Assiette de charcuterie* – cold platter of saucisson, ham and pâté.
- ☛ *Andouillettes à la Lyonnaise* – tripe sausages cooked with onions.
- ☛ *Rognon de veau à la moutarde* – calf's kidney,

cooked rare, surrounded by a mustard sauce.
- ☛ *Petit salé aux lentilles* – salt pork with lentils.
- ☛ *Escargots à la Bourguignonne* – snails in garlic and parsley butter in their shells.
- ☛ *Moules marinières* – mussels cooked in their shells in a white wine and garlic stock.
- ☛ *Gigot d'agnean rôti aux flageolets* – roast lamb with green kidney beans.
- ☛ *Tarte tatin* – upside down apple tart.
- ☛ *Paris Brest* – choux pastry filled with custard and sprinkled with almonds.
- ☛ *Ile flottante* – sweetened whisked egg whites floating in custard.

a wide variety of dishes, including some Alsatian specialities. They were introduced to the French capital in the late 19th century, at about the time when modern methods of brewing were being perfected. Cold draft beer was a novelty to Parisians then, as was *choucroute* (Alsatian sauerkraut), and both quickly became as popular as the *baguette*.

Surprisingly, given the distance of Alsace from the ocean, brasseries also specialise in shellfish platters –

A HEARTY MEAL

In a brasserie, sample the seafood as a prelude to the sauerkraut, piled high with pork and sausages, that attracts hungry Parisians on cold winter nights. Wash it down with a glass of Riesling and end with a wedge of Münster cheese.

1814. The Russian military were forbidden to drink, so whenever they dived into a bar in Montmartre, they demanded their refreshments urgently – *bistrot* – to avoid being caught.

Nowadays, any restaurant with a relaxed atmosphere can call itself a bistro (seafood restaurants are often called *bistros de la mer*).

Bistro-type food is also served in a *bar à vins* (wine bar). Although some more fashionable establishments offer smoked salmon and

baskets of oysters, clams, cockles and mussels often line the pavement outside and men in sailors' caps deftly open oysters under the admiring gaze of passers-by.

Where brasseries are generally spacious, festive and slightly "exotic", bistros are traditionally small, modest and very French, generally serving typically French fare, usually at moderate prices, although some can be as expensive as a starred restaurant.

The origin of the name "bistro" supposedly lies in the days of Allied occupation of Paris in

foie gras (fattened goose liver), the majority serve the kind of hearty food that Parisians call their own, including excellent cheeses and remarkable wines. In most wine bars, as opposed to traditional restaurants, it is possible to order one dish rather than a complete meal.

Behind the scenes

Staff who prepare food in a traditional bistro are cooks (*cuisiniers*), not chefs. Generally, a chef is more ambitious than a cook and places greater importance on innovation and technical prowess. Bistro cooks pride themselves on serving well-executed versions of traditional fare.

Chefs tend to run restaurants where the food

LEFT: dining out on a summer's day.
ABOVE: a fine array of cheeses to choose from.

reflects both changing fashion and/or personal taste. They labour in the hope that one day their talent will be discovered.

This trend grew rapidly to the fore in the 1980s with the rise of *nouvelle cuisine,* whose supporters applauded unorthodox combinations of taste and encouraged a break with routine. "*Les chefs*" listened to the message and, today, flourless butter sauces (*beurre blanc*) have replaced the *béchamel* of yore, *feuilletés* (thin layers of puff pastry) have

STAR TURNS

Of the 19 restaurants in France that earned the coveted Michelin three-star rating recently, five were in Paris, along with more than a quarter of those which were awarded two stars.

French provincial cooking

Unlike other big cities in France, Paris offers a varied and changing spectrum of foreign cuisines, as well as its own local fare, making it possible to sample not only food from the provinces, but also specialities from around the world.

The oldest and largest immigrant community in Paris is the rural French. Many a Parisian will tell you that *grandmère* came from the Auvergne, Brittany or an other distant corner of France. When times were hard,

supplanted the once popular *bouchées* (puff pastry shells), fish fillets have ousted whole fish from menus, *magret de canard* (duck steak) has displaced beef.

Tartare de poisson (raw fish) is no longer scandalous and exotic combinations or tastes (fruit with meat or fish, the use of spices such as ginger or unusual herbs like fresh coriander) no longer shock but are accepted as bold touches on the part of the chef. In short, a series of new "classics" is now being served not only in Paris but throughout France. However, remember to bear in mind that the great chefs are more interested in stimulating the taste buds than filling the belly – at a price.

they flocked to the city where the streets were supposed to be paved with gold. Restaurants sprang up around the spots where these newcomers first stood on Parisian soil. These were the railway stations.

The Gare Montparnasse is surrounded by bars, proudly draped with the flag of Brittany, and *crêperies bretonnes* (pancake restaurants or stalls) line the side streets leading to the station. The Gare de l'Est is flanked by Alsatian restaurants (and a famous Alsatian *charcuterie*), whereas, not far from the Gare de Lyon and the now-vanished Bastille station, traces of an Auvergnat community can still be seen.

Today, however, the regional cuisine most

popular with Parisians is that of Gascony, broadly referred to as the "Southwest". Throughout the city, speciality shops sell *foie gras* and even traditional Parisian bistros now offer *confit de canard* (preserved duck) and *magret* (duck steak), both literally unknown in Paris 50 years ago but adopted as enthusiastically and as quickly as sauerkraut was about a century earlier.

Couscous and phô

Of all the foreign cuisines to be found in the French capital, the two favourites are North African and Vietnamese. Modified to suit

can restaurants can be found in Belleville, northeast of Place de la République.

So Parisian fare is as cosmopolitan as the city itself. Regional produce is shipped daily to Paris and nowhere else will you find such a choice of French cheeses, wines, sausages or hams on offer. Parisians are used to this agglomeration of resources and take the exceptional variety of foods available for granted. "Their" food is the nation's finest. Going to the markets in the French capital is like taking a survey of France's agricultural wealth, while dining in Paris provides a glimpse of French cuisine at its best.

French taste, both offer emblematic dishes: *couscous* (steamed semolina served with a spicy meat and vegetable stew) and *phô* (beef and noodle soup) respectively.

Although the French do not consider any cuisine a rival to their own, they do enjoy *couscous* as a welcome change and students, in particular, are happy to find a source of inexpensive meals in the Vietnamese restaurants clustered together in the Porte d'Italie neighbourhood, not far south of their stamping ground in the Quartier Latin. A concentration of North Afri-

LEFT: bistros serve good-value, traditional fare.
ABOVE: a popular bistro in Montmartre.

COSMOPOLITAN CUISINE

As immigrants have settled in specific areas of the city, so restaurants have sprung up around them. Here is a rough guide to where they are:

- ☞ Chinese/Vietnamese: between Avenue de Choisy and Avenue d'Ivry near Place d'Italie.
- ☞ Indian: on the Rue du Faubourg St-Denis between Gare du Nord and La Chapelle.
- ☞ Middle Eastern: around Strasbourg St-Denis and Goutte d'Or, near Montmartre.
- ☞ Jewish: Rue des Rosiers in the Marais.
- ☞ Japanese: Rue Ste-Anne near Opéra.
- ☞ North African: Belleville.

Foods for thought

Not all visitors to Paris are as enthusiastic about certain classic dishes as the French. If almost everyone knows that *escargots* are snails and *cuisses de grenouille* are frog's legs, many an innocent tourist has unwittingly ordered calf's head (*tête de veau*) or calf's kidney (*rognon de veau*) thinking they were ordering veal (*veau*) or knowingly pointed to *andouillette* believing that some pork sausage would appear, only to discover a pungent tripe-filled creation instead.

The reader should not fear the above-named specialities – after all, 50 million French (and many a foreign visitor) relish their taste – but those with a meat-and-two-veg upbringing may well be shocked by the French penchant for animal organs or offal (*les abats*) and creatures that tend to hop or crawl.

Even certain favourite French fish are not to everyone's taste. *Anguille* (eel), a speciality in both the northern provinces and the southwest, is rarely served in Paris, although *oursins* (sea urchins), equally strange creatures for some, are a standard feature of most Parisian *plateaux de fruits de mer* (raw shellfish platters). *Moules* (mussels), generally cooked with a little white wine and eaten with French fries, are served in many modest brasseries and are as Parisian as

steack frites. And most Parisians prefer their herring smoked, filleted and left for several weeks with carrots and onions in a bowl full of peanut oil (this may sound terrible but, drained and served with a warm potato salad, they make an appetising first course).

Some familiar foods are presented in ways that have surprised more than one conservative diner. Steaks, lamb and duck, for example, will always be served *saignant* (rare) and those who prefer their steak medium are best advised to ask for it *bien cuit* (well done). *Confit de canard* (preserved duck) is a speciality that must be tasted to be understood and generally becomes a favourite once discovered. Squeamish visitors

DIFFERENT TYPES OF EATERIES

There is an assortment of places in which to eat, from the cheap to the expensive:

- ☞ Cafés, open from early morning until 9 pm, offer drinks (coffee, alcohol and soft drinks), snacks and light meals, outdoors or in.
- ☞ Wine bars, open all day mostly until 9 pm, serve snacks and light meals with wine.
- ☞ Brasseries offer vast menus, throughout the day until late, in a jolly atmosphere.
- ☞ Bistros, open at lunchtimes and evenings, are smaller and more intimate, offering fixed-price menus.

sometimes feel faint when they learn how this great southwestern delicacy is produced (ducks, after a life of being force-fed through funnels to fatten their livers into *foie gras*, are salted for several days, then simmered in their own fat for many hours).

Lastly, although French cheeses deserve their international reputation and are nowhere else as good as they are in France, wary first-time visitors reel from some of the more pungent ones. More specifically,

VEGETARIAN DESERT

Vegetarian dishes do not feature much in French cuisine, but you can often order two starters, instead of a main course, or phone a restaurant in advance to ask for a vegetarian meal to be prepared for you.

French etiquette

Regardless of your budget, some basic rules apply to all French meals and respecting them will help you avoid awkward situations, making you feel more comfortable, which will increase your pleasure.

Before any large meal, you will usually be offered an *apéritif*. In a French home, this can be anything from Scotch to port, but, in restaurants, a glass of champagne, white wine or a *kir* (white wine with *cassis* – a

Epoisses, Münster, Boulette d'Avènes and Vieux Lille are not for those who enjoy only mild Cheddar.

With all this in mind, don't consider France a country where bizarre food items and strange food habits make eating out a source of anguish rather than a pleasure. Raw vegetable salads (*crudités*) and omelettes are as common as smoked herring and snails, roast lamb more frequently served than calf's head and mild cheeses are as plentiful as strong.

LEFT: traditional zinc-topped bar that gave the cafés their nickname.

ABOVE: proud chefs, keeping up the style.

blackcurrant liqueur) are preferred. Don't feel obliged to order an *apéritif* if you are on your own but, if your French host offers you one, it can be taken as a (minor) insult to refuse.

French wine is, of course, the perfect accompaniment to French food. Alternatively, or additionally, you can order mineral water, sparkling or not (*gazeuse* or *plat*, respectively). Beer is drunk only with sandwiches, with very simple meals such as *steack frites*, as a thirst quencher or with Alsatian meals.

Even in extremely modest restaurants, a meal is composed of three courses: *entrées/hors d'oeuvres* (starters/salads), a *plat* (main course) and *dessert* (dessert). Americans who call their main dish an entree should beware – an *entrée* (as its name implies) is a first course in France.

Although an *hors d'oeuvre* may be a salad, a green salad with *vinaigrette* (French dressing) is never an *hors d'oeuvre*. Grated carrots or celeriac and boiled leeks with *vinaigrette* are typical *hors d'oeuvre* "salads". A *salade verte* (green salad) is often served after the main course and before cheese. Though fewer and fewer restaurants offer a green salad as a matter of course, most will be glad to prepare one and it makes a refreshing break midway through the meal.

Many Parisians prefer to end a meal with

cheese, rather than something sweet, so it's extremely common for moderately priced restaurants to offer fixed-price menus that include a starter, a main dish and cheese or dessert. When ordering cheese in a restaurant, a cheese platter will be presented. Don't hesitate to try a small slice of several cheeses (in private homes three is the polite number to try) and bear in mind that a cheese platter is almost never offered a second time.

Bread is an indispensable part of every meal. It should be on the table virtually from the time you sit down until the moment dessert is to be served. Bread is usually never eaten with butter, although some might be on the table in

LE BEAUJOLAIS NOUVEAU EST ICI!

On the third Thursday in November, the first bottles of the year's Beaujolais grape harvest arrive in Paris and the streets are festooned with bunches of grape-like purple balloons.

fancier restaurants to accommodate tourists. However, butter is served with radishes, country hams, sausages and Roquefort cheese. The French also use bread to mop up any left-over sauce on their plates – a practice considered to be bad manners in countries such as Britain.

On the menu

Good-value, fixed-price menus are common in fine restaurants and in simple eating places alike, but better restaurants tend to offer them only at lunch. If you plan on ordering the fixed menu in the evening, read it carefully to make sure that the words *déjeuner seulement* (lunch only) are not included.

Some better restaurants offer a *menu dégustation* (tasting menu) and usually everyone at table must order it to make it worthwhile, as it involves serving numerous courses and is difficult to orchestrate when some people at the table have ordered a simple three-course meal.

Coffee is never served with milk after a meal in France. *Café crème* is considered hard to digest, whereas black coffee is a stimulant to counteract that satisfied, sleepy feeling that can wash over you after a large, rich meal. This said, decaffeinated coffee (*café décaféiné, déca* for short) is available everywhere, made and served like an espresso.

Lastly, a wide range of *digestifs* (after-dinner drinks) is available in even the most ordinary of cafés. They range from the roughest of rough brandies (*grappa*) to the smoothest of cognacs. Fruit brandies are particularly good. *Poire* (pear) and *mirabelle* (plum) are two favourites. Brandies are never mixed with anything else and are always served at the end of a meal.

Voilà! You are now ready for a true dining experience. Speak slowly to your waiter (but not loudly), listen attentively, relax and *bon appétit!*

See Travel Tips *at the back of this book for restaurant recommendations – pages 271–75.*

LEFT: pavement dining at night.
RIGHT: enjoying a meal al fresco.

SHOPPING AROUND

"All that remained was the sense of an enormous Paris – one so enormous that it would always have enough to provide for shoppers" – EMILE ZOLA

In the capital of chic, even window-shopping is a more sensuous experience than elsewhere. The French call it *léche-vitrines*, literally "window-licking" and despite the city dwellers' *Métro-boulot-dodo* (commute, work, sleep) idiom, Parisians still find time for "*le shopping slow*".

Dripping with designer style, from monumental boulevards to manicured parks, from minimalist bedrooms to monogrammed boxer shorts (even Bohemianism is cultivated rather than simply born), Paris is the market leader in all that is tasteful, with tourist tackiness restricted to Eiffel Tower statuettes, Mona Lisa socks and rubber can-can dancers. As Coco Chanel said of her city, "Fashions come and go but style survives."

The French benchmarks are quality and authenticity: *la marque, la griffe* – the label, the stamp of authenticity and status. Certainly, snob appeal is part of the picture. As a rule, Parisians err on the side of conservatism, choosing a single classic item in preference to several less expensive options. This sense of conservative chic and innate good taste extends to the home. America invented the "total designer look", from co-ordinated bathrobes to bed linen and crockery, but France does it more stylishly.

Paris à la carte – by quarters

Luxury goods are a potent Parisian cultural symbol and are what the French do best. Such was the renown of Cartier in the 1930s that American designer Elsie de Wolfe dyed her hair blue at the age of 70 to match her new acquamarine tiara.

Perfumes, belts, bags, leather goods and fashionable clothes make sensible Parisian purchases. By the same token, seek out gourmet goodies such as chocolate, truffles or foie gras. Equally tempting are the quirky or classical

PRECEDING PAGES: the extravagant Art Nouveau interior of Galeries Lafayette.
LEFT: shopping in the fashionable Galerie Vivienne.
RIGHT: Parisian dolls waiting for a home.

objets d'art, from crystal and ceramics to prints and paintings. Although potential gifts are scattered throughout the *arrondissements*, there are geographical distinctions. The Right Bank, being the province of commerce and luxury, is the obvious area to shop for luxuries and status symbols, while the Left Bank, with a spirit of

culture, education and the arts, has an artistic soul and pocket.

Haute couture (*see pages 54–55*) is concentrated on Rue du Faubourg St-Honoré and Avenue Montaigne off the Champs-Elysées. Art galleries and trendy boutiques tend to be in the Marais, Bastille and St-Germain quarters. For idle window-shopping while away the day in the passages, the renovated arcades off the Grands Boulevards. For convenience or speed, plump for the *grands magasins* (department stores). For fun, visit the colourful markets or ethnic neighbourhoods, such as African Belleville. As the consummate shopping experience, stray no further than the St-Germain-des-Prés quarter, a gorgeous patchwork of galleries, bookshops, chic boutiques and twee *salons de thé*. Even non-shoppers will be converted, or at least find a café suitable for a member of the "shopaphobic" intelligentsia.

Champs-Elysées – open all hours

This grandiose part of the Triumphal Way is coolly clinical, but a mecca for late-night shopping and a magnet for sleepless tourists. The avenue is lined by endless airline offices, car showrooms, soulless and over-priced cafés and shopping arcades. **Virgin Megastore**, at Nos 52–60 (Métro Franklin D. Roosevelt) is Richard

area also includes the *grands magasins* (major department stores) and the glitzy designer paradise of **Rue du Faubourg St-Honoré** (*see page 131*) and **Avenue Montaigne**, off the Champs-Elysées. Shoppers can be easily seduced by the superficiality of wafty designer dresses, snooty shoe shops and seductive jewellers. The list of luxury boutiques on these two streets is a roll call of the top names in couture and *prêt à porter*. Aloof assistants assure a chilly reception from poorly dressed shoppers.

The city's ritziest shopping quarter is crisscrossed with passages – 19th-century arcades which have been forerunners of the ubiquitous

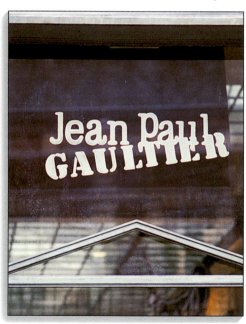

Branson's flagship store and offers the widest musical selection in Paris, from CDs, tapes and videos to tickets for concerts and Disneyland Paris (*see page 238*). Its appeal is enhanced by a late-night opening policy, a chic café and endless opportunities for people-watching. Around the corner, at 109 Rue de la Boétie, is **Prisunic**, a handy late-night supermarket. **Drugstore Publicis**, No 133 (Métro Charles de Gaulle–Etoile), is the place for late-night gifts, books and newspapers, a chemist and café.

Ritzy Right Bank

Encompassed by the broad boulevards landscaped by Baron Haussmann, this upmarket

LES GRANDS MAGASINS

Parisian department stores, or *grands magasins*, are bastions of consumer glory with parfumerie, books, fashion and food halls, alongside in-store tearooms and cafés for the weary. In Boulevard Haussmann, **Galeries Lafayette**, under an Art Nouveau dome, is a good place for an overview of designer *prêt-à-porter*. Nearby, rival **Printemps** is a domed 19th-century world within a world, with a fire station and post office to boot. Opposite Pont Neuf, **La Samaritaine** is full of bargains and supports a panoramic rooftop café. On the Left Bank, in Rue de Babylone, stands the city's first department store, **Au Bon Marché**, with a fantastic food hall – and cheaper.

shopping mall. Suffused with soft, hazy light filtering through the glass rooftops, they are ethereal, mysterious places, tinged with nostalgia. The most intriguing ones are **Galerie Vivienne** (*see page 126*) and the renovated **Passages des Panoramas** and **Jouffroy** (*see page 128*) and **Galerie Véro-Dodat** (*see page 127*).

Paris is blessed with superb specialist shops, deserving of their pretentious "temples of gastronomy" tag. There are emporia dedicated to snails, caviare, mushrooms, cheese,

MARKS ET SPARKS

Ironically, the French have fallen for Britain's Marks & Spencer, noted for its knitwear, underwear and, for Parisians, delicacies such as sliced white bread.

Les Halles – fast and furious

At the former market heart of Paris, the district around Les Halles – the first and second *arrondissements* – is the inner hub of the Right Bank. The rag trade is based in the northeast corner, around Place du Caire, and, in the grander parts to the west, designer jewellery, reputable antiques and museum shops abound.

Forum des Halles is a labyrinthine concrete shopping centre carved into the ravaged heart of the market. Essentially

honey and preserves. For a concentration of these bastions of de luxe go to **Place de la Madeleine**, where, at No 19, you will find **Maison de la Truffe**, the temple of truffles and more. The most famous is **Fauchon**, at No 26, the French answer to Harrods Food Hall, offering exotic groceries, charcuterie, its own label coffee and irresistible pâtisserie. Its rival, **Hédiard**, No 21, was founded in 1854 as a purveyor of fine foodstuffs to the upper classes. Its obsequious staff flit about the old-fashioned setting.

cheap and cheerful, the scruffy complex has been invaded by fast-food outlets and shoddy clothing stores for young people. One shining exception is FNAC (Forum des Halles, Level 2), the French institution selling maps, books, music and ticket bookings. **Mora**, 13 rue Montmartre, behind the church of St-Eustache, is where professional chefs buy kitchen equipment. The adjoining St-Denis area is good for china and crystal, as well as hookers and hoods.

Eastwards in the Opéra quarter, **Place Vendôme** has been the centre of the French jewellery district since the glamour of the *Belle Epoque*. It was here that Princess Diana acquired her "friendship ring" from Dodi al-

---

FAR LEFT: Kenzo's main shop in Place des Victoires.
LEFT: Eurotrash king's shop in the Bastille district.
ABOVE: a parfumerie – devoted to beautiful smells.

Fayed on the day of her fatal crash. The grandest house is **Cartier**, famed for the bejewelled parrot and panthers designed for the Duchess of Windsor, and for the diamond-encrusted watches which grace the wrists of Hollywood stars. Its rival, **Chaumet**, has been known as the Imperial jeweller ever since the house created Napoleon's coronation regalia. **Chanel** offers a more eclectic array of jewellery, based on Coco Chanel's original designs. Coco was the first designer to commercialise the mixing of gems and costume jewellery, with designs inspired by gifts from her English and Russian lovers.

The interminable **Rue de Rivoli**, running alongside the Tuileries and the Louvre, leads to the huge **La Samaritaine** department store and harbours the British bookshop **W.H. Smith,** at No 248, as well as the **Librairie des Musées des Arts Décoratifs**, at No 107, for a comprehensive range of books on art and architecture.

At the Louvre, beneath the inverted glass pyramid, lies an upmarket shopping mall, **Le Carrousel du Louvre**, where you can find a wide range of gifts, from designer crystal at **Lalique** to tasteful posters, books and scarves at the **Boutique du Musée**, the Louvre gift shop. Elsewhere Eiffel Tower earrings await.

Back across the Rue de Rivoli in the grounds

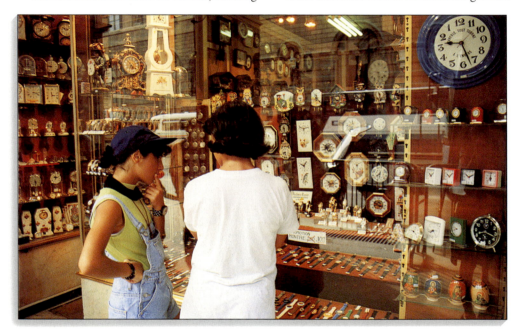

OFF THE CATWALKS, INTO THE STREETS

Ironically, the capital of haute couture is increasingly dominated by foreign designers. The Japanese have always believed in Paris and have injected a note of originality into the staid world of French design. **Comme des Garçons**, inspired by Junya Watanabe and Rei Kawakubo, provides innovative clothes. Other Japanese names include **Kenzo** and **Issey Miyake** (3 Place des Vosges). German Karl Lagerfeld has long masterminded design at **Chanel** (31 Rue Cambon).

Recently, the French fashion world has experienced the thrill or chill of a British invasion, led by John Galliano at **Dior** (32 Avenue Montaigne), the latest sensation on the Parisian scene. Stella McCartney, ex-Beatle Paul McCartney's daughter, is revitalising **Chloe** (60 Rue du Faubourg St-Honoré). However, the French are still a force to be reckoned with – **Agnès B** is a model designer of the younger school, classic yet casual and as quintessentially French as an elegant navy blue suit and **Jean-Paul Gaultier**, the ageing *enfant terrible* of the French fashion scene, presents his endearingly outrageous designs at 30 Rue du Faubourg St-Antoine.

Fortunately, Paris has numerous discount stores, called *Dépôts-Ventes*, which offer last year's stock, unlabelled stock clothes or designer seconds at up to 50 percent off. **Studio Lolita** is one such outlet. (For more shop details, see Travel Tips on pages 278–79).

of the **Palais Royal** are arcaded shops that were purpose-built in the 18th century and today harbour specialist shops. Nearby, the **Louvre des Antiquaires**, in the Place du Palais Royal, is a large antiques hypermarket, selling everything from chandeliers to chaise-longues. Art Deco mirrors and Sèvres porcelain vie with Gobelins tapestries and Post Impressionist paintings – not a place for bargain hunters.

The Marais – a new chic

The restored area of the Marais, straddling the third and fourth *arrondissements* (Métro St-Paul), is popular with the new aristocracy of

offers mouthwatering charcuterie and pâtisserie. Echoes of the Marais's old Jewish legacy survive in the Rue des Rosiers, with **Jo Goldenburg's**, *the* kosher deli (*see page 160*), and Middle Eastern street food such as falafel.

The adjacent **Rue Vieille du Temple** is the centre of the gay community and retro clothes scene, with 1950's kitsch and tasteless Abba outfits from the 1970s and period clothes from the 1920s onwards, including anything from cocktail dresses, Blues Brothers suits and hippy robes to army surplus and military wear. Nearby, **André Bissonet's** engaging musical instrument shop is the place to pop in for an

conceptual artists, fêted designers, media pundits and would-be philosophers. Although high rents have driven out many of the craft shops that once animated the area, the emerging new identity has its own charm. Workshops have been supplanted by minimalist shoe shops and quirky fashion boutiques. Many shops flout the law by opening on Sunday.

Rue des Francs-Bourgeois is the main shopping street, with its displays of designer lamps, mirrors and picture frames. **Rue Rambuteau**

18th-century piano to grace your *salon*.

Village St-Paul is an upcoming crafts centre with a villagey, arty crafty feel in the narrow streets and hidden courtyards. The cluster of workshops include antique shops, places for art and design, *objets d'art*, retro clothing and period furniture. Towards République are the rag trade wholesalers and loft-like art galleries ripe for an appearance in whimsical Eric Rohmer films. Depending on taste, the Marais shopping spree can be interspersed with visits to genteel *salons de thé*, nicotine-stained haunts or gay bars. **Les Maronniers** is an intellectual bar for floppy-haired philosophers claiming to be "counter-culturalists".

LEFT: window-shopping in the Rue de Rivoli.
ABOVE: Parisians will go to great lengths to find the right flowers.

Bastille – offbeat and funky

This hitherto working-class neighbourhood in the 11th and 12th *arrondissements* is succumbing to creeping gentrification and designer cool. Modernistic workshops and design shops reflect the Bohemian mood created by buskers, hawkers and boisterous bars and there are several funky outlets for street fashion. There is another branch of FNAC beside the Opera Bastille. **The Viaduc des Arts** conceals designer boutiques tucked into

IT'S IN THE BAG

"You may decide that instead of going on holiday twice a year to Bermuda, you only go once and buy a Hermès handbag for your wife."
– JEAN-LOUIS DUMAS HERMÈS

on the ground in the cheap and lively **Marché d'Aligre** (Métro Ledru Rollin), whose North African flavour gives it the air of a Moroccan bazaar (*see pages 78–79*).

Studious Left Bank

The **Quartier Latin**, centred on Boul' Mich and traditionally seen as the students' quarter, is – naturally – full of bookshops. **Shakespeare and Company**, 37 Rue de la Boucherie, is the place for new and secondhand English language books (*see page 188*). Around the

the railway arches on the north side of the street. While more fashionable than Les Halles, the quarter serves a bizarre mixture of tastes, with tatty ironmongers ill at ease alongside trendy computer stores and sushi bars. Canny shoppers focus on ceramics, sculpture and jewellery in sharp contemporary designs.

Cobbled alleyways lead off **Rue du Faubourg St-Antoine**, a district dotted with crafts workshops since the 18th century. Some of the best buys are from workshops which sell direct. **Prisunic**, a supermarket at 109 Rue de la Bastille, offers late-night shopping and collections of cheap clothes, crockery, kitchen equipment and foodstuffs. The Bastille keeps its feet

corner is the rival **La Librairie Canadienne**, with a good selection of American books and a warm welcome over coffee. **La Hune**, 170 St-Germain-des-Prés, is a Left Bank bookstore which is popular with night owls and city-bred *intéllos* (intellectuals).

Impoverished students head for the colourful Rue de Buci market (*see pages 78–79*), off Boulevard St-Germain, where there is a cornucopia of cheeses, fruit, chocolate and charcuterie. Further on, in **St-Germain-des-Prés**, the taste of luxury beckons at **Debauve et Gallais**, 30 Rue des St-Pères, in the guise of some of the finest chocolates in Paris.

As the home of monied opinion-formers and

power-brokers, St-Germain-des-Prés contains an eclectic array of shops. Cut by Rue Jacob, the quarter is lined with art galleries, antique shops, interior design shops and **Yves Saint-Laurent** at 12 Place St-Sulpice. The liberal, welcoming mood is echoed by the elegant but unintimidating boutiques.

Village Paris – a change of scene

Tucked into the shrinking remnants of working-class Paris, these old-fashioned yet quirky quarters, with the exception of Montmartre, are struggling to survive in the face of the city's gradual gentrification and the movement of the

figs. Although her records are not on sale locally, *chanteuse* Edith Piaf was allegedly born on the pavement of Rue de Belleville. **Place d'Italie** to the south, represents old-fashioned, ungentrified Paris. It is home to the Chinese and Asian communities, with Laotian and Cambodian specialist foodshops and Chinese eateries.

Montmartre, to the north, has a distinctly villagey feel. Although touristy, the galleries are fun and the foodshops lining hilly **Rue Lepic** (*see pages 78–79*) are delightful.

Around the Périphérique are the *marché aux puces*, or flea markets (*see pages 78–79*), fascinating places on an early Sunday morning.

proletariat to the insalubrious suburbs on the outside of the Périphérique. For shoppers in search of a Paris beyond designer shop windows, the diversity of these districts easily compensates for a certain shabbiness and a slightly above average crime rate.

Belleville, to the east, has a Jewish and North African flavour. Apart from the kosher butchers and bakers, there are *épiceries-buvettes* – old-fashioned shops-cum-cafés – as well as stalls laden with spices, artichokes and purple

LEFT: antiques and junk spill out on to the street.
ABOVE: one of the many retailers in the regal Place des Vosges, which buzzes with life at weekends.

DRESSING UP THE KIDS

Unlike leading American and British designers, who create casual clothes for children who act as children, French designers create clothes for children who act as adults. However, while unfortunate junior fashion victims may end up in tortured pinafores or frilly party frocks, not all French clothes are dressy. **Bon Point** (15 Rue Royale) is one of the smarter boutiques but more eminently practical options are offered by **Tartine et Chocolat** (66 Boulevard St-Germain) and **Petit Bateau** (13c Rue Tronchet). **Froment-Leroyer** (7 Rue Vavin) provides a comprehensive range of classic shoes.

BEST MARKET BUYS

The intimacy, vibrancy and villagey nature of neighbourhood markets act as a welcome antidote to the monumentality of "museum Paris"

Visitors who tire of the cool chic of haute couture Paris or the impersonality of the Grands Boulevards should plunge into the nearest market. The flavour of Paris is rarely further than a couple of Métro stops away. Foodies will be beguiled by the tantalising smells of Rue de Buci (flowers mingled with ripe tropical fruit and the aroma of roast chicken). Rue Mouffetard vies with Rue de Buci as the most picturesque market, enlivened by an accordionist who passes out sheet music to encourage sing-alongs. Idle browsers may prefer the *bouquinistes*, the quaint book stalls that line the banks of the Seine. Specialists are drawn to the markets dedicated to flowers, birds, postcards and stamps. For the rest, there are funky Left Bank markets selling secondhand designer clothes, rural markets laden with produce fresh from the farm, and exotic bazaars selling piles of scented mint and coriander.

FINE REGIONAL FOODSTUFFS

Marché d'Aligre is the most authentic and exotic experience, its stalls laden with olives, spices and nuts, like an Arab souk. However, the finest French regional foodstuffs (*produits de terroir*) are available from many Parisian markets. Visitors with a nose for the right stuff may be rewarded with chestnuts from Corrèze, *choucroute* from Alsace, or calvados and camembert from Normandy. Street snacks are readily available, from pastries such as *tarte tatin* (apple tart) to sweet or savoury *crêpes*. For eating on the hoof market fare includes a *baguette* (French stick) filled with *charcuterie* from the Auvergne, Alsace or the Ardennes. Foodies will also seek out honey from Provence or the Morvan, dairy produce and salad leaves from the Ile de France, and fruit and goat's cheeses brought from the Loire. Bear in mind food markets are generally closed on Monday (*see* page 279).

◁ **CAST IRON MONUMENTS**
Marché St-Quentin, built in 1910, is the quaintest remaining cast-iron hall.

△ **PLUMP FOR THE POT**
Close to the Louvre, the colourful Quai de la Mégisserie is lined with plants and pet shops, with geese, ducks, rabbits and even the odd goat often destined for the cooking pot.

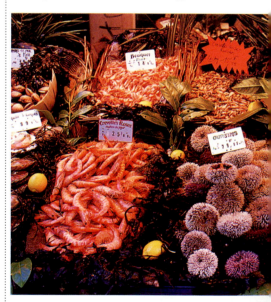

△ **FRESH FISH**
Glistening fish are displayed on the stalls of a *poissonier* (fishmonger's) on the Rue du Seine. Equally fine seafood, including tuna and turbot, lobster and fish-stuffed *rillettes* can be bought in Rue Lepic or in Rue Daguerre in Montparnasse.

◁ FRUIT AND VEGETABLES

Rue Lepic and Rue Mouffetard markets are both awash with fruit and vegetables. Although technically a street of fabulous food shops, Rue Lepic feels more like a chaotic market, with its cosmopolitan air and stalls lining the slopes of Montmartre. On the Left Bank, the chicly photogenic Rue Mouffetard market winds down the hill from the elegantly domed Panthéon.

▽ CURED MEATS

The *boucherie-charcuterie* stalls and delicatessens on Rue Mouffetard are a feast for the eyes. On display are *boudin blanc* (white pudding), *foie gras* (fattened goose liver), duck pâté and ham from the Ardennes, Burgundy or Basque country and *boudin* (black pudding). *Andouillettes* are another delicacy made from tripe.

ALL THE FUN OF THE FLEA MARKETS

Parisian flea markets, known as *marchés aux puces*, were originally clustered around the ancient city gates, and largely remain on the outskirts. At best, they offer a melange of Louis XV armchairs, Art Deco lamps, antique wrought-iron gates and rustic Moroccan pottery. Among the curios are former Soviet combat jackets, *fripes* (secondhand clothes) and general *brocante* (junk).

The best-known flea market is by Porte de Clignancourt (Sat–Mon). Set in northern Paris, this sprawling, touristy affair is home to 1,500 dealers and specialises in new, retro or period clothes, as well as books, china, linen, reproduction furniture, jewellery, junk and some genuine antiques.

Porte de Vanves (Sat–Sun) is the haunt of amateur and professional dealers. Marché d'Aligre (Métro Ledru-Rollin) is one of the most complete markets, selling food, mirrors, cutlery and clothes.

◁ BOOKSELLERS

The *bouquinistes* are second-hand and antiquarian booksellers whose stalls line the Left Bank of the Seine between the Quai d'Orsay and Ile de la Cité. They sell musty, leather-bound volumes as well as records, sheet music and prints.

▷ AFRICAN SPICE

Marché d'Aligre is a popular market with a spicy North African flavour. Olives and spices vie with mint tea, *citron pressé* and fresh fruit and vegetables.

A PARIS PORTRAIT

Soak up the atmosphere of present-day Paris – take time off to wander the streets and sit in cafés, just watching the world go by

The secret of appreciating Paris is to love life. The surest way to seize the city for yourself is to put aside its quicksand of historical facts and its overwhelming grandeur. Simply wander about down shady boulevards, or along the quiet and gritty pathways in the parks, soaking up the atmosphere created by the past, alert for those telling everyday details that make this city unique.

Indeed, the best way to start may be to stop. Watch Paris breathe – heave, rather – with an endlessly fascinating mixture of energy and relaxation, passion and disdain. Find a bench, or better still a café, and watch the world go by: the strangers wandering in awe, the chic, young woman in a hurry, groups of teenagers chattering, the impatient motorist, the lovers with eyes only for each other. Against the background of traffic noise rises the chirp of birds, the chatter of conversation and the chink of glasses at the tables on the pavements.

Zelda Fitzgerald epitomises the spirit and beauty of Paris in a letter to her husband, F. Scott Fitzgerald in 1930, "Was it fun in Paris? Who did you see there and was the Madeleine pink at five o'clock and did the fountains fall with hollow delicacy into the framing of space in the Place de la Concorde, and did the blue creep out from behind the Colonades in the Rue de Rivoli through the grill of the Tuileries and was the Louvre gray and metallic in the sun and did the trees hang brooding over the cafés and were there lights at night and the click of saucers and the auto horns that play Debussy…?"

All the pavement's a stage

Parisians live right at the very heart of Paris, which deepens the spirit, unlike a city such as London, large parts of which are only occupied during the day by a tide of commuters that ebbs back to suburban gardens in the evening. The streets of Paris are very much alive by day and

PRECEDING PAGES: merry-go-rounds pop up everywhere.
LEFT: soaking up the atmosphere at the Louvre.
RIGHT: relaxing in the Jardins des Tuileries.

by night, and in this grand theatre every pavement is a stage.

Look out for the fashionable ladies with their tiny yapping dogs and keep a sharp eye out for what they leave behind. Look out, too, for the street-cleaning machines, which resemble a cross between a golf cart and a toothbrush –

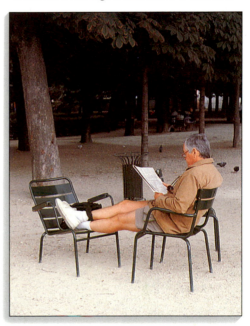

Paris, it should be said, is a much cleaner city now, an army of garish-green uniforms washes the streets endlessly – but the dogs still win. And, wherever you go, keep an eye out for the Eiffel Tower, which, thrusting skyward out of a landscape of classic architecture, was once described by writer Jean Cocteau (1889–1963) as the Notre Dame of the Left Bank.

Taking Paris easily

As a first-time visitor to Paris, you may already have a strong impression of the city from other people, literature and films, giving you high expectations. Paris can be a most daunting city, but don't be afraid to admit it, if your sense of duty to see as many sights, monuments, museums and galleries as possible is at odds with your inclination, your timetable and even your energy on what is supposed to be a holiday. Take it easy. Just as *Hamlet* is more than a sequence of quotations, so Paris is much more than a catalogue of sights.

A city of ideas

Connoisseurs of the capital often say that it is still a medieval city in essence. Some of its monuments are certainly medieval and its undying taste for bawdy high-living can be described as medieval but, essentially, it is an *everyday* city, briskly mundane in the midst of the breathtaking grandeur.

Honoré de Balzac (1799–1850), the great novelist, thought of Paris as a city of ideas, those that smile at you at street corners or splash you with mud from carriage wheels.

Where compression and excitement are concerned, the city of New York is quite similar to Paris, but this landscape of mighty monoliths gives the stroller the impression of being built from the sky down, whereas Paris was built from the pavement up. Balzac also compared Paris to an ocean, with uncharted depths ever-yielding new pearls and monsters.

PARIS EDICTS

Throughout the city streets you will come upon evidence of the essentially Napoleonic taste for edicts and statutes, simple instructions backed up by the date of the relevant law. Take, for example, the sinister and frequently encountered citation of a law preventing the pasting up of posters – it is still dated April 1943, the period of the German Occupation. Or even the prohibition against public drunkenness announced in the same edict as the forbidding of under-age drinking and displayed as a tobacco-yellowed notice in every bar, "*Protection des mineurs et répression de l'ivresse publique*". Very few take notice of the "*Défense de fumer*" (no smoking) signs.

Avoiding the traffic

Even the traffic of Paris has its place in French history. In 1610, two dozen or so attempts on his life having failed, King Henry IV was stabbed to death as his carriage was trapped in a traffic jam in Rue de la Ferronerie. Moreover, the great sweeping Grand Boulevards of Paris today were not built for the benefits of traffic, but for better control of a restive civilian population: narrow streets lent themselves nicely to barricades, whereas boulevards were better for baton charges.

The most conspicuous blockade these days is the parked car. Paris is the centre of that continental sport, which involves the nudging forwards and backwards of a line of parked cars to allow just one more to squeeze in. Among the signs you may notice on the street is the one which warns of the risk of towing away – yet all it says is that you may have your car towed away if your parking is *gênant*, a word meaning mildly annoying.

Never so hugely was a city map redrawn when Baron Georges Haussmann, Napoleon III's Prefect of the Seine, was ordered to rebuild Paris. Climactic

What's in a Sight?

In the past, sights were rarely created to be sights. Even the Eiffel Tower, built to vaunt French technology at the 1889 World Fair, was all set to be dismantled, until it was discovered that it made a perfect radio mast.

Wander the streets

Paris is a compact city, worth a good walk – just as your feet tire, your soul gasps. On a practical note, the street names are well displayed. Curiously, the name plates have been designed to look as if they were in relief, with something like a shadow marked on the borders. This is Paris seeking to "present" or thematise itself.

It is easy enough to get lost in Paris, even in Haussmann's grand scheme – possibly even more so, since his

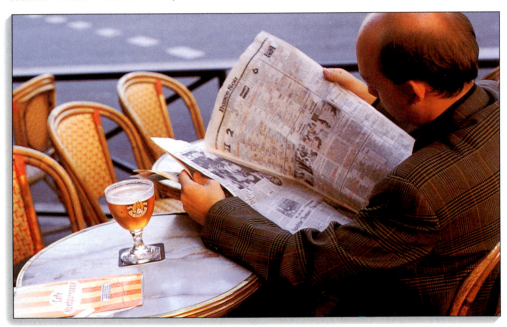

views and sweeping carriage-trots this way and that across the city were created by a splintering geometry of long avenues meeting in starburst junctions (Place de Ternes, Place Victor Hugo) or round a great building like an exuberant but organised dance (the Opéra, the Madeleine, even the Gare St-Lazare).

The most relaxing way to see the city on the move is to leave the car at home and travel around by bus (*see* Travel Tips, *pages 266–67*). From your seat by the window, you can watch Haussmann's drama unfurl around you.

Left: taking the lunch for a drag.
Above: time out for a beer with the newspaper.

passion for vista gives rise to a great quantity of extremely sharp-angled street corners, which can make you feel like a mouse lost in a mosaic of slabs of cheese, while, at the same time, may be hiding small shifts of direction in the pattern, leading you off course.

We expect old buildings to be askew or awry. Those old tall houses on the south bank of the river, by Notre Dame on the Ile de la Cité, clutter and lean in on each other like drinkers overfilling a bar, not quite all falling over. Even today this quirkiness continues.

Out just beyond the city limits, in the business area known as La Défense, the Grand Arche that is the focus of the central esplanade

– itself a perfectly straight continuation of the line, constituted by the Champs-Elysées and the Avenue de la Grande Armée, passing through the Arc de Triomphe – is at a slight angle to the rest of the Triumphal Way. In fact, La Défense itself is a phenomenon: whereas most cities could do with a dose of old Paris, new Paris wanted its own high-rise area without submerging its past. La Défense expresses the Parisian taste for high-rise technology, just as the Eiffel Tower before it – and Notre Dame before that.

As you wander around Paris, once your eye has acquired the habit, there is plenty to notice:

are now hanging in the prestigious museums around Paris.

For students, the area on the Left Bank, south of Notre Dame, is the focus of university life. It became known as the Quartier Latin as a result of a long tradition of everyone, including the servants, having to speak Latin in the university precincts, until Napoleon I stopped it at the beginning of the 19th century.

The Sorbonne is the oldest university in the world, and student life is conducted in the streets and cafés, once frequented by such literary figures as Jean-Paul Sartre and Albert Camus, by Ernest Hemingway and Henry

the grills round trees, the stray café chairs that all but block the narrowest passageway, the rolls of old carpet used to divert the morning rivers that flow down the gutters.

As for the gutters themselves, they contain numerous, alarmingly-wide drain-holes that yawn down into the underworld, which, in fact, is open to visitors – the sewers of Paris are a popular attraction.

Exploring the quartiers

For aspiring artists, this city's centre is Montmartre. Here they can tread in the footsteps of those who spent their poverty-stricken youth, a century before them, creating masterpieces that

PAVEMENT THEATRICALS

During the student riots of 1968 (violent enough but not as bad as the second lot of student riots in 1223), there was a rebellious slogan to the effect that under the pavements lay the beach – *sous les pavés la plage*. The gist of this was that freedom, symbolised by the beach, was represented by the sand, typically to be found immediately under the cobblestones. Such freedom, therefore, could be won by hoisting the cobblestones at the police. After the riots, most of the pavements were replaced by unlobbable tar. The revolutionary slogan has since been used by a car manufacturer, replacing "under" with "on", to advertise the easy ride of a new model.

Miller. Aspiring writers are still drawn to the area – every nation seems to have a poet or painter who has adopted Paris. Can you spot one?

Today's café clientele

Taking a break in a café outside on the pavement, you will see a good cross-section of Paris life coming and going alongside you. Almost every café has the paragon of fashion and the scallywag reading Nietzsche, their attention momentarily caught by the smartest of businessmen making a brief call for a snatch of coffee and a private word to each other on their way, or by old cronies arguing over politics or

pétanque. And then there are those with nothing much else to do but pass the time of day holding on to their café tables for as long as possible. All to the music of video games and, above that, the roar of the traffic.

In the Marais (the web of streets to the east of the Centre Georges-Pompidou), one of the most characteristic and varied quarters of Paris, the ancient contrasts between artisans and aristocrats can still be sensed today. Here it is quite possible for an aristocrat to find himself living next door to a carpenter or shoe mender. Wealth

LEFT: a busker playing for his supper.
ABOVE: a serious discussion in the Place des Vosges.

and a person's position in society was once defined by the width of his property in the Marais, rather than its height, as it was around the Grand Boulevards, where social standing was measured vertically – the finest apartments on the first floor, the most rudimentary on the topmost. Today, amid the resulting jumble of old aristocratic mansions and workshops, you can buy vegetables in one shop and the rarest of fashionable high-tech accessories next door.

The mish-mash of Marais streets, never quite at right-angles, almost intentionally seem to hide one of the finest, most serene town squares in Europe, the Place des Vosges, the last duelling ground of Paris.

A city to suit your mood

Most cities have a contrast between seedy and splendid: in Paris the mixture is like a chemical reaction whose by-product is energy, sheer energy. A hundred years ago, Montmartre was a seedy quarter that became the genuinely creative crucible of Europe, a shanty town that gave birth to Cubism and a gossip madhouse of chattering poets.

You will not find much of the same energy now – and the seediness lies tucked away from a rather too presentable, model village neatness – but if you take in the unique view across the whole of Paris, a swordfight splatter of roofs shimmering beneath, a capital at your feet, you may understand the vaunting, almost arrogant fertility of that creative world. To the artists of the time it made sense to live in a shack and to experience the low life, while looking down on a quilt of palaces and boulevards.

There is a street or square in Paris for every mood – and for all weathers. Paris has shifting weather, blue, fluffy-white or damnably grey. It can look its best shimmering after a downpour, or in the lazy early light before breakfast, when the smell of fresh bread and coffee lurks behind every café front. So, take a seat. Breathe in. Mind the dog. If the coffee tastes terrible, that is history, because Casanova made *exactly* the same complaint.

ARCHITECTURE

A veritable textbook of architectural history, Paris is a living museum that displays an evolving heritage in which the new complements the old

Two thousand years of history and seven centuries of artistic brilliance have made Paris a city rich in architecture. Yet invasions, sieges and insurrections have irreparably destroyed a great number of the capital's architectural masterpieces.

Fortunately, the many famous monuments that we can enjoy today had a narrow escape in 1944. As Allied troops approached Paris, Hitler gave General Dietrich von Choltitz, the occupying governor of Paris, the order to blast every single historical edifice to pieces, so that the Allies' triumphant entry would be greeted by a field of smoking ruins. Charges of dynamite were laid under Les Invalides, Notre Dame, the Madeleine, the Opéra, the Arc de Triomphe and even at the foot of the Eiffel Tower. But, at the last minute, unable to perpetrate such sacrilege, von Choltitz refused to give the order and ultimately surrendered the city intact to General Jacques-Philippe Leclerc, liberator of Paris.

Despite the various devastations in its history, Paris has retained examples of all France's architectural styles, especially from the 12th century and the beginnings of the Gothic era onwards, creating a textbook of architectural history, a living museum. It requires little imagination to conjure up a sense of the past. Over the centuries, the best architects, sculptors, masons and painters have preserved this sense, while at the same time looking forward. This explains the extraordinary juxtaposition of different styles of architecture, complementary or contrasting but seldom jarring or in bad taste.

Roman remains

Nothing is left of the wooden huts occupied by the Gallic Parisii on the Ile de la Cité. However, thanks to the Romans' development of an extremely durable concrete, from stone quarried out of Mont Ste-Geneviève, their ruins – the site of their settlement, Lutetia – can still be found in the Quartier Latin. Several streets, such as the Rue St-Jacques and the Boulevard St-Michel are built on ancient Roman roads. Lutetia was not an important city, but it was equipped with the buildings necessary to Roman civic life – a palace, forum, theatre, arena, baths and temples. The vestiges of one of these baths can be seen in the garden at the Musée National du Moyen Age – Thermes de Cluny and the ruins of the arena (Arènes de Lutèce) have also survived.

Destruction by the Vikings

Unfortunately, nothing is left of the Merovingian and Carolingian eras (6th–9th centuries), because the Vikings burnt and pillaged Paris on several occasions during this period.

Romanesque, with a propensity for ponderous and gloomy structures, hardly left a mark, either. One of the few remnants of this artistic and religious movement that spread throughout France at the turn of the first millennium is the steeple of the St-Germain-des-Prés church.

In the 12th century, Paris and the Ile de France turned to the newest rage in religious

---

NOTHING BUT THE BEST

For centuries, Paris has traditionally attracted the best architects, sculptors, masons and painters.

THROUGH THE AGES

Architecture in Paris embraces a whole spectrum of styles, which have been meticulously preserved and restored. Here are a few examples:

- ☞ Gothic: Notre Dame (1160–1345), Sainte-Chapelle (1245), Tour St-Jacques (1523)
- ☞ Renaissance: Cour Carrée facade of the Louvre (1549–56), St-Eustache (1532–1637)
- ☞ Classical: Versailles (1668), Les Invalides (1671–76), Place Vendôme (1698)
- ☞ Neo-Classical: Panthéon (1764–90)
- ☞ 19th century: Opéra Garnier (1862–75)
- ☞ Modern: La Défense, Opéra Bastille (1989)

PRECEDING PAGES: a fine example of wrought ironwork at Gare de l'Est.
LEFT: Gothic arches line the nave of Notre Dame.

architecture: Gothic. Lighter, more slender and luminous than previous architecture, Gothic coincided with the strengthening of the French crown and a fresh religious fervour inflamed by the Crusades. Gothic architecture is distinguished by pointed arches and the combined use of ribbed vaults with flying buttresses, a technique that allowed windows to replace walls and walls to soar towards the heavens.

Gothic marvels

The most beautiful religious edifice in Paris, the cathedral of Notre Dame epitomises the perfection of Gothic style. The construction of Notre

revivalist Eugène Viollet-le-Duc (1814–79) eventually started in 1841, as a result of Victor Hugo's novel, *Notre Dame de Paris* (*The Hunchback of Notre Dame*) and prodding by the Romantic movement, and took 23 years.

Close by, stands Sainte-Chapelle, a famous and fragile-looking church in the High Gothic style, which differs from Notre Dame in that the vast stained glass windows (the oldest in Paris) are supported by only a thin framework of stone. Nestled within the walls of the Palais de Justice, the church was built by St Louis (King Louis IX) in 33 months to shelter the Crown of Thorns and other so-called relics.

Dame began in 1163 on the site of a Romanesque church, which had been built on the foundations of a Carolingian basilica, which in turn had been built on the site of a Roman temple, and took 200 years and several generations of architects and craftsmen to finish it.

Like all medieval churches, Notre Dame was completely painted on the inside. The paintings were the way medieval man learned the Bible stories and the use of colour was meant to glorify God and breathe life into the sculptures. The statues over the triple front doors were once multicoloured on a gold background.

The building began to decay during the 17th century, but restoration by 19th-century Gothic

An Italian influence

War in Italy, in 1495, brought the French into contact with Renaissance grandeur and the style, characterised by a contempt for all Gothic forms and a rediscovery of antiquity, was imported to France. In architecture, the ribbed vault disappeared in favour of flat ceilings with wooden beams. Medieval fortresses gave way to genteel palaces and Greek-style colonnades were re-established.

Among Paris's main exponents of the Renaissance were architect Pierre Lescot (1510–78), whose finest work is the west wing of the Louvre, and Jean Goujon (1510–68), who sculpted the magnificent reliefs on Lescot's facade at the

Louvre and worked on the Hôtel Carnavalet (1544) in the Marais. Goujon's work can also be seen on Lescot's Fontaine des Innocents, near Les Halles, which provides an example of Renaissance sensuality jubilantly rejecting the sacred hierarchy of figures imposed by the Middle Ages.

The Classical era

At the end of the 16th century, while the Renaissance had succumbed to the Baroque movement in the rest of Europe, French architects were looking

a statue of the king in the middle of the large central garden. The Place des Vosges, commissioned by Henri IV in 1609, was the first and most elegant of the Classical royal squares. Edged with graceful arcades, the square started out as the Place Royale, until it was changed in the Revolution.

In grand style

The Sun King certainly left his mark on Paris and the Ile de France, imposing his personality in true grand style on the palace of Versailles. Started in

towards sobriety and Classicism. A desire for strength and clarity, born of rationalism, dominated architecture. The Classical style is based on symmetry, simplicity of line and wide open perspectives, and the Pont Neuf, the first bridge to be built without houses on it in 1606, and now the oldest in Paris, was one of the first examples of such architecture.

During this period, large squares were created, surrounded by uniform buildings and with

1668, the château symbolised the absolute power of the monarch and employed the top designers of the time – architects Louis Le Vau and Hardouin-Mansart, painter Charles Lebrun and landscape gardener André Le Nôtre. Other fine examples are the Palais du Luxembourg (1631) and the Hôtel des Invalides (1670).

After Louis XIV's death, building was kept to a minimum until the 1750s, when the Neo-Classical movement turned to forms lifted directly from antiquity, taking the utmost care to reproduce what recent progress in archaeology had brought to light. Jacques-Ange Gabriel built Place de la Concorde and the Ecole Militaire and Jacques-Germain Soufflot designed

LEFT: Place des Vosges, the first and most elegant of royal squares, built by Henri IV.

ABOVE: Notre Dame was black before it was cleaned in the 1960s with forceful jets of pure water.

the Panthéon, originally a church and today a necropolis for the great and good of France.

With the coronation of a triumphant Napoleon and the installation of a new Empire at the beginning of the 19th century, came the triumphal arch (Arc de Triomphe du Carrousel and Arc de Triomphe) and the triumphal Neo-Classical Rue de Rivoli.

Baron Haussmann's legacy

With the exception of a few elite neighbour-hoods, post-Revolution Paris was a squalid city. Poverty-stricken communities, with their filthy, narrow alleyways and miserable, overpopulated

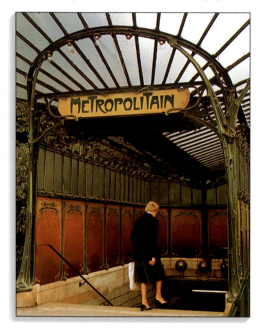

shacks, were constantly on the brink of revolt. For obvious sanitary reasons, but also to cir-cumvent the risk of riots, Napoleon III and the Prefect Baron Georges Haussmann began a sweeping urbanisation programme in the 1850s.

Medieval Paris all but disappeared. Whole quarters were razed and wide, tree-lined avenues, more difficult to barricade, took the place of grimy backstreets.

The city of Paris today is still strongly stamped with Haussmann's ideas. After clear-ing out slums and opening up the area around the Louvre, he concentrated on expanding the system of boulevards through the city centre, started by Louis XIV. A small hill then known

as the Butte St-Roch, occupied by windmills, a gallows and a pig market, was intended to be their centre. It is hard to picture that today as you stand on the level, busy Place de l'Opéra, looking at Charles Garnier's opera house, the Second Empire's most sumptuous construction.

Monsieur Eiffel's tower

The second half of the 19th century was very rich in creativity. Wrought-iron architecture made its debut with the Grand Palais, the Pont Alexandre III and, of course, the Eiffel Tower. Panned by the architectural critics during its construction in 1889 for the World Exhibition, the tower is now the universal symbol of Paris. It was originally designed to be a temporary exhibit, along with "a grotesque city of plaster, staff and pasteboard... buildings from an Asian temple to a Swiss chalet, from Kanaka hut to medieval Paris, Chinese pagoda to Montmartre cabaret", as one contemporary visitor remarked on a trip to the city. As Gustave Eiffel's contro-versial creation, symbolising the uneasy rela-tionship between science, industry and art, rose higher and higher, bets were placed on when it would topple over.

When the engineer himself climbed up to plant the French flag atop his iron latticework fantasy, the cheering crowds comprised ordi-nary Parisians who admired his vision; the snobbish aesthetes stayed away.

This was also an eclectic period. The Hôtel de Ville (city hall) on the Right Bank was rebuilt Renaissance-style, while the Sacré-Cœur was created in the antique tradition, and numerous churches toed the Gothic line. Reacting against these academic approaches and inspired by Japanese art, Hector Guimard established the Art Nouveau movement. The sinuous plant forms and curving lines, natural and Baroque at the same time, were decried by some as "noodle style". Guimard designed several buildings in the 16th *arrondissement*, including the Castel Béranger (14 Rue de la Fontaine), and also the city's Métro entrances, many of which, such as Porte Dauphine and Abbesses, still remain.

The modern age

Both the modern movements of the 1920s and 1930s and Art Deco were born in the 16th *arrondissement*. Mallet-Stevens (Rue Mallet-Stevens) and Le Corbusier (Maison Jeanneret, 8 Square du Dr Blanche) were the main artisans of the Cubic style of architecture, all pure line and concrete. The Palais de Chaillot is a typical example of the grandiose, Neo-Classical architectural style that made a great impression, particularly on the Third Reich and Soviet Russia.

From the 1960s, Paris underwent a transformation. Facades were cleaned, the Métro was modernised and old parts of the city, such as Les Halles, were demolished. New architectural projects were developed, keeping up with technical advances by building upwards (La Défense and Tour

glass, in the Cour Napoleon, is already world-famous. Generally lauded for its beauty and efficiency, the largest, central pyramid has earned its place on the architectural stage of Paris.

The new Opéra Bastille, like Peï's pyramid or the Géode at La Villette, exemplifies the harmony of modern architecture in Paris by reflecting the neighbouring buildings and the ever-changing Parisian sky. Gothic architecture, in its time, held a mirror to society in much the same way.

Montparnasse), expanding indoor space (Centre Georges-Pompidou, La Villette, Bercy) and experimenting with new materials that capture, reflect and admit light.

In the 1980s, the Chinese-American architect I.M. Peï was employed to design a new entrance and orientation centre for the Louvre. His solution, an illusionistic "landscape" of pyramids in stainless steel and specially created polished

LEFT: Guimet's original Art Nouveau Métro entrance at Porte Dauphine.
ABOVE LEFT: one of the 1,600 light screens that filter light into the Institut du Monde Arabe.
ABOVE RIGHT: Reflections in the Parc de la Villette.

MITTERRAND'S GRAND POLICIES

When François Mitterrand came to power in 1981, he initiated a *grands projets* scheme ensuring his mark would be left on the city:

- ☛ Le Grand Louvre (1981–97) renovation
- ☛ Cité des Sciences at La Villette (1986)
- ☛ Institut du Monde Arabe (1987)
- ☛ Gare d'Orsay conversion to museum (1986)
- ☛ La Grande Arche at La Défense (1989)
- ☛ Opéra Bastille (1989)
- ☛ Finance ministry building at Bercy (1989)
- ☛ Bibliothèque Nationale de France relocation to new buildings at Tolbiac (1998)

PARIS THROUGH PAINTINGS

The French capital has been a honeypot to artists for centuries, providing an
infinite source of material for their canvases

For the Russian painter Marc Chagall (1887–1985) Paris was "my heart's image – I should like to blend with it and not be alone with myself". In many paintings, especially those portraying lovers sky high in serene embrace, he did just that, wrapping the couple in warm colours as if in the evening air over

and provincial country, with a city which is sophisticated and worldly-wise.

Yet in the 18th century, the young artist's greatest ambition was to win the *Prix de Rome* with the long study in the Italian capital, in a country steeped in historical art, as the prize. However, few of the names of the winners mean

Paris and giving flight to their calm passion across the rooftops of the capital.

A city of painters

Paris's reputation has not only developed as the city of lovers – if lovers need any city in particular – but more importantly as the city of painters. Apart from the obvious justification that it is a lovely place to paint, there are special reasons for this. Perhaps no other capital city has been the centre and focus of its whole nation's identity to such a degree for so long a time. Nor does any comparable country have such a unique divide between town and country as exists in France – a quintessentially rural

much to us today, which points to the discrepancy between the official, sanctioned opinion of the establishment and the verdict of history.

In France, the establishment was rooted in Paris, epitomised by the annual *salon* exhibitions, set up by Louis XIVth's Académie Royale de Peinture et de Sculpture in the uninhabited Louvre in 1734. These exhibitions were all-powerful – sometimes an artist who had sold a given picture to a customer shortly before the opening of a *salon* would be obliged to take the picture back if it failed to be selected for the exhibition. Nevertheless, over the years, the *salon* jury continuously overlooked many great talents: Cézanne (1839–1906) was never accepted.

Paris as an artist's model

Thanks to the Montgolfier brothers' hot air balloon flight in 1783, Paris was the first city to be seen from the air and, 75 years later, to be photographed from on high – by French pioneer photographer and novelist Gaspard Nadar. Moreover, with the reshaping of the city along starburst lines of avenues and junctions, an artist in Paris around 150 years ago may have felt that, as he created his Paris on canvas, the city itself was still being created around him.

PISSARRO'S VIEW

Towards the end of his life, Camille Pissarro (1830–1903) used to sit at windows on the top floors of houses, painting the busy scenes below. His famous *Boulevard des Italiens*, bathed in morning sunlight, is full of atmosphere.

palaces and avenue apartments of Paris, stood out like a nude at a dinner party, and the sight of so blatant and jagged a thing, that was yet so characterful, appears to have had a surreptitiously liberating effect on all sorts of art styles associated with Paris, be it Cubism, Vorticism or Futurism.

Studio life

In today's Paris, there is nothing like the system of studios that existed in the 19th century, when painters

Technology has always fascinated the French and the Eiffel Tower has not only provided a worthy subject for painters, but has also afforded an easily accessible aerial view as in no other city. For the Impressionists the railways were important, partly because they could take the train from the Gare St-Lazare up the Seine, but partly also because steam makes such a splendid haze over a field of vision.

The Eiffel Tower, placed beside all the other

were apprenticed to masters. At that time, they learned to paint in an atmosphere sometimes deeply serious to the point of stuffy, or hilarious to the point of bawdy. Drawing was at the centre of the training, the nude the central subject of draughtsmanship. Mythological and generally heroic and historical subject matter was emphasised to such an extent that we may wonder that anyone ever thought of painting a simple view of a street.

Common sense did not always mix with high principles: Gustav Courbet (1819 –77), who broke away from Classicism to lead a Realism movement, only wanting to paint what he could see with his own eyes, thought that life classes

PRECEDING PAGES: art on the Pont des Arts.
LEFT: Monet's Impressionist painting of Gare St-Lazare.
ABOVE: Edgar Degas's ballerinas.

should extend beyond the human nude, to take in animals as well. However, instead of making excursions to the country, he had the animals brought to the studio – horses, cattle, the lot.

The aim of Edouard Manet (1832–83) was to make art belong to his own time and he became a forerunner for the Impressionists. But he did not like his studio, "I don't know why I come here, everything that meets the eye is ridiculous – the light is wrong, the shadows are wrong…" So he went out and about, painting life exactly and simply as he saw it, producing such masterpieces as the *Buveur d'Absinthe*, a true character study, and *Musique aux Tuileries*, a realistic portrait of Paris in the 19th century.

It was after Manet, at the turn of the century, that French painting – and the paintings of the many foreigners who came to live and work in Paris – became so domestic, be it rural or urban. From then on, studio life changed, artists rented their own space where they lived, worked and discussed ideas together.

First they gathered in Montmartre in a ramshackle building called the *Bateau Lavoir*, because it looked like an old Seine laundry boat, where Cubism was born. Then they went to *La Ruche* (beehive) in the more sophisticated Montparnasse. Built from remnants of the 1900

AN EYE FOR THE DANCING GIRLS

The most popular artist associated with Paris has to be Henri Toulouse-Lautrec (1864–1901), an aristocrat who led a Bohemian lifestyle in Montmartre. His artist's eye was a street eye, sharper than any in cafés, theatres, bars and brothels. And where was his art seen most of all? In the street. His colourful and vibrant posters led the way as they replaced layers of print wrapping the ventilation shafts and urinals of the capital. The painter loved to entertain, too, always concocting new cocktails for his guests. His lover was Suzanne, the model for Renoir and Degas and whose son, Maurice Utrillo (1883–1955), became famous for his scenes of Montmartre.

World Exhibition, the collection of studios was opened in 1902 and housed the likes of Picasso, Modigliani, Léger, Chagall, Soutine and the poet Apollinaire.

The lure of the French capital

From the 1890s, many artists flocked to Paris, a city of taste and filth, style and vulgarity, romance and prostitution – a city of energy. Talking of that time, one writer described the successful artist's lot: "A painter can become established more quickly than a notary's clerk: he does watercolours in albums, dresses like the Prince of Wales, paints slick portraits of ladies, leads the dancing. He pays his colour merchant in cash in order to get a discount, invests his money in the railways and, as soon as he is *hors concours*, marries the daughter of a wealthy if unscrupulous banker."

So obvious was Paris as the place to be, that Pablo Picasso (1881–1973) used to claim that his journey there in 1900 was, in fact, just a halt on the way to London. It was as if he could not dare to admit to something as *obvious* as the lure of the French capital.

Although neither Picasso nor, to a lesser

THE EIFFEL GARTER

Gustav Eiffel was also the inventor of the garter belt, which seems perfectly logical when you imagine his tower upside down. Doesn't it look like a stockinged leg?

of his most abstract works, lush in its austerity.

Picasso's scenic paintings are mostly of the city during World War II, reflecting either the grey quality of life under an occupying army or the frantic relief of hope or news of victory. In his paintings of Notre Dame and the Ile de la Cité, we can detect his sensitivity to the church's unique position, dominating an island. He evokes from the church not only the intimate image of a woman, but also the inviolable heart of a nation.

extent, Henri Matisse (1869–1954), the greatest painters of the 20th century, were known for landscape painting, concentrating more on line and the human form, they could not resist Paris as a subject, especially Notre Dame.

Both artists' work tackles something of the intimate grandeur of the building, which is imposing not by size but by detail, not by scale but by rhythm. Clearly, these aspects of the church fascinated Matisse as he looked out at it from his studio and, from this, he produced one

---

FAR LEFT: Matisse's portrayal of Notre Dame.
LEFT: Toulouse-Lautrec focused on Parisian society.
ABOVE : Raoul Dufy's vision of Paris.

A charming vision

Raoul Dufy's vision of Paris is perhaps the most charming of all, for with deft simplicity he is able to conjure up the sheer jumble of impressions that is Paris. It is a touch as brisk as the traffic but as certain as the *joie de vivre* peculiar to the place.

It seems typical that while Picasso travelled all the way from Barcelona to Paris to attend the Universal Exhibition of 1900, Dufy (1877–1953) did not even take the trouble to stroll down the street to visit it. Dufy's pictures saunter in the shade, bask in the sun; his understanding is lazy, but it is understanding for all that and perfect for this romantic French city.

THE LOUVRE AND THE GRAND BOULEVARDS

The royal part of Paris offers the world's largest museum of art, the ornamental Jardin des Tuileries, the elaborate Palais Royal, the opulence of the Opéra and elegant Champs-Elysées

Map, pages 114/5

On the Seine's Right Bank expanses of beautifully laid out gardens stretch into ostentatious squares and wide tree-lined boulevards overflow with designer boutiques and department stores, interspersed with royal palaces, the world's most famous museum and an opulent opera house. The lairs of the most fashionable of fashion houses hide inbetween. Meticulously planned by Prefect Baron Haussmann, the elegant buildings, boulevards and open spaces engulf the visitor in 19th-century grandeur.

In this self-contained world, you can buy your luxurious outfit to wear to the luxurious restaurant which serves food bought from luxurious shops. At night, however, apart from the expensive sparkle of the Champs-Elysées and the area around the Opéra, this historically royal region is empty and strangely forlorn.

The Louvre – grand palace of art

Once the seat of royalty, the **Musée du Louvre ❶** (open daily; Wed till 9.45pm; closed Tues; entrance fee) has been the home of fine art since a colony of painters and sculptors moved into the empty halls after Louis XIV decamped to Versailles in 1682. The Louvre's art collection goes back even further, to 1516, when François I invited Leonardo da Vinci to be the Royal Court painter and he brought with him his masterpieces of the *Mona Lisa* and *Virgin of the Rocks*.

Originally built as a fortress in 1190 by King Philippe-Auguste to protect a weak link in his city wall, the Louvre was transformed into a royal château in the 1360s by Charles V, who established his extensive library in one of the towers. Successive monarchs added to it and destroyed parts until Louis XIV moved out leaving his extensions partly built. The squatters who consequently took up residence in the palace included Guillaume Coustou, sculptor of the *Marly Horses*, now one of the Louvre's main exhibits. A fine artistic reputation grew out of the decaying passageways and galleries and, in the 18th century, the fine arts academy, which had joined the Académie Française (*see page 197*) and other academic bodies in the royal apartments, set up a tradition of *salons* (*see page 98*) for artists to exhibit their work, lasting for more than 120 years.

During the Revolution, in a rare moment of creative fervour, the rebels decided to inaugurate the palace as a museum, ironically fulfilling the plans of Louis XVI, the king they had just beheaded. Opened in August 1793, the museum benefited greatly from the steadily growing collection of royal treasures, which were augmented by Napoleon's subsequent efforts to relocate

LEFT: the Champs-Elysées from the Arc de Triomphe. **BELOW:** postcards of turn-of-the-century art.

much of Europe's artistic wealth, following victories in Italy, Austria and Germany. After Napoleon lost at Waterloo in 1815, many of the stolen masterpieces were reclaimed by their rightful owners.

Modern-day museum

In 1981, President François Mitterand began a vast renovation of the museum, calling it the *Projet du Grand Louvre*. His first step was to move the Finance Ministry out of the **Richelieu Wing** to Bercy, in eastern Paris, to create more museum space. Opening in 1993, it doubled the size of the already enormous museum to make it unquestionably the world's biggest. Four years earlier, the controversial **Louvre Pyramid**, designed by the Chinese-American architect I.M. Peï over the new main entrance, was opened. A celebration of angles, the pyramid's 666 panes of glass are held together with stainless steel nodes and cables, reflecting and contrasting with and, to some minds, complementing the ancient curves of the surrounding main building. However, to traditionalists such modernism amid such historic beauty is a heresy. Occultists take comfort in the fact that the number of panes in the pyramid matches the sum of the numbers in the sun's magic square, advocating that it is a solar temple. It also forms part of the Royal Axis, or Triumphal Way, which lines up monuments, regal and triumphal, from the Louvre's Cour Carrée to the Grande Arche in La Défense.

Practical, as well as sparkling, the pyramid allows light to flood into the new underground area where you buy your ticket – if you don't already have a *Carte Musées* (*see page 275*) – and where there are shops, a restaurant, cafés and an exhibition area, called the Medieval Louvre, which shows the palace at different stages of its development. It is also the new location for the Paris fashion shows

ABOVE: foundations of the Louvre fortress and keep discovered in 1984. **BELOW:** underneath the Pyramid in the Louvre entrance hall.

(*see pages 54–55*). However, the pyramid entrance does become very congested, so try toavoid peak times such as Sundays, when ticket prices are reduced after 3pm, or use the entrances at 99 Rue de Rivoli or Porte de Lions on the Quai des Tuileries, through which cars pass, and go down through the shopping arcade, **Galeries du Carrousel** under the arch, or approach it from the Palais-Royal–Musée du Louvre Métro. There is an underground car park (open daily 7am–11pm) off Avenue du Général-Lemonnier.

A tour of the treasures

From the central **Hall Napoléon**, escalators whisk visitors off to various parts of the building, which is divided into three separate sections: Sully (east wing), Denon (south wing) and Richelieu (north wing), with the exhibits on three levels in numbered areas. Although star attractions are well signposted, the free map provided is essential.

A good exhibition to start with is the **Medieval Louvre** *en route* to the Crypte Sully under the Cour Carrée, where the remains of **Philippe-Auguste's fort and keep**, and some of the artifacts discovered in the recent excavations to build the underground complex, can be seen. Pieces of Charles VI's parade helmet were found at the bottom of the well in the keep in 1984 and a replica of the helmet is now on display in the **Salle St-Louis**.

Up on the ground floor of the Sully and Richelieu Wings are the **Oriental Antiquities**, which include the Mesopotamian prayer statuette of Ebih-il (around 2400 BC), with striking lapiz lazuli eyes, and the black basalt Babylonian Code of Hammurabi (1792–1750 BC), one of the world's first legal documents.

On the south side of the Sully Wing, you will find the graceful Hellenic statue

Map, pages 114/5

ABOVE: *Venus de Milo* in Sully Wing.
BELOW LEFT: Louvre and Triumphal Way.
BELOW RIGHT: the Gallerie d'Apollon.

The enigmatic smile of the Mona Lisa *was described by Lawrence Durrell as that "of a woman who has just dined off her husband".*

Venus de Milo (2nd century BC), purchased by the French government for 6,000FF in 1820 from the Greek island of Milos. From here, head on into the Denon Wing to see the Etruscan *Sarcophagus of the Reclining Couple* (*see pages 134–35*). Continuing along the ground floor level, you will reach the Italian sculpture section and its famous masterpieces, such as Michelangelo's *Slaves* (1513–1520), sculpted in marble for Pope Julius II's tomb but which was never finished, and Canova's delightful Neo-Classical *Psyche Revived by the Kiss of Cupid* (1793).

In the **Grande Galerie,** immediately above on the first floor, is the work of art that everyone wants to see for themselves, the *Mona Lisa* (1503) – *La Joconde* in French. The first incumbent in the Louvre, Leonardo da Vinci's small painting of a Florentine noblewoman rests securely behind glass since her knife assault several years ago. But don't ignore the many other masterpieces hanging in this gallery, including more by Leonardo and works by Raphael, Titian and Veronese, as well as Caravaggio's *The Fortune Teller* (about 1594).

On the same floor is the **French School of 19th-century painting**, with work by Romanticist Eugène Delacroix (*see page 192*), which starts at the top of the Escalier Daru opposite the *Winged Victory of Samothrace* (2nd century BC), the Hellenistic stone figurehead commemorating a victory at sea. The Spanish School, with masterpieces by El Greco and Goya, can be found close by.

The second floor of the Richelieu and Sully wings are completely given over to paintings and include Rembrandt's masterpiece of his second wife, *Bathsheba Bathing* (1654), and the Dutch painter Jan Vermeer's telling portrayal of domestic life in the 1660s, *The Lacemaker.*

BELOW: view of the Jardin des Tuileries.

The beautifully renovated Richelieu Wing houses a vast collection of French sculpture on the ground floor and is focussed around two splendid sculpture courts, starring Guillaume Coustou's two giant *Marly Horses*.

Also part of the Louvre collection, with renovation due to be completed before 2000, is the **Musée des Arts Decoratifs ❷** (open daily; closed Mon; entrance fee) in the northwest wing. It presents an exhaustive survey of interior design from medieval tapestries to extravagant Empire furniture and a marvellous exhibition of 20th-century design including Art Nouveau and Art Deco. Note especially the wonderful Art Nouveau bedroom by Hector Guimard, designer of the Métro entrances (*see page 133*). Further along in the Pavillon de Marsan, which with the Pavillon de Flore on the south side is all that is left of Catherine de Médicis' Tuileries Palace, is the **Musée des Arts de la Mode et du Textile ❸** (open daily from 11am; Wed till 10pm; weekends 10am–6pm; closed Mon; entrance fee). Here on display are the fruits of Paris fashion from the 16th century until today as well as a large turnover of temporary exhibitions.

A walk in the Tuileries

The **Jardin des Tuileries ❹** offers shade, statues, fountains and a place to relax and pretend to read *Le Monde*. Once a rubbish tip and a clay quarry for tiles (*tuiles*, hence the name, the Tuileries), the garden was initially created, in 1564, for Catherine de Médicis in front of her palace, to remind her of her native Tuscany. In 1664, Louis XIV's celebrated gardener André Le Nôtre, redesigned the park with his predilection for straight lines and clipped trees. It was then opened to the public and quickly became the first fashionable outdoor area in which to see and be seen in, triggering the appearance of the first deckchairs and public toilets. One of the earliest hot-air balloon flights was launched from this garden

Aristide Maillol (1861–1944) started sculpting at the age of 40, concentrating his efforts on large, bronze, nude women – 20 of which adorn the Tuileries.

BELOW: drama in stone in the Tuileries.

André Le Notre (1613–1700) is France's most celebrated gardener. Creator of the French formal garden, he designed those at Versailles, the Champs-Elysées and the Tuileries, where his family had gardened for three generations.

BELOW: part of Monet's *Les Nymphéas* hanging in the Orangerie.

in 1783. Now, after several years of disruption, the Tuileries have been renovated as part of the *Projet du Grand Louvre*, reflecting Le Nôtre's original design and incorporating a new sloping terrace and enclosed garden.

Approaching the gardens from the Louvre, you pass through the **Arc de Triomphe du Carrousel**, the smallest of the three arches (the others being the Arc de Triomphe and Grande Arche at La Défense) on the Triumphal Way. Erected in 1808 by Napoleon, to commemorate his Austrian victories, this arch is a garish imitation of Roman arches and the four horses galloping across its summit are copies of four gilded bronze horses, stolen by Napoleon from St Mark's Square in Venice to decorate his memorial. After his downfall in 1815, the originals were returned.

In front of the arch, where the Tuileries Palace used to stand linking the Pavillon de Marsan and the Pavillon de Flore, is a collection of sculptures of sensuous nudes, produced between 1900 and 1938 by Aristide Maillol (*see page 209*), adorning the ornamental pools. More works by sculptors such as Rodin and Le Pautre, along with copies of ancient works, can be found scattered around.

Continue westwards along the Terrasse du Bord de l'Eau, where Napoleon's children played under the watchful gaze of their emperor father, to the hexagonal pool – still a favourite spot for children with boats and ducks with attitudes. Here, facing each other across the wide, sweeping steps, leading to Place de la Concorde, are the twin museums of the **Galerie National du Jeu de Paume ❺** (open daily; weekday afternoons; Tues till 9.30pm; closed Mon; entrance fee) and the **Musée de l'Orangerie ❻** (open daily; closed Tues; entrance fee).

Built by Napoleon III as a real tennis court, the Jeu de Paume, following the Impressionists' migration to the Musée d'Orsay (*see pages 211–12*), now houses temporary modern art exhibitions. The Orangerie is one of the city's hidden gems, a beautifully harmonious museum, containing some of the world's finest paintings. If the big museums are full, come here for peace, quiet and exhilaration. The list of canvases is impressive: 22 Soutines, 14 Cézannes – including one of *The Bathers* which was cut into three, then stuck back together again (look for the joins) – 24 Renoirs, 28 Derains and a pile of Picassos, Matisses and Utrillos. Yet the masterpieces of the museum are, undoubtedly, Monet's *Les Nymphéas* (*Waterlilies*), paintings of the Impressionist leader's waterlily pond in his beloved garden at Giverny (*see page 253*). Eight huge canvases drown the spectator in colour and movement, subtly displayed in a room purposefully built for them after Monet's gift to the state at the 1918 Armistice.

Down the Rue de Rivoli

The arcaded **Rue de Rivoli**, topped with Neo-Classical apartments, was built to commemorate Napoleon's victory over the Austrians at Rivoli, north of Verona, in 1797 but was completed well after the Emperor's demise. Planned for victory marches along the Triumphal Way, the street now contains luxury and souvenir shops, cafés and bookstores, including **W.H. Smith**, for English books and newspapers, and Angelina, a turn-of-the-century Viennese *salon de thé*, which once played host to the likes of intellectual novelist Marcel Proust and fashion icon Coco Chanel.

From the Place de la Concorde head east towards Rue St-Roch, or you can take the Métro to the Tuileries. The harmonious church of **St-Roch ❼** is on the corner of Rue St-Honoré, running parallel with Rue de Rivoli. André Le Nôtre and Denis Diderot (1713–84), the philosopher, writer and critic, are buried here

Map, pages 114/5

The Tuileries Palace, which had housed Louis XIV, Napoleon Bonaparte, Louis-Philippe and finally Napoleon III, was burnt down by members of the Paris Commune in 1871 (see page 36), when three centuries of art went up in smoke.

BELOW: Rue de Rivoli, named after one of Napoleon's victories in 1797.

TIP

Each evening, 45 minutes before curtain-rise at the Comédie Française, 112 tickets are sold at low prices at the booth just off the square on Rue de Montpensier behind the theatre.

alongside one of the Comédie Française's favourite playwrights, Pierre Corneille (1606–84). In 1795, Royalist insurgents were shot dead on the church steps on the orders of a young, up-and-coming artillery general, named Napoleon Bonaparte and you can still see the bullet holes today.

A few minutes walk further on, you reach **Place André Malraux**, which has been a focal point of Parisian life since the Middle Ages. It was here that Joan of Arc stood at the gates of Paris in 1429, attempting to win back the capital from the English. She was struck by a sniper's arrow, and taken to a nearby house (No 4 on the square) to be bandaged. Her quest was in vain and 10-year-old Henry VI of England was crowned King of France in Notre Dame in 1431, while Joan was burnt at the stake in Rouen.

Adjoining the square, on Place Colette, stands the illustrious **Comédie Française ❽**, the French national theatre. Originating from Molière's acting troupe, the company has been established on these premises since 1799. Napoleon passed a decree in 1812, still applicable today, placing it under state control with a director nominated by the government. But his interest in the theatre was far from passive, as he was having an affair with the company's leading lady, Mademoiselle Mars.

The Palais Royal – den of state

Stretching its elegant columns and arcades away from the Louvre, the **Palais Royal ❾** is a place of repose and refinement. Built on the site of a Roman bath house by Cardinal Richelieu, prime minister from 1624, as a palace for himself, he willed it to the Crown in 1642, when it became the childhood home of Louis XIV. At the beginning of the 18th century, the dukes of Orléans took up resi-

BELOW: playing on Daniel Buren's columns in the courtyard of the Palais Royal.

MOLIÈRE – A GREAT MAN OF COMEDY

Born Jean Baptise Poquelin in Paris in 1622, Molière, playwright, actor, director and stage manager, created 12 of the most durable satirical comedies of all time, including *Tartuffe* (1669) and *Bourgeois Gentilhomme* (1671). After studying law, he formed an acting troupe with members of the Béjart family in 1643, whose daughter he was in love with. The troupe had an unsuccessful start, but after Molière polished up his act in the provinces, they became Louis XIV's official entertainers. In 1673, at 51, Molière collapsed on stage while acting the title role in his play *Le Malade Imaginaire,* in which an old man feigns death, and died a few hours later. In 1680 the King merged his company with a rival's, creating a united Parisian theatre called the Comédie Française. The great thespian lived at 40 Rue de Richelieu and is commemorated by the **Molière Fountain** close by.

dence and the palace became a den of debauchery, as a result of the infamous "libertines' suppers" regularly thrown by the Regent, Philippe d'Orléans. Gambling and prostitution became commonplace as, by order of the Dukes of Orléans, police were forbidden to enter the palace precincts. In 1780, to compensate for his family's free spending, Louis-Philippe built shops around the palace, to let at exorbitant prices. After the Revolution, the palace was turned into a gaming house and, although Louis-Philippe moved back in 1815, gambling continued until after he became King in 1830. The Commune (*see page 36*) almost destroyed the palace in 1871 and the state took control, starting restoration work the following year.

Today, it houses government offices and in the Cour d'Honneur, the main courtyard, stand 250 black-and-white striped columns of varying heights, erected by artist Daniel Buren in 1986. Once a meeting place for some of the most important protagonists of the Revolution, the garden is a tranquil oasis populated by nannies, children and tourists and in the arcades are art galleries and specialist shops, including costumes, coins, porcelain and antiques. Hiding shyly under the arches, at 17 Rue Beaujolais, is the most beautiful restaurant in Paris, **Le Grand Véfour** which opened in 1784 and has fed the likes of Revolutionary Camille Desmoulins, the Emperor Napoleon and writers Alphonse Lamartine and Victor Hugo.

Exploring the palace streets

Directly north of the Palais Royal, beyond the crumbling, alluring facade of the Palais Royal vaudeville theatre, sits the **Bibliothèque Nationale de France - Richelieu ❿** (open daily; closed Sun and pub. hols; free). Containing every

Map, pages 114/5

By 1830, suicides in the garden of the Palais Royal were commonplace, as gamblers sought certain escape from their huge debts. Prostitution was so rife that guidebooks were produced detailing the wares on offer.

BELOW: browsing in the arcades of the Palais Royal.

book published in France since 1500, the library's book collection is one of the biggest in the world and includes original manuscripts from Rabelais, Villon, Hugo and Proust and Charlemagne's illuminated Bible. Now in the process of being rehoused in the massive, new, ultra modern premises at Tolbiac, near the Gare de Austerlitz, to be completed by the end of 1998, the Richelieu building is keeping the specialised departments of prints, drawings, maps, music and manuscripts. The main reading room, designed by Henri Labrouste in 1863, is an architectural masterpiece. Downstairs, the permanent museum, **Cabinet des Médailles et Antiques** (open afternoons; entrance fee), contains *objets d'art* from the royal collections taken during the Revolution.

Opposite the library, across Rue de Richelieu, is the charming small **Square Louvois**, containing one of the most beautiful fountains in Paris, which represents the four "female" rivers of France – La Loire, La Seine, La Garonne and La Saône. East of the library are the early 19th-century, aristocratic, covered arcades **Galerie Colbert** and **Galerie Vivienne ⓫**. Recently renovated, both arcades hint of past grandeur, fitted out with intricate brass lamps, graceful glass canopies and marbled mosaic floors. Sip a strong coffee at the expansive copper counter of the refurbished Le Grand Colbert, an 1830s' brasserie at 4 Rue Vivienne and pop into No.6 to check out Jean-Paul Gaultier's latest creations. Tea addicts will find a welcome repose at A Priori Thé, in the Galerie Vivienne, a *salon de thé* which spreads out into the gallery.

ABOVE: a hard day's shopping.
BELOW: the stylish, 19th-century Galerie Colbert.

From the Galerie Colbert, the Rue des Petits-Champs points eastward to the 17th-century crescents of **Place des Victoires ⓬**. This genteel square, guarded by a mounted Louis XIV, is now home to the elite of the Parisian fashion world such as Kenzo, Stefan Kelian and Thierry Mügler. On your way there, look out for **Willi's Wine Bar** (13 Rue des Petits-Champs), which offers a fine selection of wines and cheeses.

Heading south down Rue Croix-des-Petits-Champs for about five minutes, you will reach the most beautiful and atmospheric passageway in Paris, **Galerie Véro-Dodat ⑬** (opposite Rue Montesquieu), with its polished mahogany facades, brass lamps and musty skylights. When it opened in 1826, the arcade was fitted with the new technology of the day, gas lighting. Le Véro-Dodat Bistro serves wholesome dishes, expertly executed by Monsieur Gomond and served by his wife.

A little further south on the Place du Palais-Royal is the massive **Louvre des Antiquaires ⑭**. Once a department store, it is now packed with antiques shops. This area, once so congested, was cleared on the orders of Napoleon following an attempt on his life in 1800, when he was First Consul. Two Royalists planted explosives in a cart, but the bomb missed his carriage. Not wishing to repeat the experience, when he became Emperor, Napoleon razed 50 houses.

Along the Grands Boulevards

Stretching from the Opéra to the Place de la République, the Grands Boulevards is a 3-km (2-mile) run of wide avenues incorporating Boulevards Haussmann, Montmartre, Poissonière, St-Denis and St-Martin. The city's strolling ground since 1705, the boulevards are tree-lined, bustling and endowed with huge department stores, cinemas and cafés that spill out on to the pavements.

The Grands Boulevards have a colourful past. When Louis XIV tore down Charles V's walls around Paris, he created wide, open spaces, bordered with trees, for his subjects. A raised road was constructed, four carriages wide, which

Map, pages 114/5

ABOVE: exotic sculpture for sale.
BELOW: the genteel Place des Victoires.

Shirley MacLaine roamed the red light district around Boulevard St-Denis, observing Parisian low life for her role as a prostitute in the film Irma la Douce.

BELOW: publicity for the wax museum, Musée Grévin.

became known as the "boulevard". By the 19th century, the west end of the thoroughfare was the reserve of the rich, and the east had become the playground of the workers of industrial Paris – vaudeville theatres, circuses, waxworks, bars and brothels competed side by side. By 1830, the theatres played so many tumultuous melodramas that the area became known as the "Boulevard du Crime".

This end still maintains a nefarious reputation – the area around Boulevard St-Denis hosts 80 percent of the capital's prostitutes. Actress Shirley MacLaine, perfecting her role for Billy Wilder's *Irma la Douce*, spent a week here, observing the life of a Parisian prostitute among the neon sex shops and massage parlours. Paradoxically, Rue St-Denis was the road taken by the Kings of France to Notre Dame for their coronation, as well as their final route north, for burial in the basilica of St-Denis (*see page 250*).

Starting on the Boulevard Montmartre, vestiges of popular 19th-century entertainment can be found at the **Musée Grévin** ⓯ (open daily during school holidays; afternoons otherwise; entrance fee). A light-hearted waxwork museum, full of cheerfully incompatible figures – Marie-Antoinette, Michael Jackson, National Front leader Jean-Marie Le Pen and a less charming display of Revolutionary justice – and a hall of mirrors, it is set in an old theatre, whose original decor of sumptuous upholstery and polished brass has been preserved.

To the right of the museum is the **Passage Jouffroy**, with gift and bookshops. Across the boulevard, the **Passage des Panoramas** ⓰ is a bustling network of arcades, lit by 100 lamps. Stop at the window of Stern, the engraver, whose decor has not changed since 1840. The **Galerie des Variétés** still shrills to operatic tenors, reliving the golden years of the 1806 **Théâtre des Variétés** close by, and of Offenbach's finest arias. On emerging from the arcades head south

COUR DES MIRACLES

Place du Caire (off the Rue d'Aboukir) is rich in mementoes of Napoleon's campaign in Egypt, including sphinxes and hieroglyphics. It was here that the Cour des Miracles was established In the 1600s, described by Victor Hugo in his famous novel *The Hunchback of Notre Dame*, as the central meeting point for Parisian beggars. By day, these ruffians went out on the streets convincingly handicapped, blind and deaf. At night, they returned, shed their wooden legs and eye patches, and embarked on riotous orgies – hence the ironic miracles. The police did not dare enter this criminal enclave until 1667, when one brave police chief emptied it of the scurrilous beggars in 10 minutes, by threatening that the last nine to leave would be hanged.

Today, the square, just across from Métro Sentier, is the centre of a clothes manufacturing area and contains countless low-cost clothing shops.

MUSÉE GREVIN

THE GREVIN WAX MUSEUM

10, bd Montmartre 75009 Paris Tél. (1) 47 70 85 05
Métro : Rue Montmartre

Map, pages 114/5

towards the French stock exchange at the Neo-Classical, colonnaded **Bourse des Valeurs** ⓱ (afternoon guided tours daily; entrance fee) built in 1808 to Napoleon's favourite specifications.

Going to the Opéra

Behind the Opéra runs the busy **Boulevard Haussmann**, which is laden with shopping, including two large resplendent *grands magasins* (department stores). The green domes of **Printemps** compete with the sparkling cupola of **Galeries Lafayette** and indeed the two giants seem to fight a constant battle for the title of "Most Parisian of Department Stores" (*see page 72*).

You can either approach the Opéra from here or from the Boulevard des Italiens, which still retains some of its old charm and which was a centre of fashion in its heyday. On the left is **L'Opéra Comique** ⓲, once home to the popular 19th-century operetta composers of Offenbach's generation. In the adjoining Boulevard des Capucines, where the first motion pictures were shown in 1865 and where the music hall star Mistinguett used to live, is the **Musée du Parfum** ⓳ (open daily; closed Sunday; free). Here, in the former Théâtre des Capucines, is a beautiful collection of rare *objets* retracing 5,000 years of perfume.

Place de l'Opéra is not just a setting for Charles Garnier's magnificent opera house. Laid out by the hand of town planner Baron Haussmann during the Second Empire and criticised for being too grandiose, this square is the intersection of six roads, which is now a nonstop contest between pedestrians and traffic. Luxury shops line the square and the **Café de la Paix** is one of Paris's most fashionable, most expensive and most crowded watering-holes.

Opened in 1875, the **Opéra** ⓴ is predictably resplendent, with a team of gold

BELOW: the Opéra lords over the chic Café de la Paix.

Beneath the auditorium of the Opéra lies an underground lake, draining water from the foundations. This inspired Gaston Leroux to write The Phantom of the Opéra *in which Erik, while working on the foundations, creates an underground palace on the lake.*

BELOW: Napoleon looks down over the Place Vendôme.

leaf statues perched on the roof and monumental steps. Garnier, who won the commission to build an opera house in a competition, intended it to be the model for a Napoleon III style of architecture but, as it broke away from the normal Classical vein of that time, it didn't get much of a following.

On the Rue Scribe side of the building, the Emperor's Pavilion now houses a library and museum. Initially, it enabled direct access from carriage to the royal box, thus reducing the risk of assassination. Underneath is an underground lake, providing a perfect setting for many a tale – true or legendary. Inside, the decor is thickly ornate. If you cannot attend a performance, a tour of the interior will give you a glimpse of the pomp – Garnier's grand marble staircase and the masterpiece of a ceiling, painted by Marc Chagall in 1964. Now referred to as the Opéra Garnier since the opening of the Opéra Bastille in 1989 (*see page 165*), the theatre is the home of the Ballet de l'Opéra National de Paris, with opera and concert performances divided between the two opera houses.

From here, the Avenue de l'Opéra yawns widely down to the Palais Royal. Once the site of a slum neighbourhood, razed in the replanning of Paris, the avenue soon became a prestigious thoroughfare after it was completed in 1878. Today, it contains tourist shops offering perfume, scarves, Paris T-shirts and other souvenirs, whereas Rue de la Paix, which leads south to Place Vendôme a short distance away, is one long, dazzling shop window for gold cards, where Cartier rubs shoulders with airline offices and the Hotel Westminster.

The recently renovated expanse of **Place Vendôme** ㉑, dominated by Napoleon on top of his milky-green column, is ornamentally chic, resounding with every step of Italian shoes on polished marble. The 17th-century facades remained mere facades for half a century, following the construction of the

AUSTERLITZ COLUMN

Napoleon had 1,200 cannons, captured in 1805 at the Battle of Austerlitz, melted down to make the column (right), which stands in the Place Vendôme, after the statue of Louis XIV was torn down during the Revolution. A copy of Trajan's Column in Rome, with Napoleon as Caesar on top, the 44-metre (140-ft) monument, decorated with battle scenes has proved a political yardstick. The fall of the First Empire brought the fall of the statue and, during the 100 days that Napoleon tried to regain power, a statue of Henri IV was erected there. Louis XVIII then hoisted a huge *fleur de lys* flag up on top of the column. Louis-Philippe reinstalled Napoleon, in military garb, to his perch, only for him to be toppled, supposedly by the painter Gustav Courbet, into a carefully arranged pile of manure during the 1871 Commune. The Third Republic restored it, requisitioning the exiled Courbet's paintings to pay for it.

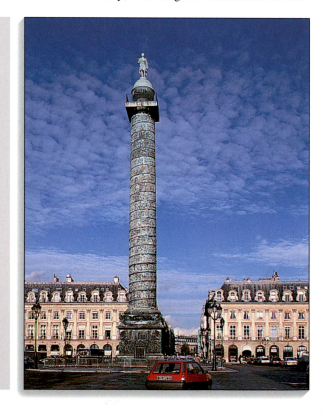

square in 1685 as a display case for Girardon's statue of Louis XIV, replaced by Napoleon's Austerlitz Column. Like a film set, the walls had no buildings behind them, until, gradually, the rich and influential filled up the empty spaces.

Today, the square exudes concentrated wealth. Here are jewellers Boucheron, Van Cleef and Arpels. Here, too, are banks, such as J.P. Morgan, and **The Ritz** at No 15. Hemingway once hoped that heaven would be as good as the Ritz; his ghost still haunts the bar which is named after him (prices have risen since Ernest's day). Now the hotel has earned worldwide notoriety through being where Diana, Princess of Wales, spent her last hours before her fateful car journey with the hotel owner's son, Dodi al-Fayed, in August 1997.

Place de la Concorde via La Madeleine's luxuries

Close to Place Vendôme and reached via the chic Faubourg St-Honoré, the church of **La Madeleine** ㉒ rises classically from the midst of the roaring traffic and expensive shops. Its temple facade is Athenian, its interior gloomily Italian and its history very French in that, after a couple of false starts, it was nearly a bank and a railway station, before being dedicated in 1842.

In the surrounding Place de la Madeleine are the food halls of the rich and famous – Fauchon, Hédiard and La Maison de la Truffe (*see page 72*). On the eastern side of the square is the charming Marché aux Fleurs Madeleine (open daily; closed Mon) and Marcel Proust spent his childhood at No 9.

From La Madeleine, Rue Royale runs past the bullet-proof security of Maxim's restaurant to Place de la Concorde. In the **Hotel de Crillon** on the right, Benjamin Franklin signed the Treaty of Friendship between the newly formed United States of America and King Louis XVI in 1778. A few minutes away,

Map, pages 114/5

*A flock of fashion designers have their principal houses in **Rue Faubourg St-Honoré** (see page 72): Christian Lacroix at No 73, Sonia Rykiel at No 70, Yves St Laurent at No. 38 and Japanese Ashida at No 34. For the best in scarves and leather goods, Hermès at No 24 is worth saving up for.*

BELOW: Mohamed al-Fayed's Ritz Hotel in Place Vendôme.

Map, pages 114/5

ABOVE: guarding the Palais d'Elysée.
BELOW: the Unknown Soldier lies under the Arc de Triomphe.

around the corner from Avenue Gabriel, is the **Palais d'Elysée**, home of the French president.

Place de la Concorde ㉓ was originally marshland, which offered the architect, Jacques-Ange Gabriel, much scope for grandeur. His square has been the site of grand events since its completion in 1763, most importantly, the decapitation of Louis XVI by Revolutionaries in January 1793.

The guillotine stood near the statue of Brest, representing one of the eight largest towns in France, where, despite the onslaught of traffic and tourists, it still is possible to imagine Louis's calm words as the blade was raised: "May my blood bring happiness to France."

Standing majestically in the middle of chaos, the central obelisk was a gift from the Viceroy of Egypt in 1829, attempting to gain favour with Charles X. The 3,300-year-old column originated in the Temple of Thebes and, weighing 220 tonnes, took four years to reach its destination in Paris.

The Champs-Elysées – the world's most famous street

Since its recent facelift, with a new row of trees, underground parking and legislation banning the tacky facades of fast-food joints, the **Champs-Elysées** (Elysian Fields), the vast avenue from the Place de la Concorde to the Arc de Triomphe on the Triumphal Way, is looking more elegant again. Once a bog, until Marie de Médicis cut a carriageway through it in 1616, the avenue was landscaped 50 years later by Le Nôtre but, in 1814, the occupying Russians made firewood out of all the trees. To the left, the unmistakable greenhouses of the **Grand Palais ㉔** and **Petit Palais ㉕** are remnants of the *Belle Epoque*, built for the 1900 World Exhibition. The big one holds conferences and exhibitions and contains the **Palais de la Découverte** (open daily; closed Mon; entrance fee), Paris's less interesting science museum, in comparison with the one at La Villette (*see pages 229–30*). The little one houses the **Musée des Beaux-Arts de Paris** (open daily; closed Mon and pub. hols) with medieval *objets d'art*, 18th-century furniture and Impressionist paintings.

Crowning the Champs-Elysées is a massive memorial to megalomania, the **Arc de Triomphe ㉖**. Commissioned by Napoleon in 1806, the ornately carved arch wasn't completed until after his death. When he married Marie-Louise of Austria in 1810, a mock-up of the arch had to be put up for the wedding procession to pass through. Napoleon's chance to pass under the real thing came when his body was triumphantly returned to Paris for reburial in Les Invalides in 1840. The Allies marched through victoriously in 1919 and 1944.

Beneath the ample armpit of the arch, the Unknown Soldier was laid to rest in 1920 and, in 1923, the eternal flame was lit. It is rekindled each evening at 6.30, with a wreath-laying ceremony. In 1962, a man was arrested for frying eggs over the flame, but more daring deeds date back to 1919, when a biplane flew through the arch.

From the top of the Arc de Triomphe, the view is breathtaking. Look out west to the futuristic skyscape of La Défense and east over the graceful parks of the Louvre. Paris stretches to the horizon, humming, sparkling and enticing.

The Métro

Deep beneath the streets of Paris there exists another city, a subterranean society with its own shops, cafés, market stalls, hairdressers, banking facilities, musicians, artists, beggars and pickpockets, even its own police force and its own micro climate. Temperatures here occasionally exceed 30°C (86°F), while wind speeds through the tunnels can reach up to 40 km (25 miles) per hour.

In Luc Besson's 1985 thriller, *Subway*, audiences had a glimpse of this surreal world and the kind of eccentric characters who have made the Métro their home. In real life, it is a sad statistic that every night around 1,000 people take refuge underground, most because they have nowhere else to go.

Construction of the Métro began in 1898. The first line, precisely 10.3 km (6.4 miles) long between Porte de Vincennes and Porte Maillot, opened on 19 July 1900. Within a year it had carried over 15 million passengers. Since then, the Métro has extended its routes in every direction and, today, it is widely hailed as the world's cheapest, cleanest and most efficiently run underground system, carrying over 3.5 million passengers daily along 200 km (124 miles) of track to 370 stations on 15 lines.

The massive station at Châtelet–Les Halles is the hub of the whole network. Four Métro lines and three RER commuter lines meet here, disgorging a quarter of a million passengers daily into its labyrinth of corridors. As you search this nightmarish warren for the exit, you may wonder if you will ever come up for air. Trudging the 75 km (47 miles) of corridors and 60 km (37 miles) of platforms, it seems unsurprising that the Parisian's average body weight is among the lowest in the industrialised world.

Métro stations abound in the city with no point being further than 500 metres (550 yds) away. Many entrances retain their Art Nouveau features, designed by turn-of-the-century architect Hector Guimard, whose work is recognisable by flowing lines evoking the growth of plants. Two notable entrances still covered by his beautiful cast iron and glass pavilions are at the stations of Porte Dauphine and Abbesses. The modern Métro sign is a circled large yellow letter M.

Underground, the walls are mostly covered in white tiles, apart from a few stations such as St Michel, which has a mozaic ceiling, and Bastille whose platforms are decorated with scenes from the Revolution (*see page 164*).

The average Parisian commuter spends a year and four months of his or her life below ground. In an attempt to make this time slightly more bearable, the RATP (the organisation which runs the Métro network and the buses) organises a diverse programme of cultural events, from photography exhibitions to fashion shows, classical concerts to puppet theatre. Less organised are the buskers, profiting from the perfect acoustics.

Back home in Birmingham, England, or Knoxville, Tennessee, you may find yourself missing the whiff of that distinctive aroma of gorgonzola and old socks, so redolent of the Métro. Then you will know that Paris has truly worked its way into your heart.

RIGHT: many of the Métro entrances retain their distinctive Art Nouveau features.

TREASURES OF THE LOUVRE

The largest palace in Europe, the Louvre has assembled an incomparable collection of old masters, sculptures and antiquities

One of the world's greatest museums, the Louvre is immense in scale, the size of its collections (well over 200,000 pieces) and the crowds that invariably throng its galleries (5 million visitors each year), make it one of the more challenging Parisian sights. It is impossible to try to see everything in one visit, although many people manage to cram in the edited highlights in one morning. This, however, does little justice to the wealth of exhibits, which range from European sculpture and painting to antiquities, decorative arts and objects.

HISTORY OF THE COLLECTION

The Louvre's collection was built up through patronage, gift-giving, requisition and other methods of appropriation. François I (pictured above, by Jean Clouet) was a Renaissance king who amassed a superb array of mostly Italian contemporary and classical works, and patronised artists such as Leonardo da Vinci. Louis XIV similarly made patronage a royal duty and added to the collection. Nationalisation of most French works of art after the Revolution led to the Musée de la Rèpublique being opened to the public in 1793. The greatest contribution to the Museum was made by Napoleon I, who brought back the spoils of his various campaigns. Louis XVIII acquired works including the Venus de Milo, but in 1848 the Louvre once again became the property of the State.

◁ **DYING SLAVE**
One of a pair of sculptures by Michelangelo, thought to represent the Arts, held captive by Death, after the death of Pope Julius II, a great arts patron.

▷ **THE BATHERS**
It is thought that Fragonard painted this canvas in the 1760s following his first trip to Italy. Fragonard was greatly influenced by Rubens in his use of colour, the fullness of his figures, and the painting's sensual and joyous theme was enhanced by the use of scumbles and glazes. Donated in 1869, the canvas is today part of the museum's comprehensive collection of European painting.

△ **OBJETS D'ART**
This 13th-century reliquary of St Francis of Assisi is one of the fabulous items found in the eclectic department of Objets d'Art.

▷ **ANTIQUITIES**
During the 18th and 19th centuries, antiquities were seen as the greatest art form, although the Louvre's core collection contains pieces which belonged to François I.

▷ FONTAINEBLEAU SCHOOL
This 16th-century painting of the Duchess of Villars and Gabrielle d'Estrée, attributed to the School of Fontaine-bleau, is a fine example of the then popular portrait genre. It shows the two sisters taking a bath. The Duchess, in a symbolic gesture, is announcing the future birth of her sister's child, the illegitimate son of Henry IV.

◁ TOMB OF PHILIPPE POT
A star of the collection of European sculpture is this unusual late 15th-century piece by Antoine le Moiturier. Philippe Pot was the Great Seneschal of Burgundy, an official of considerable rank. His imposing tomb, which was formerly in the Abbey of Citeaux, shows him dressed in armour, being carried on a shield and supported by eight weeping figures dressed in mourning garb.

▽ SARCOPHAGUS OF THE RECLINING COUPLE
Standing more than a metre high, this painted terracotta sarcophagus is one of the most impressive of the museum's Etruscan treasures. It depicts in detail everything from the folds of the garments to enigmatic smiles. The base of the sarcophagus is a couch, used by guests at an Etruscan banquet.

CASTLE, PRISON AND PALACE

The Louvre building, thought to be named after an area where wolves were hunted, has been enlarged and remodelled by French rulers for more than 800 years. The first building on the site was Philippe-Auguste's 12th-century fortified castle, known popularly as the "Tour de Paris", which contained the state treasury, archives and the royal storeroom. It also served as a prison. As medieval Paris grew, and the monarchy established other residences, the Louvre's importance declined.

In 1527, François I commissioned a Renaissance palace – the first example of French Classical architecture – to replace the château. By the end of the 17th century there was hardly an original stone left standing. The buildings surrounding the Cour Carrée predate 1715, and comprise the oldest parts of the building. In the 19th century, Napoleon I added the Galerie du Nord, and the buildings which flank the north and south sides of the Cour Napoleon date from the time of Napoleon III. The most recent addition to the Louvre's landscape is I.M. Pei's dramatic glass pyramid, which has become the museum's 20th-century emblem.

THE HEART OF THE CITY

The Gothic edifices of Notre Dame and Sainte-Chapelle rub shoulders with the dour Conciergerie on Ile de la Cité, at odds with the genteel mansions of Ile St-Louis and the fine modernism across the Seine

Map, page 140/1

T he Ile de la Cité in the middle of the Seine is the birthplace and topo-graphical centre of Paris and has been its spiritual and legislative heart for more than 2,000 years. Invading the Parisii settlement already established there in 53 BC, the Romans built a prefect's palace, law court and temple to Jupiter on the island. Across the river on the Right Bank, the Hôtel de Ville has been the cauldron of political debate since the Middle Ages, while just to the north, the area of Les Halles fed the city's stomachs from AD 1110 until 1969. This is the core of the capital, an area which, in many ways, embraces the essence of Paris.

Notre Dame – seven centuries of magnificence

"The bells, the bells," shout crowds of giggling schoolchildren from the towers of the cathedral of **Notre Dame de Paris** ❶ (open daily; free), echoing the cry of Victor Hugo's infamous hunchback, Quasimodo. Gazing up at the cathedral's finely sculptured facade, it is hard to imagine the building's poor condition when Hugo (*see page 159*) wrote the *Hunchback of Notre Dame* in 1831. He and his Romantic followers (*see page 35*) were so appalled at the state of the building that, in 1841, they succeeded in triggering a massive restoration programme, headed by Viollet-le-Duc (*see page 92*). Taking 23 years, the meticulous architect repaired the cathedral's structure literally from the foundations to the roof tiles, recreated stained-glass windows by copying remaining ones and replaced sculptures destroyed in the Revolution, such as the Gallery of Kings, by studying those of other Gothic cathedrals. He scrubbed the whitewash off the interior walls and administered a protective coating to the exterior. He also added a sacristy to the south side, now the **Trésor de Notre Dame** (open daily; closed 11.45am–12.30pm; entrance fee) housing the alleged Crown of Thorns, other relics and manuscripts.

The church of "Our Lady" was built on the site of ear-lier pagan fertility worship by the Romans, venerating a black Virgin. The conquering Frankish king, Clovis, erected a suitably impressive Christian basilica in the 6th century, which was replaced by a Romanesque church. By 1159, a young bishop, Maurice de Sully, decided that Paris deserved bigger and better. Work on the cathedral began in 1163 and took just under 200 years to complete, following plans drawn up by Pierre de Montreuil, Sainte-Chapelle's architect.

Even before it was finished, Notre Dame had become the venue for national ceremonies: state funerals, thanksgivings and, in 1239, St Louis deposited in the cathedral the Crown of Thorns, and other relics acquired on a Crusade, while Sainte-Chapelle was being built. Since then, Notre Dame has been witness to a string of

PRECEDING PAGES: imposing towers of the Conciergerie. **LEFT:** sculptured facade of Notre Dame by night. **BELOW:** one of the cathedral's exquisite rose windows.

historical events: in 1572, the cathedral's strangest wedding took place. The bride, Marguerite de Valois (a Catholic), stood at the altar, while the bridegroom Henri de Navarre (a Protestant), called in his vows from the doorstep. Later, in 1589, Henri was crowned in the cathedral, having decided to convert to Catholicism saying, "Paris is well worth a Mass".

Come the Revolution, Notre Dame was ravaged by enthusiastic citizens, melting down and destroying anything that hinted of royalty, including lopping off the heads of the kings of Judah, along the top of the main portals – Viollet-le-Duc replaced the statues with copies in 1850 and the original heads were discovered in a cellar of a bank in 1977. They now reside in the Hôtel de Cluny (*see page 183*). The cathedral was then turned into a Temple of Reason and by the end of the Revolution was being used for wine storage.

By the time Napoleon decided to crown himself Emperor in 1804, the cathedral was in such a shabby state that bright tapestries were hung up to cover the crumbling decor. Pope Pius VII attended with reluctant obedience and, when he hesitated at the altar, Napoleon snatched the crown and to the crowd's cheers of *"Vive l'Empéreur!"* placed it on his head himself. In August 1944, at the thanksgiving ceremony for the Liberation of Paris, the Resistance hero and leader of the new provisional government, General Charles de Gaulle, was shot at during the *Te Deum*.

Grand architecture

Notre Dame is magnificent from any angle, but its Gothic facade is particularly impressive. Viewed from out front on the **Place du Parvis**, the twin towers soar to the heavens with dramatic grace. The cathedral's three doors each have a distinct design – an asymmetry typical of medieval architecture. Originally, the stone figures were finely painted against a gilt background and were designed to illustrate the Bible to an illiterate populace. On the left, the **Portal of the Virgin** depicts the ark of the covenant and the coronation of the Virgin. The **Portal of**

The devilish gargoyles scowling down from the upper gallery are not medieval nightmares but the playful creations of the 19th-century Gothic revivalist architect Viollet-le-Duc.

BELOW: high-vaulted elegance of the central nave.

the Last Judgement, in the middle, shows the Resurrection, weighing of souls and their procession to heaven or hell. The **Portal of St Anne** portrays the Virgin and Maurice de Sully. Above the doorways, the **Rose Window**, showing the Virgin and Child in deep blues and rich reds, is a miracle of engineering. Picture the rickety scaffolding and the armies of stonemasons, who with simple measuring techniques constructed an intricate masterpiece that has lasted for 750 years. The glass, however, has been restored.

The ascent of the **Tours de Notre Dame** (open daily; closed some pub. hols; entrance fee) is a religious experience for those who love heights and a taste of hell for claustrophobes with vertigo. From the top of 387 steps Paris stretches to the horizon. "Emmanuel", the 13-tonne bell of Notre Dame, is pealed only on state occasions. Dating from the 17th century, legend has it that the purity of the bell's tone is due to the gold and silver jewellery cast into its heated bronze by the most beautiful women of Paris.

A medieval cavern

Inside, edged with 37 side chapels, the cathedral is enough to inspire the most hardened atheist. Supported by flying buttresses, the vault of the chancel seems almost weightless, with stained glass windows distributing rays of coloured light into the solemn shadows. The exquisite 13th-century north and south rose windows are the transept's two star attractions. The most spectacular north window still has most of its 13th-century glass but the south rose had to be reconstructed completely by Viollet-le-Duc. The 18th-century carved choir stalls, depicting the life of the Virgin Mary, were commissioned by Louis XIV, who was fulfilling the vow his father made 60 years earlier that he would build a high altar and devote the east chancel to the Virgin, if he were to have an heir. Louis XIII's statue stands behind the high altar, along with Guillaume Coustou's *Pietà*.

Outside on Rue du Cloître-Notre-Dame is the **Musée de Notre Dame de Paris ②** (open Wed, Sat, Sun; 2.30pm–6pm; entrance fee) which charts the history of the cathedral and has exhibits of ancient pottery found beneath the parvis, Gallo-Roman artifacts, works of art and a cup, dating from the 4th century. In the **Crypte Archéologique ③** (open daily; entrance fee), underneath the parvis, are excavations of buildings dating back to the 3rd century, including parts of a Lutetian house inhabited by the Gallic Parisii.

Sainte-Chapelle – a venerable shrine

Across from Notre Dame rise the imposing walls of the Palais de Justice and the Conciergerie. At one time, the **Palais de Justice ④** (open daily; closed weekends; free) was a royal palace and St Louis had his bedroom in what is now the First Civil Court. In the 14th century, Charles V moved out, installing his parliament there with full judiciary rights. A wander around the hushed corridors, past fleeting black-robed figures, is a reminder of the tense days of the Revolution when a new judicial system was imposed and the public prosecutor, Fouquier-Tinville, sent thousands to the guillotine. The present legal system has been passed down from Napoleon Bonaparte.

Confined within the walls of the Palais de Justice, **Sainte-Chapelle ⑤** (open daily; closed some pub. hols; entrance fee) stands like a skeletal finger pointing heavenwards – an ethereal counterpoint to the stones of the establishment. This miracle of High Gothic ingenuity is an obligatory pause on any visit to Paris. Completed in just 33 months by Pierre de Montreuil and consecrated in

Map, page 140/1

TIP

Each Sunday at 5.45pm, the organ master fills Notre Dame with classical music, soaring to paradise out of the 112-stop instrument. Classical concerts are also given in Sainte-Chapelle.

BELOW: the lower chapel of Sainte-Chapelle.

1248, the chapel was built to house the Crown of Thorns, bartered from the Venetians by St Louis. Seemingly constructed without walls, the chapel's vaulted roof is supported by a thin web of stone, from which descend veils of richly coloured stained glass. A symbolic, sculptured Crown of Thorns decorates the top of one of the pinnacles.

Built in two tiers, the lower chapel was designed for the palace staff and is consequently smaller and gloomier. From the shadows, climb the spiral staircase into the crystalline cavern of the upper chapel. The soaring windows catch the faintest of lights, creating kaleidoscopes of colour. The 13th-century colours are sharply vivid and depict 1,134 scenes from the Bible, which begin by the staircase with Genesis and proceed round the church to the 15th-century rose window. Regular orchestral concerts are held in the chapel.

The Conciergerie – a place of retribution

Occupying the northeast wing of the Palais de Justice, the **Conciergerie** ❻ (open daily; closed pub. hols; entrance fee) looks like an intimidating castle, its four towers rising insolently above impenetrable walls. It isn't hard to imagine this fortress as a merciless medieval prison – which it was (although much of the pitiless facade is 19th-century). Originally, it housed the Comte des Cierges, who was in charge of the king's lodgings and taxes, until it became a prison in the 14th century, when his job changed to that of chief gaoler. The Capetian palace came into its own during the Revolution, when it housed nearly 2,600 prisoners awaiting the guillotine, including Marie-Antoinette. Ironically, her prosecutor, Danton resided in the next cell before his trip to the guillotine, as, in turn, did his nemesis Robespierre. In the merry-go-round of retribution, 1,306

ABOVE: stained-glass perfection at Sainte-Chapelle.
BELOW RIGHT: replica of Marie-Antoinette's prison cell.

NOTABLE INMATES

A prison for four centuries, the medieval Conciergerie was host to many an inmate before the onslaught of the Revolution. Among those who were forced to take up residence there were the Scottish captain Montgomery, who fatally wounded Henri II during a tournament in1559, Ravaillac, who assassinated Henri IV in 1610, and the famous robber Cartouche (1693–1721).

During the Revolution, inmates included Madame du Barry, Louis XV's favourite mistress, Marie-Antoinette, Louis XVI's wife (above), Charlotte Corday, who murdered the Revolutionary leader Marat, the poet André Chenier; and, finally, the public prosecutor himself and the judges of the Revolutionary Tribunal.

heads rolled in one month at Place de la Nation. To the west is the **Cour des Femmes**, a rough courtyard where the women were allowed during the day.

The tower at the back is called **Bonbec** (the squealer), for it was here, from the 11th century, that torture victims told all. At the front is the 14th-century **Clock Tower** containing the first public clock in Paris, still ticking today.

Inside, the original kitchens are still intact. They were built to feed up to 3,000 using four huge fireplaces and have a Gothic canopied ceiling supported by buttresses. The adjacent **Salles des Gens d'Armes** is a magnificent four-aisled Gothic hall where the royal guards, or men-at-arms, used to live.

Exploring the island and river

Escape the shadows of the Revolution on **Quai des Orfèvres**, along the south bank of the island, now home to the *Police Judicaire* (CID), where goldsmiths once fashioned Marie-Antoinette's jewellery. Beyond the Square du Vert-Galant and the statue of Henri IV, the river slides silently past the tip of the island, caressing wistful willows. **Pont Neuf**, bisected by the island, is the oldest surviving bridge in Paris and the first to be built without houses on it. Here the first folk singers of the capital congregated to lampoon the aristocracy. In 1985, the American artist Christo wrapped up the whole bridge in brown paper.

Return to the east end of the island via the colourful **Marché aux Fleurs** in Place L. Lepine opposite the **Préfecture de Police** and Haussmann's **Hôtel Dieu**. Built on the site of a medieval hospital, which was the recipient of generous donations from Louis IX, the Hôtel Dieu, now a city hospital, was the scene of intense battles when the police resisted the Germans in 1944. In contrast to these forbidding structures, the market is a joyful array of small glasshouses

Map, page 140/1

Vedettes du Pont Neuf (tel: 01 46 33 98 38) run cruises along the Seine lasting about an hour. Boats leave from the Square du Vert-Galant every half hour in the high season (see page 275).

BELOW: a river view of the Conciergerie.

Scooping the Poop

Since 1977, when opinion polls revealed that the cleanliness of the streets came top among Parisian concerns, the then new mayor, the proud and energetic Jacques Chirac, made it a priority to overhaul Paris's entire waste disposal and street-cleaning system. The city cleaners' distinctive green uniform and vehicles were introduced in 1980. An *école de la propreté* was added to teach new recruits the finer elements of street cleaning and, today, the green, gnashing wagons have become a symbol of the city.

Paris has one of the world's most efficient clean-up services, employing around 4,500 people to collect 3,500 tonnes of rubbish daily at an annual cost of 2 billion francs – about 10 percent of the city's annual budget. And representatives from abroad, including officials from Tokyo and New York, have rushed over for cleaning lessons.

The fact is that Paris faces a singularly challenging obstacle to maintaining clean streets:

déjections canines, of which no less than 20 tonnes are vacuumed off the streets daily by a team of mobile pooper-scoopers. The annual bill amounts to 42 million francs. Spread among the city's 200,000 dog population, that's 210 francs per dog.

Paris has an unusually large canine population – but then the Parisian pooch is not merely man's best friend, he is also an essential fashion accessory. Just as residents of Los Angeles define themselves by their cars and Italians by their wardrobe, so Parisians tend to express their personalities through their dogs. From the toy poodle prancing along the Faubourg St-Honoré in a tartan raincoat and matching ribbon to the muzzled German shepherd dozing on the Métro after a night's guard duty, Parisian dogs are as diverse and eclectic a breed as their owners.

In fact, the distinction between animal and human often seems blurred in a city where it is not uncommon to see dogs seated at café tables. Far from being banned from shops and restaurants in France, almost every boutique or eating establishment worth its salt has its resident canine character, whose acquaintance it is advisable to make if you plan on becoming a regular customer.

Needless to say, this indulgence towards their pets does not translate well when it comes to teaching Frou-Frou the toutou (bow-wow) how to use the gutter.

Signs bearing sausage dogs and arrows have appeared at regular intervals on the capital's pavements, pointing to doggy latrines. When they failed to give results, a system of hefty fines was introduced. The new law is now enforced by an undercover cleanliness squad, the plainclothes *agents de propreté*, who patrol the streets and are instructed to swoop on sight – presumably watching where they put their feet.

Despite their valiant efforts, Paris remains a city where canny pedestrians keep an eye on the pavement. An estimated two serious falls a day are the result of what a man's best friend leaves lying around. If, during an unguarded moment, you too find yourself thus inconvenienced, take comfort: Parisians believe it brings good fortune.

LEFT: praise for an essential Parisian fashion accessory.

selling flowers and plants underneath classical black streetlamps. On Sunday, the stalls become a bird market and the jabbering of parakeets fills the air.

On the north side of Notre Dame is the **Quartier des Anciens Cloîtres** (Ancient Cloister Quarter), one-time home and study area for 12th-century monks and scholars, belonging to the cathedral chapter, including the controversial philosopher and theologian Pierre Abélard, who got himself into hot water with Eloïse (*see page 27*). Around here used to be a warren of houses, until Haussmann razed the brothels, pawnbrokers and taverns, moving 25,000 inhabitants to the suburbs, to provide the present vista. As you pass along Rue de la Colombe, note the remains of the Gallo-Roman wall in the pavement.

On the eastern tip of the island lies the **Mémorial de la Déportation** ❼ (open daily; closed noon–2pm; free). Within this rather bleak structure 200,000 crystals commemorate the 200,000 French victims of the concentration camps, overlooking the quays across the river where many of them lived.

Ile St-Louis – 17th-century elegance and tranquillity

Far from the madding video cameras, across the pedestrian Pont St-Louis, **Ile St-Louis** is a privileged haven of peace and wealth. The island's elegance is 17th-century and its mansions are home to Paris's elite. Turning right along the south bank, you will reach the **Musée Adam Mickiewicz** ❽ (open afternoons; morning only Sat; closed Mon; entrance fee). Adam Mickiewicz (1798–1855) was a Polish poet, living in Paris, who devoted his work to helping oppressed Poles. The 17th-century building includes the Polish Library and memorabilia of the Polish composer Frédéric Chopin.

Continuing eastwards round the island to the north bank, you will pass **Hôtel**

Map, page 140/1

ABOVE: a decorative drainpipe on the Hôtel de Lauzun. **BELOW:** a wider view of the *hôtel*.

The Tour St-Jacques was the belfry of a church on the pilgrimage route to Santiago de Compostela in Spain, in the Middle Ages. Pilgrims (above) carried gourds and a scallop shell with them as a symbol of St Jacques (St James).

BELOW: inside-out building of Centre Georges-Pompidou.

Lambert. Built in 1640 by Louis Le Vau, an advisor to Louis XVIII, it is the finest residence in the city, now owned by the Rothschilds. Further on, in **Hôtel de Lauzun**, fellow poets Théophile Gautier and Charles Baudelaire formed a hashish smoking society in 1845. Ironically, the house now belongs to the City of Paris, reserved for official guests. Behind, on **Rue St-Louis-en-l'Ile**, the church of the same name contains a plaque from the city of St Louis, Missouri, in America. Ile St-Louis's favourite attraction is edible: **Berthillon**, opposite the Pont St-Louis, purveys 100 flavours of the most delicious ice cream. **Brasserie de l'Isle St-Louis**, on Quai de Bourbon, is an institution among institutions, serving the likes of pop stars and politicians.

On the Right Bank of the Seine

To explore the Right Bank **Place du Châtelet** is a good place to start. Flanked by its two theatres, the square is a meeting place for lovers above one of Paris's biggest Métro and RER stations. Northeast of the square stands the **Tour St-Jacques**, seemingly dropped there by mistake, but its chapel was destroyed during the Revolution. Scientist Blaise Pascal (1623–62) experimented with the weight of air from the top and it is now used as a weather station.

Opening out at the eastern end of Avenue Victoria is the wide esplanade of the **Hôtel de Ville 9** (guided tours, Mon only; tel: 01 42 76 50 49), which was the site of the Liberation of Paris celebrations in 1944 and, in medieval times, the scene of hangings and macabre executions. Flanked by bare-breasted maidens in characteristic French style, the 19th-century building contains the majestic Salles des Fêtes (ballroom), a magnificent staircase and lots of chandeliers.

Heading north up Rue St-Martin, towards the Centre Georges-Pompidou

Map, page 140/1

about five minutes away, you pass the richly adorned church of **St-Merri ⑩**. The bell is the oldest in Paris, dating from 1331, and the 17th-century organ used to be played by the French composer Camille Saint-Saëns (1835–1921). Behind the church, the modern **Fontaine de Stravinski** is home to a colourful herd of spouting creatures – innovative fountains which suck and spit water, each named after a piece of music by the Russian composer (*see page 37*). **Le Café Beaubourg**, nearby, offers a trendy tipple in *avant-garde* surroundings. Westwards, down **Rue de la Ferronnerie,** is the spot where Henri IV was stabbed to death by Ravaillac.

Centre Georges-Pompidou – a modern experience

Known locally as Beaubourg and officially as the Centre National d'Art et de Culture, **Centre Georges-Pompidou ⑪** (open all day weekends; afternoons weekdays; closed Tues; entrance fee to galleries; closed for renovation until January 2000, although you can still go up to the viewing area), looking like an airport terminal with the skin stripped off, caused an uproar when it was finished in 1977. But it has since attracted nearly 8 million visitors a year (the most-visited cultural site in the world), who marvel at its pipes, tubes, scaffolds and the external escalators. The pipes are not just for show: the blue convey air, the green transport water, the yellow contain electricity and the red conduct heating. The slightly sunken forecourt is a stage for street entertainment.

Inside, the centre is cavernous, as all the infrastructure is part of the outer structure. The **Musée National de l'Art Moderne**, on the fourth floor, is the jewel in this crown of tubes. Far less frequented than the escalators leading to the expensive roof café, the museum's displays are addictively humorous, bright

ABOVE: viewing from the top of the Centre Georges-Pompidou. **BELOW:** looking down on the entertainment outside.

and airily presented. The colourful Fauvists – Dufy, Derain, van Dongen and early Matisse – are here, alongside the Cubism of Picasso and Braque, abstract childlike canvases of Kandinsky and Klee, and hallucinogenic surrealism of Miró and Dali. Here, too, are Warhol's *Boxes* and Lichtenstein's cartoon-like dot paintings. The outdoor terrace looks over towards Les Halles, displaying sculptures by Tinguely. During the renovation period, temporary exhibitions will be staged in different locations such as La Samaritaine department store in the Rue de Rivoli. A large teepee in the forecourt houses an information office.

Dotted around the Beaubourg quarter are numerous modern art and photographic galleries, inspired by the Centre. Wander the side streets, in particular Rue Beaubourg on the east side and Rue Quincampoix towards Les Halles.

Les Halles – a futuristic marketplace

West of Beaubourg, **Les Halles** (pronounced *Lay Al*) has been a market area since 1183, when Philippe-Auguste erected permanent halls and ordered the city traders to close their shops for two days a week to do business at his own market. Reorganised under Napoleon III, who demanded that his architect, Baltard, build with "iron, nothing but iron!", the market consisted of 10 halls, resembling small railway stations, which were fed by vast underground storehouses, dark kingdoms of death and decay where cages of animals were piled amongst rotting fruits, ruled over by blind storekeepers. Up above, stallholders, restaurant owners, pickpockets, artists, prostitutes and police crowded the market, shouting obscenities as colourful as the food.

The last night of the market, Thursday 27 February 1969, was a sad occasion for Parisians. The animated halls, so lovingly described by Emile Zola

In the Quartier de l'Horloge, a pedestrianised area just north of Centre Georges-Pompidou, is a huge Defender of Time clock in brass and steel. On the hour, a life-size soldier does battle with either the dragon of earth, the bird of the air or the crab of the sea. At six and 12, all attack.

BELOW: the Forum des Halles with St-Eustache behind.

FOUNTAIN OF INNOCENTS

The sole Renaissance fountain in Paris, the Fontaine des Innocents, created by Pierre Lescot and Jean Goujon, sits on the one-time site of the city's infamous cemetery, Les Innocents, just southeast of Les Halles.

Filled with corpses since the 12th century, the graveyard, with a high wall around it, had become a putrid metropolis by the 18th century, as the dead – mostly paupers – were carried there amongst produce bound for the market at Les Halles. Gruesome tales abound about how people ground up the bones for bread, when Paris was under siege in 1590, and how they used the skeletons for firewood.

By 1780, the corpses were overflowing above street level and were teeming with rats, so the cemetery was finally closed and its inmates moved to the Catacombs, where their bones can still be visited (*see page 181*). Today, the square is a meeting place for the city's youth.

Map, page 140/1

(1840–1902) in his novel *Le Ventre de Paris* (*The Belly of Paris*), were no longer suitable for 20th-century commerce and trading was moved to Rungis, near Orly Airport. Vestiges of the past survive in the scattered 24-hour bistros of the area. Make for Au Pied du Cochon (6 Rue Coavillière) for onion soup, snails and pig's trotters at six in the morning, or La Poule au Pot (9 Rue Vauvilliers) for tripe with film directors and singers.

The present-day **Forum des Halles** ⓬ filled the large hole left after the market buildings were demolished. This vast underground commercial centre, four floors beneath Paris, is a monument to modernism. Above ground are glass and steel mushrooms housing cultural centres for contemporary arts and poetry, the **Pavillon des Arts** and **Maison de la Poésie**, created to offset the commercial tone of the Forum. The central courtyard hosts the odd concert around a suggestive Pygmalion statue by Julio Silva. Inside, the **Musée Grévin** (open daily, afternoons Sun and pub. hols; entrance fee), a subsidiary of the larger Grévin museum on Boulevard Montmartre (*see page 128*), has waxwork displays illustrating the *Belle Epoque*, with a talking Victor Hugo and Gustav Eiffel, and the **Musée de l'Holographie** (open daily, afternoons, Sun and pub. hols; entrance fee) provides miraculous holograms to wonder over.

Back to the Seine

Outside the Forum, a pleasant park stretches westward towards the Bourse. In the northeast corner, a giant head and cupped hand, by Henri de Miller, attract children and pigeons to its benign seat, beneath the Gothic gaze of **St-Eustache** ⓭. The 100-metre (330-ft) long church, with Renaissance decoration, is one of Paris's most beautiful, resembling a pregnant Notre Dame. Berlioz and Liszt played premieres here, and music still fills the huge interior during concerts.

To the left, glass pyramids recalling the new Louvre entrance reflect the stones of St-Eustache. This is a new hothouse full of palms, papayas and banana trees. Metal walkways traverse the glasshouses to the **Bourse de Commerce** ⓮ (open daily; closed weekends; free), a circular commercial exchange built in the 18th century on the site of a luxurious brothel and renovated in 1889.

Head back towards the Seine through narrow streets, crossing **Rue St-Honoré**, a major 12th-century thoroughfare, at the **Fontaine de la Croix-du-Trahoir**. Here, in 613, Frédégonde, Queen of Austria, was tied by her hair to a wild horse and dragged to her death. A little further on, the church of **St Germain-l'Auxerrois** ⓯ is another example of Gothic finery with an impressive collection of gargoyles and devils. At midnight on 24 August 1572, the church bells rang as the signal to start the St Bartholomew's Day Massacre (*see page 29*), when thousands of Protestants were butchered on the orders of Catholic Catherine de Médicis and her sons, Charles IX and the future Henri III.

Behind, the edifice of **La Samaritaine** ⓰, one of the biggest and oldest department stores in Paris, spreads over five buildings joined by overhead walkways (*see page 72*). On the roof of the second building, which has an Art Nouveau facade, the terrace restaurant provides one of the finest views of Paris – at a reasonable price.

An ancient edict of Les Halles, stating that nothing hard could be thrown in the market – only mud and detritus – was obeyed with gusto. Dairymaids accused of giving short measures were stood in the square with a slab of the offending butter on their heads.

BELOW: organ grinder on the pedestrian Pont St-Louis.

THE MARAIS AND THE BASTILLE

Steeped in royal and Revolutionary history, these two lively villages within a great metropolis offer medieval streets, museum-filled mansions and the city's oldest and most beautiful square

Map, page 140/1

On the Right Bank of the Seine, tucked behind the Hôtel de Ville and hiding away from the extravagance of the Grands Boulevards, the Marais and the area of the city around the Bastille are both proudly independent districts, possessing an intimate, animated charm that sets them apart from the more grandiose expanses to the west. Here live small communities with their own traditions, folklore and heroes.

The Marais (literally the swamp) was notable in the 13th century for the mosquitoes and frogs that infested the bogs on either side of Rue St-Antoine, the old, raised Roman eastern highway. First, Philippe-Auguste built a defensive wall, then with the arrival of monks and monasteries, the marshes were drained and Charles V constructed a new wall around Paris, which ended at the forbidding, newly completed Bastille fort, bringing the area into the city. When, as Regent, in 1358, Charles V moved from his royal palace on Ile de la Cité, as a result of the *Jacquerie* uprising (*see page 28*), he set up one of his residences on the Seine at St-Paul's, establishing the start of a royal influx into the quarter.

In 1609, Henri IV decided to build a sumptuous nest for his court at the present-day Place des Vosges, shifting the political and financial focus from the Louvre. As a result, the finest architects and stonemasons in Europe descended on the Marais, building countless grand residences, or *hôtels*, for the nobility, each more impressive than the last. These classical walls sheltered *salons* – living-room intellectual societies – where the bright and beautiful of the day would pontificate, lounging on ornate divans.

The fall and rise of the Marais

The pendulum of fashion swung away from the Marais after Louis XIV moved his court to Versailles in the 1680s and the nobility moved to the Ile St-Louis, then westwards to the Faubourg St-Honoré and the Boulevard St-Germain. During the Revolution, the area was abandoned to the people and the Marais's graceful *hôtels* tumbled into disrepair alongside the narrow streets, which became dens of iniquity.

In the 19th and 20th centuries, the quarter became a centre for small industries and craftwork, and successive developers dug up and widened its picturesque streets. In 1962, André Malraux, President de Gaulle's Arts Minister, set wide-scale renovation work in motion to preserve the Marais. Today, many of the *hôtels* are beautifully restored and, although the area maintains a rougher edge which adds to its charm, its former elegance is returning.

Contained by **Rue Beaubourg** to the west and by

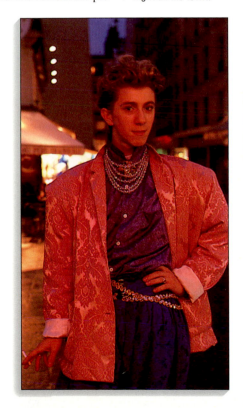

PRECEDING PAGES: Hôtel de Ville in all its glory. **LEFT:** absorbed in a Picasso. **BELOW:** poised for a night on the town.

Boulevard Beaumarchais to the east, the Marais is the historic home of the city's Jewish community and attracts a large number of gays; local cafés, bars and restaurants are animated day and night. Modern art galleries pepper the side streets and passageways, enticing the curious, and at night the ancient lamps exude a romantic glow.

A tour of the old *hôtels*

Behind the Hôtel de Ville (*see page 148*) stands the church of **St-Gervais-St-Protais** (open daily; closed Mon; free) with a flight of Italianate steps and some monstrous-looking gargoyles. The church is famous for sacred music, possessing an 18th-century organ played by eight generations of the Couperin family and François Couperin (1668–1733) composed his two Masses for it. Named after the martyrs Gervase and Protase, two Roman officers who were executed by Nero, the church was shelled by Germany's Big Bertha as a parting shot at the end of World War I in 1918, killing over 100 worshippers.

Rue François-Miron leads away from the Place St-Gervais into the heart of the Marais. Houses along here were nearly demolished by World War II, but with careful restoration are now creeping back to their former glory. At the corner of Rue Cloche-Perce is a half-timbered medieval house and, at No 68, stands the **Hôtel de Beauvais** built by Catherine Beauvais, in 1654, with money and land from King Louis XIV, who had greatly enjoyed her favours as a teenager. She is also said to have entertained archbishops. More innocently, the composer Mozart stayed here on his first visit to Paris at the age of seven – before he too became considerably more profligate.

Neighbouring Rue de Jouy contains **Hôtel d'Aumont** , designed by the

Catherine Beauvais, known as One-eyed Kate, was 40 when she "educated" 16-year-old Louis XIV under the benign gaze of his mother, Anne of Austria. When Louis's marriage procession passed under the balcony of the Hôtel de Beauvais many years later, Kate tipped the bridegroom a wink.

BELOW: a village tempo pervades the Marais.

Map, page 140/1

Versailles architect Louis Le Vau (*see pages 254–255*), renovated and enlarged by the French Classical architect François Mansart (1598–1666) and decorated by Versailles painter Charles Le Brun (1619–90). With a formal garden designed by Le Nôtre (*see page 122*), the mansion is now the city's administrative court.

Further on down Rue Figuier, stand the château-like turrets of one of Paris's few medieval residences, the **Hôtel de Sens** ⓴ (open weekday afternoons; all day Sat; closed Sun and pub. hols; entrance fee) which now houses the city's historical and fine arts library, the Bibliothèque Forney. Built at the end of the 15th century for the Archbishop of Sens, who was a soldier and a cleric, the mansion is military in style, with simple but immaculate gardens. Henri IV lodged his first wife, Marguerite de Valois (Reine Margot), in the *hôtel* when he could no longer put up with her promiscuity. Here she continued her active social life, leaving a trail of broken hearts. When a jealous ex-lover murdered her current *beau*, Marguerite had him beheaded outside the house.

Looking behind the Hôtel de Sens back along the river, the stark contrast of the resolutely modern **Cité Internationale des Arts** can be seen in the midst of antiquated refinement; the building provides studios and a year's lodging for artists from around the world.

The Village St-Paul – a romantic spot

Opposite the Hôtel de Sens, the Rue de l'Ave-Maria intersects with the Rue des Jardins St-Paul, a block away. This leads into the **Village St-Paul** past two towers and ramparts, the remnants of the **Enceinte de Philippe-Auguste** (Philippe-Auguste's city wall), shadowing the antics of local schoolchildren. The restored village consists of a series of small courtyards and fountains, sheltering bustling

In the 18th century, Hôtel de Sens was the departure point for the Paris-Lyon stage-coach run – a route deemed so unsafe that passengers were encouraged to make a will before setting out on a journey.

BELOW: a trendy shop for those in the know.

For a true Parisian meal, Le Temps des Cerises in Rue de la Cerisaie, where 1,000 cherry trees used to grow, is a bistro that hasn't changed with the times, providing fresh market produce served by endearing, jocular waiters.

BELOW: Place des Vosges – a sought-after address.

antique shops and secondhand stalls. At night, it is romantically tranquil, beneath the halo of diffused light from the old streetlamps.

On **Rue Charlemagne**, wooden walkways between the buildings have been restored as they were in the Middle Ages. Left along Rue St-Paul is an ancient passageway leading to the church of **St-Paul-St-Louis** ㉑, an amalgamation of two parishes and constructed by Jesuits, in 1627, copying the Gesù church in Rome. Here, the hearts of Louis XIII and Louis XIV were embalmed and kept as relics until the Revolution, when they were removed and sold to an artist, St-Martin, who crushed them to mix with oil for a varnish for one of his pictures. Later he gave what was left of Louis XIII's heart to the newly installed King Louis XVIII, in return for a golden snuffbox.

Before plunging into the area north of Rue St-Antoine, this may be a good point to stop for a meal, either at **Le Temps des Cerises** (*see left and page 273*) near the Place de la Bastille, or at **Le Beautreillis** (18 Rue Beautreillis). This is where Jim Morrison, deity of the Doors rock band, drank his last bottle of wine with his girlfriend Pamela Courson. He was found dead in the bath in her apartment across the street on 3 July 1971, officially from a heart attack. Unofficially...

To the Place des Vosges – an enchanting square

Rue St-Antoine is the ancient jugular of the Marais. Built wide and straight in good old Roman fashion, from the 14th century, the road became a site of jousting tournaments until, in 1574, Henri II was knocked off his horse by his Scottish Captain of the Guard, Montgomery, with a blow to his eye. In a drastic bid to save his life, the King's physician, Ambroise Paré, ordered the immediate decapitation of every prisoner on death row and had their heads rushed to the surgery so that he could experiment on them in a bid to rescue his monarch. Needless to say he didn't succeed and Henri died 10 days later. The unfortunate Captain Montgomery lost his head, too.

Hôtel de Sully ㉒ (open daily; closed public hols; entrance fee) in Rue St-Antoine is one of the finest in the Marais. Under the courtyard's grumpy statues, Voltaire was beaten with clubs by followers of the Count of Rohan, following a slanging match between the two at the Comédie Française (*see page 124*). Through the courtyard, temporary art exhibitions are housed in what is now known as the **Caisse Nationale des Monuments Historiques** (Historic Monuments Commission; tel: 01 44 61 21 50), which organises walking tours of Paris and guided tours of monuments and museums. Behind, the intimate garden is an unexpected surprise with clipped privet hedges *à l'anglaise*. A small door in the back right corner leads to the **Place des Vosges** ㉓.

This enchanting 17th-century square, with a garden surrounded by 36 arcaded residences, was constructed by Henri IV as a showcase for his court. Here courtiers paraded, preened and pranced. After the Revolution, when the melted down statue of Louis XIII had been reforged and replaced, the square was named after Vosges, the first *département* to have paid its taxes promptly. Today, this is the most beautiful square in Paris and one of the capital's most sought-after addresses. The arcades house chic cafés, as well as Issey Miyake's boutique.

In the southeast corner is the **Maison de Victor Hugo** ㉔ (open daily; closed Mon and pub. hols; entrance fee). The Romantic writer's house is a museum to the great man, containing manuscripts, pen-and-ink drawings and pieces of furniture knocked together by Hugo in his spare time.

On Sundays, the gardens are a playground for children and lovers, while ducks

Map, page 140/1

Madame de Sévigné was born at No 1 bis Place des Vosges in 1626. Her claim to fame is through the letters written to her daughter, first published in 1726. She lived her final years in the Hôtel Carnavalet (see page 161).

BELOW: Victor Hugo's home in Place des Vosges is now a museum.

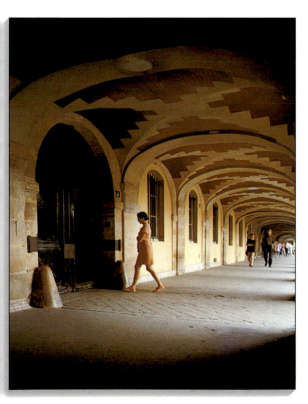

HUGO – MAN OF WORDS

Poet, dramatist, novelist, politician and leader of the Romantic movement, Victor Hugo (1802–85) lived at 6 Place des Vosges from 1832 to 1848. This was a very creative period of his life in which he wrote critical essays, reviews and the major part of his dramatic works, including *Lucrèce Borgia* (1833) and *Angelo* (1835). In 1841, after two attempts, Hugo was elected a member of the Académie Française (*see page 197*) and, in 1845, he accepted a political post under King Louis-Philippe. The 1848 Revolution threw Hugo into the thick of political struggle and he became a chief in the Democratic party against Louis-Napoleon. In 1851, he went into exile to the Channel Islands, where he wrote *Les Misérables* (1862). At the fall of the Empire in 1870, Hugo returned to Paris and continued writing there until his death.

The Mémorial du Martyr Juif Inconnu (Memorial to the Unknown Jew) *stands on Rue Geoffroy l'Asnier, south of the Jewish Quarter. Its eternal flame in an underground crypt is a poignant reminder of the Holocaust.*

BELOW: a beautifully preserved shopfront in the Marais.

happily waddle in the dancing fountains. In summer, the arcades host classical concerts where, in 1763, Mozart gave his first recital. If you are hungry, and not poor, **L'Ambroisie** at 9 Place des Vosges is one of Paris's Michelin three-star restaurants. To be sure of a table you should either book a long time in advance or become a famous politician.

A turn around the Jewish Quarter

One of the city's most colourful areas, the Jewish Quarter is well worth a visit. Turning left from the Place des Vosges, Rue des Francs-Bourgeois leads a short way along sculptured walls past the Musée Carnavalet to Rue Pavée and the **Hôtel de Lamoignon** ㉕, where 60 people were murdered during the massacres of 2 September 1792 (including the Princess of Lamballe, whose head was presented to Queen Marie-Antoinette on a spike). Built in 1584 for the Duchesse d'Angoulême, the *hôtel* now houses the city's historical library, which includes documents from the Revolution.

Rue des Rosiers, a little further on, is the heart of the district: a narrow extravaganza of kosher delis, falafel stands, old men on motorbikes selling watermelon and tiny shops packed with religious artifacts. In the 13th century, King Philippe-Auguste moved the Jewish community living by Notre Dame to the Marais and more arrivals came from Russia, Poland and central Europe in the 19th century. After the Holocaust in World War II, numbers swelled again in the 1960s, when Algeria became independent and immigrants from North Africa moved in.

Here, on 16 July 1942, French police arrested every man, woman and child in the district and sent many of them to concentration camps. More recently, in 1982, the world-renowned **Jo Goldenberg's** restaurant and deli, at 7 Rue des

Rosiers, suffered a bomb attack, for which France's extreme right got the blame.

For less expensive fare and a bustling ambience turn the corner to **Chez Marianne** (2 Rue des Hospitalières-Saint-Gervais), where the owner André Jornot writes his saying-of-the-week on the restaurant window. Gems include: "Man is a dung-heap where the Lord seeks to grow a rose". Next door, children kick footballs on a small square – the site of a primary school whose pupils were all sent to Buchenwald camp.

Map, page 140/1

The mansions of Carnavalet and Picasso

To experience the diverse collection of museums in the Marais retrace your steps back to the **Musée Carnavalet ㉗** (open daily; closed Mon and pub. hols; entrance fee). Occupying two mansions, the main 16th-century Hôtel Carnavalet and the neighbouring 17th-century Hôtel le Peletier, the museum covers the history of Paris and contains well displayed exhibits that trace the evolution of the capital in paintings, sculpture and costume. Madame de Sévigné, who wrote the illuminating *Letters* (*see page 159*), lived in the Hôtel Carnavalet between 1677 and 1696 and there is a gallery devoted to her life. From here, organised walking tours of the Marais visit those parts other guides do not reach.

Head northwards to Rue du Parc Royal, lined with magnificently restored 17th-century mansions, and in Place de Thorigny, a few minutes' walk away, is the **Musée Bricard ㉘** (open daily; afternoon Mon; closed 12–2pm and at weekends, Aug and pub. hols; entrance fee) in an elegant house built by Libéral Bruand, the architect of Les Invalides (*see page 210*). A fascinating lock and key museum, exhibits include knobs and knockers from Roman times.

Opposite, Rue de Thorigny leads to the **Musée Picasso ㉙** (open daily; closed

ABOVE: a reminder of the German occupation.
BELOW: Hôtel Carnavalet – home to the museum of the history of Paris.

Tues and pub. hols; entrance fee) in the beautifully restored Hôtel Salé. Following his death in 1973, Pablo Picasso's family was faced with an enormous inheritance tax bill and so, in lieu of payment, they donated to the nation a large collection of his works, comprising 200 paintings, more than 3,000 drawings and 88 ceramics, along with sculptures, collages, illustrated books and manuscripts, plus his own private collection of work from contemporary artists. Laid out in chronological order, the exhibition covers his long and prolific career in a superb setting and provides a conclusive tour around the genius of this greatest of 20th-century artists whose motto was, "I do not seek, I find". Giacometti's stunning ironwork completes the artistic decor. In the summer, among the statues in the garden, a small outdoor café serves tea to weary art lovers.

A cluster of museums

Passing back through Place de Thorigny, down Rue Elzévir, **Musée Cognacq-Jay** ㉚ (open daily; closed Mon and pub. hols) can be found a few minutes' walk away in the exquisite Hôtel Donon. The mansion houses the art collection of Ernest Cognacq, founder of the Samaritaine department store (*see page 151*), and his wife Louise Jay and includes works by Rembrandt and Canaletto. Each room evokes a facet of 18th-century life, with lavish furnishings and decoration.

A little further west, at the end of Rue Barbette, is the stunningly restored **Hôtel de Rohan** ㉛, which is unfortunately only accessible when housing temporary exhibitions. If closed, take a look in the courtyard at the magnificent sculpture of the *Horses of Apollo* over the stables.

Turning right on to Rue des Francs-Bourgeois a few minutes' walk southwards, you will see, on your left, the austere facade of the **Crédit Municipal**, the

ABOVE: *Portrait of Marie-Thérèse Walter*, in the Musée Picasso.
BELOW: children's hour, Musée Picasso.

A SPANISH GENIUS

Born in Malaga in Spain, Pablo Picasso (1881–1973) finally settled in Paris at the age of 23, having studied art in Barcelona and Madrid. However, he never lost his Spanish touch as his work so often revealed. A leading figure in modern 20th-century art, his work developed through many phases, including a Blue Period, when he painted his *Self Portrait* (1901), and Cubism, a primitive and monumental form of art, which he also explored in sculpture. In the 1920s and 1930s, Picasso produced his most abstract work and, in 1937, he painted his famous *Guernica*. He remained in Paris, in the Rue des Grands-Augustins, during World War II moving to the South of France afterwards.

Picasso died in Mougins, leaving a massive collection of paintings, sculptures, drawings and ceramics, along with a large collection of works by his contemporaries such as Matisse, Braque, Cézanne and Rousseau.

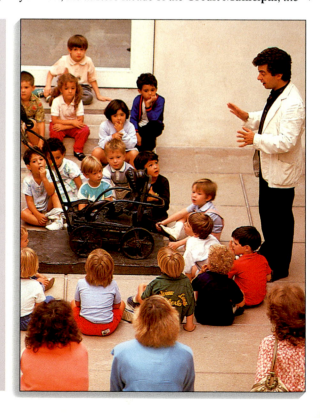

state pawnbroker. Nicknamed *Ma Tante* (My Aunt), the lending facility was opened in 1777 and you can still obtain cash on the value of objects surrendered to its charge.

Opposite the house of the poor stand the houses of the rich, namely the **Hôtel de Soubise**, home to the **Musée de l'Histoire de France** (open afternoons; closed Tues and pub. hols; entrance fee). This early 18th-century mansion has rooms handsomely decorated in the Rococo style. Here, too, are the **National Archives** in which over 6 million official documents, on 290 km (180 miles) of shelving, demonstrate the French nation's love affair with the rubber stamp.

Rue des Archives leads up to Paris's finest collection of stuffed animals in the **Musée de la Chasse et de la Nature** (Hunting Museum) ㉝ (open daily; closed 12.30–1.30pm; closed Tues and pub. hols; entrance fee) in one wing of Hôtel Guénégaud, which bears witness to the French aphorism: "If it moves, shoot it".

Quartier du Temple – a town within a town

To the north of the Marais, about a 10-minute walk up Rue des Archives, the **Quartier du Temple** was once the headquarters of the Knights Templar, where 4,000 people lived in a safe haven, out of bounds to the authorities. A 13th-century secret society of soldiers, originally formed to protect pilgrims in the Holy Land, the Knights Templar owned much of France and were in charge of the royal treasury until 1307, when Philippe the Fair burnt their leaders at the stake on an island in the Seine and the society was forced to go underground.

With the Revolution, the Temple Tower (no longer standing) became the most famous prison in France and was where the Royal Family was imprisoned, at first in luxurious apartments and later in the dungeons. It was from here,

Map,
page
140\1

TIP

Le Domarais, at 53 bis Rue des Francs-Bourgeois, is a French restaurant that offers spectacular decor and unique dinner entertainment; its circular 17th-century dining room is overlooked by a balcony where musicians perform.

BELOW: 17th-century Hôtel Salé, housing the Musée Picasso.

When the victims of the 1830 and 1841 revolutions were lying in state in the Louvre before burial under the Colonne de Juillet, legend has it they were joined by two Egyptian mummies, surplus to the museum's needs, who subsequently also received full military honours…

ABOVE: plan of the Bastille prison.
BELOW: in the Métro.

in 1793, that Louis XVI went to the guillotine. His son, Louis XVII, stayed on, but mysteriously disappeared, aged 10, in 1795.

The Temple Tower was eventually razed by a superstitious Napoleon and Haussmann replaced it with a wrought iron, covered market, the **Carreau du Temple**, which still sells inexpensive and secondhand clothes and cloth by the metre. Along the tree-lined Rue Perrée lies all that remains of the Temple fortress, the **Square du Temple** ❸❹ garden, which resounds to the sound of ping pong balls on two outdoor tables.

Not far from the Temple district, about another 10 minutes along Rue Réaumur, is France's most prestigious technical college, the **Conservatoire National des Arts et Métiers**, which houses the **Musée National des Techniques** ❸❺ (National Technical Museum, opening after refurbishment in 1998). Immortalised in Umberto Eco's finale to his novel *Foucault's Pendulum*, in which bizarre ceremonies take place under the pendulum, the museum includes such innovations as Volta's battery, Pascal's adding machine and Blériot's aeroplane.

To end a visit to the Marais head down Rue du Temple past the jewellery boutiques (about a 10-minute walk) to No 41 and its courtyard. Once the headquarters of the Aigle d'Or, the last stagecoach company in Paris, it is now a seductively bustling corner, where the **Café de la Gare** puts on alternative theatre and music and **Le Studio** is one of the better, and most fun, of the Tex-Mex restaurants in Paris.

The infamous Bastille

To the east of the Marais squats the **Bastille** district. Once a fearsome bastion of royal strength, the *quartier* fell into disrepair and disrepute after the prison

Map, page 140/1

was destroyed during the Revolution. On 14 July 1789, when crowds stormed the prison, freeing the inmates – all seven of them – Louis XVI was unimpressed, recording in his diary, "Today – nothing." Following the dismantling of the Bastille, an enterprising workman made sculptures of the prison from the rubble and sold them to local councils, who were denounced as anti-Republican if they refused the high price demanded.

The medieval Bastille covered the present day **Place de la Bastille** ❸❻ and the **Arsenal** complex to the south, at the junction of the Seine with the Canal St-Martin. The modern square is a wide, busy thoroughfare with the usual tall column in its midst – **Colonne de Juillet** – erected to victims of the 1830 and 1848 revolutions, who are buried underneath.

Dominating the square, the huge modern **Opéra Bastille** ❸❼ has been the victim of much polemic from politicians, art critics and public alike. Although its appearance (half a goldfish bowl attached to a black triumphal arch) has shocked traditionalists, the opera house is gradually creeping into Parisian hearts. Opened on the bicentenary of the Revolution, recent seasons have included works by Wagner, Verdi and Puccini.

A buzzing mecca by night and by day

The Bastille is one of Paris's most rapidly changing quarters. Old crumbling streets are being gentrified and the old crumbling inhabitants are moving out. Some of the rebellious charm remains in streets such as Rue de Lappe and Rue de Charonne to the east of the square, yet the influx of the upwardly mobile has led to an epidemic of dimly lit bistro-bars which are full of serious souls dressed in black. Countless modern art galleries have sprouted, particularly on Rue

Table tennis is the number one sport for the Chinese and Vietnamese who live in the Quartier du Temple. In 1914, the French government brought in 100,000 Chinese to replace the workers gone to war, among them was a boy named Deng Xiao Ping.

BELOW LEFT: in the spirit of Bastille Day.
BELOW: symbolic Colonne de Juillet.

BELOW: Frédéric
Chopin's grave in
the Cimetière du
Père-Lachaise.

Keller and Rue de Lappe. At night, Rue de la Roquette becomes a buzzing mecca for the fashion gurus of Paris as they roar up and down on their Harley Davidsons, oblivious to the past when this street echoed to the cries of prisoners being beheaded at the corner of Rue de la Croix-Faubin – five stones from the guillotine block remain.

Le Balajo (9 Rue de Lappe) is a hot, trendy Latin dance hall, but be prepared to stand in line to get in. The **Théâtre de la Bastille**, on Rue de la Roquette (nothing to do with the Opéra – as the tatty decor proves), currently offers Paris's most challenging dance works. At 17 Rue de la Roquette, **La Rotonde** is a young, chic bar – a far cry from its past life as a brothel whose owner was shot dead by a blind accordion player. The elegant **Bofinger** (*see page 272*) (3 Rue de la Bastille), off the Place de la Bastille, claims to be the city's oldest brasserie, magnificently decorated. Get here early for a seat under the glass cupola.

The area is still lively during the day and addictive for anyone who likes people-watching. Off Rue du Faubourg-St-Antoine, you can wander through numerous passages of small workshops manufacturing furniture, rugs and jewellery, as they have for centuries. **Passage du Cheval Blanc** leads off from the Bastille, with courtyards named after the months of the year. **Passage de la Main d'Or**, five minutes further on, is equally charming.

Wine lovers should not miss **Bistrot Jacques Mélac** (42 Rue Léon-Frot – *off the map*), towards the Cimetière du Père-Lachaise in the east. The vine that sprouts proudly from the bar sets the tone, and two signs on the wall state categorically, "Here, water is for cooking potatoes", and "Do not drink water, fish make love in it". The *patron*, Monsieur Mélac, produces 40 litres of wine annually, most of which he seems to consume himself, and The Wine Growers of

Paris have their meetings here. Recently, they have produced an average of around 600 litres a year and the association is still growing.

A trip to the Cimetière du Père-Lachaise

End your day as thousands of Parisians have ended theirs – in the **Cimetière du Père-Lachaise** (Métro Père-Lachaise). In the 17th century, a retirement home for old priests stood here and Louis XIV's confesser, Père Lachaise, was a generous benefactor. When the cemetery was built in 1803, the people were reluctant to be buried in it, as it was far from the city centre and far from fashionable. Napoleon promptly dug up Molière and La Fontaine and buried them with pomp at Père-Lachaise, with the result that today the guest list is endless. A wander among the ornate graves is a unique experience, if only to watch the living who frequent this municipality of the dead.

Probably, the most visited grave is Jim Morrison's – graffiti ensures you will not miss it and security has had to be implemented to protect it from further vandalism. Other graves are harder to find, but a map purchased at the entrance on Boulevard de Ménilmontant will aid the confused pilgrim: here lie Chopin, Rossini, Bizet and Colette; there Victor Hugo, Balzac, Apollinaire and Oscar Wilde, the latter under a fittingly inscrutable sphinx. Also at rest are Edith Piaf and American expatriates Isadora Duncan, Gertrude Stein and Alice B. Toklas.

The cemetery was the site of the last battle of the Paris Commune (*see page 36*) against French troops from Versailles on 27 May 1871. At dawn the next day, the remaining Communards were lined up against a wall and shot. They were buried in a ditch where they fell and the **Mur des Fédérés** (Federalists' Wall) is now a socialist shrine. Nearby are monuments to both world wars.

ABOVE: the French novelist Colette, one of the famous residents in Père-Lachaise.
BELOW: Jim Morrison's grave is the most popular.

Map, page 140/1

MONTMARTRE AND PIGALLE

Map, page 172

Renowned for a colourful nightlife revolving around the Moulin Rouge, Montmartre, once a haunt for writers and artists, still hums with life in the steep, narrow streets under the opulent Sacré-Coeur

The "village" of Montmartre occupies the highest point of Paris, nestling into a small hillside in the 18th *arrondissement*, north of the city centre. Extending from the sometimes seedy yet vibrant Place Pigalle in the south to the white cupolas of Sacré-Coeur, the village is an alluring huddle of small steep streets and hidden steps.

In parts, Montmartre resembles a country hamlet with its cobbled squares and gnarled inhabitants. Elsewhere, neon, fast-food, sex shows and tourist buses have tarnished the Bohemian atmosphere. Follow the golf hats and Montmartre will seem predictably commercial. Enter a narrow side street, down a deserted flight of steps and you will be alone, wandering in Paris's least Parisian and most charismatic quarter. Away from the crowds and indifferent food on Place du Tertre, numerous inexpensive restaurants greet the hungry wanderer.

How Montmartre got its name

Montmartre has always liked to be different. Legend has it that, in AD 287, the Romans decapitated St Denis, the first Bishop of Paris, and two priests on the hill. St Denis calmly picked up his head and walked off with it to where the basilica of St-Denis (*see page 250*) now stands. The hill became known as *Mons Martyrium* (Martyrs' Mound). As local bar owners point out, people have been picking their heads out of the gutters of Montmartre ever since.

In the 12th century, a Benedictine convent settled on the hill and 400 years later, Henri IV took shelter in it when laying siege to Paris in 1589. His only conquest of the campaign, it appears, was the 17-year-old abbess of the time. The last mother superior here was guillotined during the Revolution at the age of 82, despite her deafness and blindness, and the convent buildings were destroyed.

Revolution has been the district's speciality ever since St Denis's rebellious behaviour and, in 1871, its inhabitants seized 170 cannons to defend themselves after the fall of Paris to the Prussians. The Thiers' government sent in troops to recapture them but the generals were overwhelmed, lined up on the hill and shot – so beginning the Paris Commune (*see page 36*).

For much of the 19th century, Montmartre was mined for gypsum and still retained a country charm with its vineyards, cornfields, flocks of sheep and 40 windmills. It was this charm and the lofty isolation of the hill that attracted artists and writers during the latter part of the century. Painters and their models frolicked on Place Pigalle, and everyone flocked to the Moulin Rouge. Impressionism, Fauvism and Cubism were conceived in the lofts, bars and dance halls of Montmartre.

When the Bohemians migrated to Montparnasse, the

PRECEDING PAGES: one of the many caricaturists in Place du Tertre. **LEFT:** Sacré-Coeur on the Butte de Montmartre. **BELOW:** notorious Moulin Rouge.

TIP

The ideal way to see Montmartre is on foot, but the Montmartrobus and tourist train provide a less exhausting slice of the district and start from Place Blanche.

ABOVE: nightlife in *Gai Paree*.

district was left to sex-shop owners, pawnbrokers and cheap hotels and, for many years afterwards, Montmartre was synonymous with sleaze. Yet, today, the village is suddenly fashionable once more. Dingy strip bars are being transformed into chic rock clubs, peep shows are becoming American-style diners and the narrow streets roar with BMWs and Porsches.

The Moulin Rouge – a notorious dance hall

At Place Blanche, the **Moulin Rouge ❶**, with a red neon windmill, provides a taste of tourist France to wealthy foreigners (the "French" dancers are selected from auditions in the US and the UK). The club's history is gloriously scandalous: Toulouse-Lautrec (*see page 100*) sat here during the *Belle Epoque* (*see pages 36–37*), sketching the energetic cancan of Jane Avril. In 1896, the annual Paris Art School Ball at the Moulin Rouge was the scene of the first fully nude striptease, by one of the school's prettiest models. She was arrested, imprisoned and students went to the barricades in the Quartier Latin, proclaiming "The battle for artistic nudity" – two students died in subsequent scuffles with police. The **Folies-Bergère** (Métro Cadet), about 2 km (1 mile) further south on Rue Richer (*see maps on pages 112–15*) has much the same fare. Next door to the Moulin Rouge, modern hedonists gather at **La Locomotive**, a huge, train-shaped disco, ringing to rock, roll, and Europop. And a few doors away, on the Boulevard de Clichy, the **Théatre des Deux Anes** offers typical Parisian cabaret.

The changing face of Pigalle

A little further east along Boulevard de Clichy lies **Place Pigalle ❷**, the gateway to Montmartre. Less artistic attractions abound in Pigalle, or "Pig Alley", as it

Map, page 172

was once known to American soldiers, for it has been the core of the Parisian sex trade for several decades. Around the streets of Pigalle, tassled curtains provide glimpses of smoky interiors, slashed signs promote live sex shows and aggressive bouncers attempt to persuade tourists into "naked extravaganzas". Beware – prices quoted are much lower than you will pay inside. Things are changing, however. The advent of Aids has drastically reduced custom, and a hefty increase in value-added tax, from 18.6 percent to 33.3 percent, has been aimed deliberately at the sex trade.

The cabarets, which once occupied half the houses along Rue des Martyrs in the 18th century, are being taken over by hip clubs and trendy bars. At 72 Boulevard Rochechouart, the **Elysée Montmartre** ❸ has come out of retirement to host up-and-coming rock groups. The old hall greeted Russian soldiers during the Allied occupation of 1814. As they ordered their drinks (forbidden by the Russian military authorities) they shouted "*bistro*" meaning "quickly", thereby creating a Parisian institution. The *Belle Epoque* facade alone is worth the visit.

Sacré-Coeur – a church with a view

From Boulevard Rochechouart, Rue de Steinkerque leads up to Square Willette at the foot of the hill, the top of which is called the "butte" of Montmartre. Here in front is the **Marché St-Pierre** ❹, specialising in clothing and cheap textiles that often attract the professional designers. Close by is the 1868 market hall designed by Baltard, the original architect of Les Halles (*see pages 150–51*). Now a cultural centre, it houses the **Musée d'Art Naïf Max Fourny** ❺ (open daily; closed Mon; entrance fee), an unusual museum exhibiting contemporary paintings from around 30 countries, recognisable by their simple themes and

TIP

If you plan to stay out late, remember the Métro closes at 12.30am, but for the all-nighters it is open again after 5.30am. Night buses run on some routes (*see pages 266–67*).

BELOW LEFT: a popular subject for artists.

NIGHTSPOTS OF PIGALLE

A n area that never sleeps, Pigalle, with the Boulevard de Clichy running through it, is the centre of Paris nightlife. Popular venues are Folies Pigalle (11 Place Pigalle), once a strip club and now one of the most entertaining nightspots; Le Dépanneur (27 Rue Fontaine), the place to slam tequilas around the clock in an imitation American diner; Le Moloko (26 Rue Fontaine) is the hang-out for models, bad boys and transvestites – the kitsch dance floor, smoking room and cocktail bar are open all night. La Cigale (120 Boulevard de Rochechouart) offers jazz, and for a transvestite version of the Folies Bergères go to Chez Madame Arthur (75 bis Rue des Martyrs). Numerous clubs in the area offer a "Parisian atmosphere" with striptease and very expensive drinks.

bright colours. The building also includes a children's **Musée en Herbe**, focussing on green issues, with changing exhibits.

On the summit of the hill stands the white bulk of the basilica of the **Sacré-Coeur ❻** (open daily; entrance fee for dome and crypt). Either walk up through the Square Willette, laid out in terraces in 1929, or take the *funiculaire* (cable car – Métro tickets are valid on it) alongside. The domed basilica was conceived by a group of Roman Catholics in 1870 who vowed to build a church to the Sacred Heart if Paris was delivered safely from the Prussian siege – the heart of one of the men, Alexandre Legentil, has been preserved in a stone urn in the crypt. The Church took on the responsibility of the project in 1873 and work started two years later, with Paul Abadie as architect, basing its design on the Romano-Byzantine cathedral of St-Front in Périgueux.

The bone-white colour of the building is due to its Chateau-Landon stone, which secretes calcite when it rains, bleaching the walls. Its Byzantine austerity, added to its symbolic censure of a popular uprising, has rendered Sacré-Coeur one of the Parisians' least favourite monuments.

Completed in 1914 but not consecrated until after the war in 1919, the dome offers a stunning view over Paris, up 237 narrow spiral steps (this is the second highest vantage point over the city, after the Eiffel Tower) and from the stained-glass gallery beneath there is a good view of the cavernous interior which, apart from the massive Byzantine mosaic of Christ (1912–22) by Luc Olivier Merson on the chancel's vaulted ceiling, has little else to offer.

Outside on the terrace, crowds gather together in the early evening to drink wine, strum guitars and watch the glittering lights of Paris, overlooked by statues of Joan of Arc and St Louis on horseback.

The Sacré-Coeur is dominated by an 83-metre (262-ft) high belltower, built in 1895, holding one of the heaviest bells in the world at nearly 19 tonnes. Its clapper weighs 850 kg (1,900 lb).

BELOW: art and food in Place du Tertre.

On the "butte"

Next to the exotic Sacré-Coeur, the simple church of **St-Pierre de Montmartre** ❼ is the second oldest in Paris (after St-Germain-des-Prés, *see page 192*), dating from 1133, and the only remaining vestige of the Abbey of Montmartre, where the Bendictine nuns used to live. After the Revolution, the church was abandoned, until it was reconsecrated in 1908. If you are here on *Toussaint* (All Saints' Day – 1 November), visit the small, romantic graveyard behind the church, because this is the only day of the year that it is open.

Just to the west, **Place du Tertre** ❽ is the tourist honeypot of Montmartre, with its "authentic" bistros, and even more "authentic" craft shops. The square was once the site of the village hall and today it is ruled by the mighty franc. In the 19th century, artists began exhibiting their work here and now there are legions of mediocre artists on the square (two per square metre) who are voluble when selling their wares. Yet, despite this oppressive commercialisation, the square retains an animated excitement at night, lit up by fairylights.

From the Place du Tertre quiet, winding Rue Poulbot leads through **Place du Calvaire** – the smallest square in Paris, which offers a spectacular view and is the intimate home of lovers and drinkers – to the **Espace Montmartre Salvador Dalì** ❾ (open daily; entrance fee). A select collection of 330 sculptures and drawings of the surrealist Catalan painter are exhibited in unusual settings here, including his famous clocks representing "the fluidity of time".

A few minutes' walk further on, Rue des Saules passes the top of Rue St-Rustique, a quiet, rustically ancient street leading away from the buzz of the Place du Tertre, which contains the **Auberge La Bonne Franquette**, originally called Le Billard en Bois, where Vincent Van Gogh and Auguste Renoir both painted. The

Map, page 172

On Christmas Eve in 1898, Louis Renault drove the first petrol-driven car to reach the top of the "butte".

BELOW LEFT: getting together in a bar in Montmartre.

A MASTER OF SURREALISM

An eccentric, extrovert Catalan painter, Salvador Dalì (1904–89) was desparate to go to Paris in the 1920s, considered to be the art capital and already conquered by fellow Catalan artists Picasso and Joan Mirò. After studying art in Madrid and mixing with such Spanish modernists as film director Luis Buñuel, he finally made it to Paris in 1929. With the help of the two established, older artists offering him introductions and motivated by his "Catalan sense of fantasy", Dalì held his first Surrealist exhibition that same year. Through Mirò, the Spaniard with the flowing cape and handlebar moustache met other Surrealists, with whom he was to quarrel later. Picasso once said that Dalì's imagination reminded him of "an outboard motor continually running", the painter himself wanted to "systemise confusion".

Auguste Renoir (1841–1919) was an Impressionist who loved to paint the joyful and attractive sides of Paris, mainly using pretty girls in colourful clothes as subjects.

BELOW: art for sale in Montmartre.
BELOW RIGHT: sightseeing the easy way.

crossroads outside the inn and other Parisian street scenes were immortalised by Utrillo (*see page 100*) in his paintings. Other frequent vistors were Cézanne, Toulouse-Lautrec (*see page 100*), Monet (*see pages 122–23, 253*) and Zola.

Old Montmartre

In Rue Cortot, the next street along, is the **Musée du Vieux Montmartre** ❿ (open daily; closed Mon; entrance fee) which chronicles the life and times of the "butte", in an old rural residence. Originally the country home of Rozimund, an actor in Molière's theatre company and whose death in 1686 was similar to Molière's while acting in *Le Malade Imaginaire* (*see page 124*), it also housed Renoir, Dufy (*see page 101*) and Utrillo. The museum is an evocation of past simplicity, gaiety and Bohemian living, with pictures by Kees van Dongen (1877–1968) and Dufy, reconstructions of Utrillo's favourite café and an artist's studio, yellowing photographs and a wonderful view over Paris. Composer Erik Satie (1866–1925) lived in the same street. His house is now a small museum and a seven-person concert hall.

Nearby is the famous **vineyard of Montmartre**, cultivated since the Middle Ages. At the beginning of October, the grape harvest attracts hundreds of volunteers and the streets host processions and parties. Around 300 litres of wine are sold at auction, with the proceeds going to Montmartre pensioners.

The famous inn **Au Lapin Agile** ⓫ (open evenings; closed Mon; entrance fee) stands opposite the vineyard on the Rue des Saules. This was the haunt of the bright and beautiful at the turn of the century: a restaurant-cabaret, where Renoir and the symbolist poet Paul Verlaine (1844–96) laid tables and Apollinaire sang with fellow Surrealist poet Max Jacob. Picasso paid for a day's meals at the Lapin with one of his *Harlequin* paintings – today worth several million pounds. The name of this small hut on the hill, shrouded with trees, originated from humorist André Gill's 1880 wall picture of a rabbit jumping over a cooking pot, which people called the "Lapin à Gill". Today, a tourist attraction, the rabbit, with smoked-stained walls, original paintings by Cubist Fernand Léger (1881–1955) and Gill, and the old wooden tables, is still going strong. Get here by 9pm, and imbibe, sitting in the corner once inhabited by Picasso or Verlaine. A cabaret is provided, taking you back in time and encouraging audience participation.

Passing the **Cimetière St-Vincent** where Utrillo lies in peace, Rue des Saules leads to the **Musée d'Art Juif ⑫** (open afternoons; closed Fri and Sat; entrance fee), a collection of Jewish art, containing works by Soutine (1894–1943) and Pissarro, along with a Bible illustrated by Marc Chagall.

Tranquil Montmartre

Far from the helter-skelter animation of Pigalle and Place du Tertre, the west of Montmartre, on the other side of St Vincent cemetery, is a puzzle of small old streets and tumbledown houses. Take the steps from Place Constantin-Pecqueur, off Rue Caulaincourt to **Square Suzanne-Buisson ⑬**, one of the most romantic corners of Montmartre with a terrace and antiquated lamps.

The square occupies the former garden of the **Château des Brouillards**, an 18th-century folly once inhabited by Renoir and the mad, symbolist poet Gérard de Nerval (who hanged himself in 1855, leaving a note saying, "Don't wait for me, for the night will be black and white") and later turned into a dance hall. During the 19th century, the "château" could only be seen when the *brouillards*

Map, page 172

ABOVE AND BELOW:
Au Lapin Agile where artists and intellectuals used to congregate.

The Dutch painter Vincent Van Gogh (1853–90) lived in Rue Lepic between 1886 and 1888. Here, he painted his Self-Portrait with a Gray Hat. *While in Paris, he taught himself the French Impressionist techniques, breaking away from his dark painting to make better use of colour.*

(thick fogs) of Montmartre lifted, hence the name. In the middle of the square, a statue of St Denis washes the blood off his head while watching the old men playing *boules*.

From the square, **Avenue Junot** is one of the widest and most expensive streets in Montmartre. Constructed in 1910, the avenue cut through the ancient *maquis* scrubland which used to cover the hillside, where windmills turned their graceful sails and goats scampered among the trees. The street's 1920s' Art Deco elegance has attracted the cream of Montmartre society – the singer Claude Nougaro lives in the big ochre house. **Le Hameau des Artistes** (No 11) still provides artists' studios. **Maison Tristan Tzara** (No 15) is named after the eccentric Romanian Dadaist poet who once lived there and was designed especially for him by the Austrian architect Adolf Loos.

Below, on the corner of Rue Girardon and Rue Lepic, is the last of the great windmills of Montmartre, **Moulin de la Galette** ⑭. Built in 1604, the windmill became an illustrious dance hall in the 19th century. The artists and writers living in Montmartre often held parties here and it was during one of these occasions that Auguste Renoir began sketches for his famous painting *Le Moulin de la Galette* (1866). Emile Zola held a party here to celebrate the success of his novel *L'Assommoir* (1877), set in La Goutte d'Or to the east of Montmartre. (The novelist lived just below the village on Boulevard de Clichy.) Earlier, in the 1814 siege of Paris, the four Debray brothers had fought fiercely to save their windmill from the Russians – one of them was subsequently crucified on its sails. Today, the windmill is better protected, as a notice proclaims "Residence under electronic, radar and guard-dog surveillance".

Picturesque Rue Lepic, leading from the windmill and past the Moulin de

BELOW: an antique bookstall in Montmartre.

Map,
page 172

Radet, descends to Place Blanche. The old quarry road housed Vincent Van Gogh and his brother Theo, an art dealer, at No 54 for two years in the late 1880s. During that time, Van Gogh is said to have presented his paintings at Le Tambourin, a seedy cabaret on Boulevard de Clichy, until the owner demanded that he remove them, as they disturbed her customers.

Au Virage Lepic (No 61) is an ancient bar-restaurant which preserves the traditions of Montmartre – busy, inexpensive and animated by local singers and poets. Further down the hill, where the lively Lepic food market is held each morning, stop at **Le Lux** (No 12) for a white wine or hot chocolate beneath the beautiful 1909 facade. **Le Restaurant** on Rue Véron, just off Rue Lepic, provides food as stylishly simplistic as its name and is much loved by the young and beautiful of the district.

The **Cimetière de Montmartre** ⑮, just west of Rue Lepic, reflects the artistic bias of the area. The tombs are elegantly sculpted and their inmates appropriately famous: here lie the 19th-century writer Stendhal, whose real name was Henri Beyle, novelist Alexandre Dumas, poet and critic Théophile Gautier, painter Edgar Degas, dancer Waslaw Nijinsky, composers Hector Berlioz and Jacques Offenbach, and Zola's bust (his body was moved to the Panthéon). Film director François Truffaut was buried here in 1984.

On your way back to Pigalle, cut down Rue des Abbesses and turn left into Rue Ravignan, just before Place des Abbesses, for a small detour to **Place Emile-Goudeau** ⑯, a particularly attractive square. At No 13, modern art studios have replaced the wooden ramshackle building called **Le Bateau-Lavoir,** so named because it resembled a floating laundry. This artists' den housed Picasso and fellow Cubists Georges Braque and Van Dongen in the narrow ship-like corridors. Picasso painted *Les Desmoiselles d'Avignon* (1907) here in his chaotic studio, recalling the prostitutes of Barcelona, and Apollinaire and Max Jacob liberated verse-form in the rooms alongside. Unfortunately, the building burnt down in 1970 just as it was about to be renovated.

Turning left out of the square, take the Passage des Abbesses, a little further on, down to the picturesque **Place des Abbesses** ⑰ and the remarkable Art Nouveau Métro station, designed by Guimard (*see page 94*). Alongside the spiralling steps into the station is a mural painted by local artists. Just east of the square at 9 Rue Yvonne-Le-Tac, on the site of St Denis's decapitation, Ignatius Loyola and François Xavier founded the Jesuit order of the Society of Jesus in 1534.

Cosmopolitan Montmartre

To the east of Montmartre is the district of **La Goutte-d'Or** ⑱, vividly described by Zola in *L'Assommoir*. This close-knit quarter is undergoing rapid renovation and the old workers' hovels are being razed for new developments. The conglomeration of Islamic butchers, African grocers, West Indian bakers, Jewish jewellers and Arab tailors is a never-ending spectacle of sight, sound and smell. More than 30 nationalities live side by side in the streets around Rue de la Goutte-d'Or, Rue de la Charbonnière and Rue des Poissoniers. **Tati** on Boulevard Rochechouart sells cut-price clothes.

In 1911, novelist Roland Dorgelès played a joke on the Bateau-Lavoir Surrealists by tying a paintbrush to a donkey's tail and calling the result Sunset over the Adriatic, *which he sold for 400F. Apollinaire, a keen follower of Cubism and an art critic, was not amused.*

BELOW: oysters on the hoof.

THE LEFT BANK AND MONTPARNASSE

Writers, artists and thinkers have left their indelible mark on these areas since Roman times. Places to see include the Hôtel de Cluny, Panthéon and the Jardin des Plantes, an oasis of natural history

Map, pages 184/5

Extending southwards, the Rive Gauche, or Left Bank, comprises several well defined areas, with the Quartier Latin, an intimate puzzle of small streets and historic architecture between Boulevard St-Michel and the Jardin des Plantes, at its ancient heart. This has been the stamping ground of students for nearly eight centuries and, thanks to the concentration of academic institutions which grew up in the area, Latin was virtually the mother tongue until Napoleon put a stop to it after the Revolution. The elegant and chic hide in neighbouring St-Germain-des-Prés, the historical centre of literary Paris and existentialism on the west side of the Boulevard St-Michel. The once Bohemian Montparnasse, to the south, is now host to a modern business centre, but still preserves its lively atmosphere at night.

The Rive Gauche maintains a roguish charm in its beautiful tree-lined boulevards, ancient, narrow streets, manicured parks and imposing monuments, as well as an intellectual arrogance that manages to stay just the right side of pretentious. This is the place in which to stroll, imbibe and look cool. Sit in the shaded parks by day and scan the menus in the fairylit streets by night. Be warned, though, this is not the area to go looking for typical Parisian cuisine.

PRECEDING PAGES: summertime on the Left Bank.
LEFT: a chic student.
BELOW: inside the Hôtel de Cluny.

The Quartier Latin – an area of rebellion

Settled by the Romans in 53 BC and a cradle of philosophy and art since the Middle Ages, the Quartier Latin conjures up contradictions and delights in paradox, as student and poet François Villon wrote in 1456, "I laugh in tears." Villon debated with professors at the Sorbonne by day and drank with thieves in the brothels of St-Michel by night.

Villon's legacy of rebellion has survived. In 1871, the Place St-Michel was the headquarters of the Paris Commune (*see page 36*). Then in May 1968, demonstrations against deteriorating conditions in the Nanterre faculty led to students tearing up the old cobblestones of Boulevard St-Michel to hurl at the riot police. Hundreds of students were arrested, the University of Paris was decentralised, and the ancient cobblestones were buried under concrete forever (*see pages 39–40*). Protests, albeit subdued, still take place when roads are sometimes blocked by squatting students, eager to relive the glorious past of their revolutionary predecessors.

However, the Quartier Latin still remains a place of happy incongruity, where countless Greek *souvlaki* vendors stand amid traditional cafés spilling over the pavements, and new wave cinemas front ancient academic facades.

Along the Boul' Mich

Across the river from the palaces of justice and salvation (the Préfecture de Police and Notre Dame), **Place St-Michel** ❶ revels in recklessness. The fountain depicting St Michael and a surprised dragon often seems buried under scooters, lip-locked lovers and the ubiquitous *clochards* (tramps), sitting philosophically amid youthful chaos. Extending south, the grand **Boulevard St-Michel** ("Boul' Mich" to the initiated) will nourish the senses, the mind and the stomach, with an assortment of stalls, bookshops, alternative cinemas and fast-food joints.

By the crossroads of Boul' Mich and Boulevard St-Germain stands the 15th-century **Hôtel de Cluny**, housing the **Musée National du Moyen Age – Thermes de Cluny** ❷ (open daily; closed Tues and pub. hols; entrance fee). Once the residence of the Abbots of Cluny, who rebuilt the mansion to how it is today, these Gothic walls house one of the world's finest collections of medieval artefacts. Many of the treasures reflect life in the religious communities such as illuminated manuscripts, embroideries, stained glass, liturgical vestments and church furnishings.

Among the numerous tapestries is the exquisite, 15th-century **La Dame à la Licorne** (The Lady and the Unicorn) on the first floor of the rotunda. The six panels are beautifully worked in the *mille fleurs* style of design, using rich, harmonious colours. The museum also includes 21 of the original heads of the Kings of Judah, dating from 1220, from Notre Dame cathedral, which were vandalised during the Revolution (*see page 141*).

Here, too, are the remains of a huge **Gallo-Roman bath house** complex, believed built in AD 200 by the guild of boatmen (*nautes*), as their unusual symbol of carved ships' prows were found on the arch supports of the *frigidarium* (cold bath house). As elsewhere in their empire, the Romans decided to civilise a barbarian people with hot baths in the *caldarium* and mindless violence, but the barbarians got the better of them 100 years later when they ransacked the joint.

ABOVE: a section of
the six-panel, 15th-
century tapestry, *La
Dame à la Licorne,*
in Hôtel de Cluny.
BELOW: university
chapel in Place de
la Sorbonne.

The Sorbonne – the oldest university in France

In a reversal of history, Greeks now seem to have overrun Romans in the streets leading from the Cluny baths, where Greek restaurants of dubious pedigree vie for custom with a ferociousness rarely seen outside Athens. Continue south down Boul' Mich a little way to the eternal pulse of the Quartier Latin, the **Sorbonne** ❸ (open daily; closed weekends and pub. hols; free). Established in 1253 by St Louis and his confessor Robert de Sorbon, the oldest university in France has been rebuilt many times since its inception as a dormitory for 16 theology students, when it soon started to attract great thinkers from all over Europe.

In 1469, France's first printing press was set up by three Germans summoned by Louis XI, which encouraged the growth of intellectual life (*see page 29*). During the Revolution, the university was closed and allowed to become run down but, afterwards, Napoleon revitalised it and it grew once again to be the most important university in France. Now, since decentralisation in 1970, there are 13 universities in Paris and the Sorbonne has lost its force.

Entering from Rue des Ecoles, you can wander through the corridors and galleries of academe, lined with meaningful paintings reflecting the university's history, soaking up the academic atmosphere. The 17th-century **chapel**, commissioned by Sorbonne alumni Cardinal Richelieu and containing his marble tomb, overlooks the university's main courtyard. Above the tomb, beautifully carved by François Girardon, hangs a hat believed to be the cardinal's. Legend has it that the hat will fall when Richelieu's soul is released from hell.

Across Rue St-Jacques, in the next block, is the **Collège de France** (open Oct–Jun daily and Sat morning; closed Sun; free), set up by François I in 1530 on the inspiration of the great humanist Guillaume Budé, to offer an unexpurgated

Map, pages 184/5

education, unfettered by the intolerance and dogmatism of the Sorbonne. Today, the college still has its own say academically, although it is financially dependent on the state, and lectures are open to the public without charge. Next door, the **Lycée Louis-le-Grand** is the school in which Jean-Paul Sartre taught and from which the 19th-century poet and art critic Charles Baudelaire was expelled. Other old boys include Molière, Victor Hugo and Georges Pompidou.

Panthéon – the ultimate resting place

A little further on, dominating the summit of Mont Ste-Geneviève, the **Panthéon** ❹ (open daily; closed pub. hols; entrance fee) is the sort of domed and colonnaded monument famous people would die to be buried in. Inspired by Rome's Panthéon, it was conceived following Louis XV's rash vow to build a church should he recover from illness in 1744. Money was short, however, and so public lotteries were organised to raise funds. Designed by Neo-Classical architect Jacques-Germain Soufflot (1713–80), the building was finished after his death but just in time for the Revolution, when in 1791 the church was designated a pantheon for the "Founders of Liberty", a monument to rival the royal mausoleum at St-Denis (*see page 250*). Thus Voltaire, who was transferred from the country, and Jean-Jacques Rousseau came to lie in the crypt and later Victor Hugo, Emile Zola and Louis Braille, inventor of writing for the blind, and Nobel Prizewinning scientists Pierre and Marie Curie joined them. The body of the World War II Resistance hero Jean Moulin was reburied here in the 1970s.

After the Revolution, the use of the Panthéon yo-yoed from church to necropolis to church to headquarters of the Commune, until it finally became a civic building and lay temple in 1885. The interior is laid out in the shape of a Greek cross with the iron-framed dome towering above the centre. Frescoes depicting the life of Ste Geneviève line the south wall and her glorification is portrayed on the inside of the upper section of the dome.

Across Place Ste-Geneviève rises the richly ornate church of **St-Etienne-du-Mont** ❺ (open daily, closed noon–2pm and pub. hols; Jul–Aug closed Mon; free), which has a wonderful Renaissance rood screen. Playwright Jean Racine (1639–99) and the scientist Blaise Pascal (1623–62) are buried here and a marble slab near the entrance marks where the Archbishop of Paris was stabbed to death by a priest in 1857. To the right of the chancel is the shrine of Ste Geneviève who saved Paris from Attila the Hun in AD 451 (*see pages 25–26*).

Latin lanes

Heading back towards the Seine for a little way, the **Musée de la Préfecture de Police** ❻ is just across the Rue des Ecoles. This houses an intriguing jumble of macabre objects, weapons and documents, including a menu proposing "rat stew à la Robert". Cinema aficionados should pop into *Action Ecoles* or *Action Rive Gauche* (23 and 5 Rue des Ecoles) for quirky film classics, both in American and French.

Continuing on towards the Seine, you will reach **Place Maubert**, from where there is a network of small, medieval streets, lined with a jumble of boutiques revealing their shadowy interiors to the curious. Quiet

By hanging his pendulum from the top of the Panthéon's dome in 1851, Léon Foucault (1819–98) publicly proved that the world was round and rotated. The pendulum is kept in the Musée National des Techniques (see page 164).

BELOW: a student meeting outside the Panthéon.

The original Shakespeare and Company bookshop was founded in 1921 in Rue de l'Odéon by American Sylvia Beach, who shockingly published James Joyce's Ulysses. *Throughout the 1920s and 1930s, her bookshop and library was at the hub of the literary world, with regulars such as Gertrude Stein, Ernest Hemingway, T.S. Eliot and Ezra Pound. It closed down in 1941 during World War II.*

BELOW: a bookshop for English readers.

repose is to be found in the church of **St-Julien-le-Pauvre** ❼ (open daily; closed 1–3pm; free) on the tiny Square Viviani, off Rue Lagrange, overshadowed by Notre Dame. In the garden, you can sit under a 300-year-old false acacia, the second oldest tree in Paris (*see page 196*) and contemplate those who have done the same over the centuries. Behind is Rue du Fouarre, named after the bales of hay on which students used to perch during open-air lectures in the Middle Ages. The Italian poet Dante sat here in 1304.

Shakespeare and Company, at 37 Rue de la Bûcherie parallel to the Seine, is Paris's most famous English bookshop, containing a menagerie of literature from the Bard to Beatniks. Founded in 1956 by American George Whitman on similar lines to Sylvia Beach's original in Rue de l'Odéon, the shop attracted writers such as William Burroughs and James Baldwin. Today, it still closes at midnight, too soon for the addicted.

Le Petit Pont close by is a perfect spot from which to see the lights of the Seine at night. Here, the Quais St-Michel and Montebello combine picture-book views of the Ile de la Cité, with a ramshackle riverside charm. By day, ancient bookstalls line the riverbanks, offering overpriced, antique volumes. Not far, trial by Revolutionary council has been replaced with trial by jazz at **Caveau de la Huchette** (5 Rue de la Huchette). Danton and Robespierre selected guillotine victims in the cellars where jazz musician Maxim Saury now executes dixie stomps to great acclaim. At No 10, a young Napoleon dreamed of power.

The beautiful Flamboyant Gothic church of **St-Séverin** ❽, in the next street, is famous for its mighty organ loft. The church has been a place of pageantry since the Fourth Crusade set out from St-Séverin to conquer the Holy Land in 1204. In the adjacent cemetery, in 1744, the world's first gallstone operation was carried out on a death-row criminal, who was pardoned following the operation's success.

Odéon – a bustling nightlife

Across Boul' Mich from St-Séverin, the Odéon district nestles between the boisterous Quartier Latin and the refined elegance of St-Germain-des-Prés. The antiquated charm of the streets that fan out from St-Michel Mètro belie the area's bustling nightlife, which is as inspired and dedicated as any in the city.

A short walk along Rue St-André-des-Arts will take you to Rue de l'Ancienne-Comédie, the next street along, where **Le Procope**, the first café to open in Paris and introduce coffee in 1686, is still doing good business. From here, it's worthwhile looking in at **Cour de Rohan** to see its picturesque courtyards with Renaissance facades. Behind is Rue du Jardinet, where the composer Camille Saint-Saëns was born in 1835.

Across Boulevard St-Germain stands the Revolutionary leader Georges Danton's statue at the **Carrefour de l'Odéon** marking his old house. Fellow Revolutionary Camille Desmoulins lived at No 2 before storming the Bastille in 1789. Others plotted in neighbouring streets to the north, which now host some of the more bourgeois boutiques and apartments in Paris.

From here, Rue de l'Odéon, the first street in Paris to have pavements and gutters, runs parallel with Rue de Condé, where Beaumarchais wrote *The Barber of Seville* in 1773, a play whose theme of a common man usurping the nobility prefigured the rebellion of the man in the street.

Place de l'Odéon is one of the livelier squares in Paris, especially at 2am. Here the **Théâtre National de l'Odéon** ❾ presents large-scale productions of

Map, pages 184/5

ABOVE: the guillotine, invented by Dr Guillotin near the Odéon.
BELOW: café *branché* on the Left Bank.

F. Scott Fitzgerald finished his most famous novel, The Great Gatsby *(1925), portrayed on screen by Robert Redford and Mia Farrow (above), at 58 Rue de Vaugirard, just south of the romantic Jardin du Luxembourg.*

BELOW: drawing in the Jardin du Luxembourg.

foreign language theatre, from the likes of Henrik Ibsen and Arthur Miller, while the smaller **Petit Odéon** within features *avant-garde* works. In 1968, the theatre was occupied by students who donned Roman helmets from the props department to protect themselves during battles with the police (*see pages 39–40*).

Jardin du Luxembourg – a Parisian favourite

No statistics exist relating exactly how many people have fallen in love in the **Jardin du Luxembourg** ❿, but if poets as miserable as Baudelaire and Verlaine had a good time here, the garden's magic is evidently potent. Young couples meet under the plane trees by the romantic Baroque **Fontaine de Médicis** and stroll to the pool to watch children sail boats across the carp-filled water. Statues of the queens of France gaze down from the terrace, while the thwack of tennis balls disturbs the reverie of nannies pushing designer babies in designer prams.

On Wednesdays and weekends, the famous Guignol puppet show takes place in the **Théâtre des Marionettes**. More serious entertainment is located at the corner with Rue de Vaugirard, where wise old men take on earnest students at chess among the fragrant orange trees. There are 200 varieties of apple and pear trees in the garden and the beehives produce several hundred kilos of honey a year. Here, in the middle of the city, you can take bee-keeping lessons.

The Luxembourg neighbourhood used to be terrorised in the 13th-century by a bandit called Vauvert, who operated from his lair in an old ruin, until he was kicked out by Carthusian monks in 1257. As a result, they founded a monastery there, creating a wonderful vegetable garden and establishing the tree nursery still at the south of the garden.

The **Palais du Luxembourg** ⓫ (guided tours by arrangement in advance, tel: 01 44 61 21 69) was built for Marie de Médicis on the site of a mansion belonging to Duke François of Luxembourg (hence the name), in the style of the Pitti Palace in Florence. But she was banished by Cardinal Richelieu before it was completed in 1631. During the Revolution, the palace was used as a prison and in World War II the Germans made it their headquarters.

Now fortunate French Senators enjoy its Restoration interior and luxurious views of the gardens, for it is the seat of the *Sénat* (the Upper House of Parliament, as chosen by an electoral college of politicians). The even luckier President of the Senate gets to live next door in the **Petit Luxembourg**. American novelist Ernest Hemingway adored the Jardin du Luxembourg. His three principal residences during the 1920s neatly circumscribe the park, where he would saunter each afternoon. As he wrote later: "It was sad when the park was closed, and I was sad walking around it instead of through it."

From Petit Luxembourg, the Rue Garancière leads north to the imposing church of **St-Sulpice** ⓬, a short walk away. Apart from one of the finest organs in Paris and Eugène Delacroix's *Jacob Wrestling with the Angel,* modelled on the painter's own struggle with Art (*see page 192*), the great cavern of a church has little to offer. In front of the huge collonaded facade, with mismatching towers, is a large square with an amusing fountain made by Joachim Visconti in 1844.

St-Germain-des-Prés – an elegant neighbourhood

The historical heart of literary Paris, St-Germain-des-Prés is an area stretching roughly from St-Sulpice to the Seine and encompassed to the west by Boulevard St-Germain. Its elegant streets house elegant boutiques, yet it still retains a sense of animation, passed down from the 1950s (*see pages 198–99*), with

Map, pages 184/5

In Place St-Sulpice the Fontaine des Quatre Points Cardinaux shows four bishops at the cardinal points of the compass. A play on words, the name can mean the Fountain of the (compass) Cardinal Points or the Four Cardinals who Never Were.

BELOW: the odd towers of St-Sulpice.

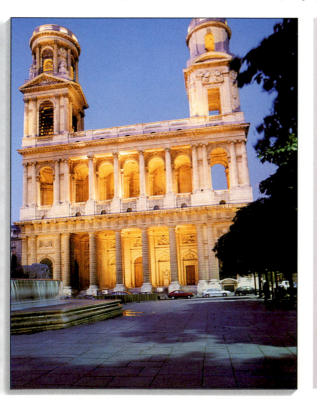

LEFT BANK RENDEZVOUS

Café Voltaire (1 Place de l'Odéon), named after its most famous regular, was where, in the 18th century, Voltaire used to meet fellow philosopher Diderot to discuss their Enlightenment theories. The tormented 19th-century poets Verlaine and Mallarmé threw Symbolist ideas at each other there and, much later, the lost American writers Hemingway and F. Scott Fitzgerald extolled the café's "sudden provincial quality".

Writers between the two world wars spent hours at their favourite tables in Le Procope (13 Rue de l'Ancienne-Comédie) and existentialist writer Jean-Paul Sartre and his lover Simone de Beauvoir (*see pages 198–99*) consolidated the highbrow reputation of Les Deux Magots (6 Place St-Germain-des-Prés) in the 1950s. The Art Deco Café de Flore (172 Boulevard St-Germain) was another Sartre favourite. Today, politicians congregate at Brasserie Lipp across the road.

Place de Fürstenburg is one of the most romantic corners of Paris. The antique, white-globed street lamps and paulownia trees inspire poetry and black and white photography.

ABOVE: not everyone is academic on the Left Bank.
BELOW: all set for a good meal.

crowded cafés spilling out on to the pavements. From St-Sulpice, head north to Boulevard St-Germain and the covered **Marché St-Germain** in Rue Mabillon, where both the vegetables and characters are colourful.

The church of **St-Germain-des-Prés ⓮**, close by, is the oldest in Paris, dating from 542 when it was originally a basilica for some holy relics. Ransacked and rebuilt over centuries, the resulting, heavily restored 11th-century building is an unsubtle blend of simple Romanesque and pretentious Baroque. In the small square alongside, Picasso's tribute to his friend, *Homage to Apollinaire*, stands under the steeple. Across the square, **Les Deux Magots** serves the best hot chocolate in Paris. Once the favourite haunt of the literati, the café is still popular – apparently, the waiters cover 12 km (about 7 miles) a day.

From the square, take Rue de Fürstenburg to the **Musée Delacroix ⓮** (open daily; closed Tues; entrance fee), where Romantic painter Eugène Delacroix (1798–1863) lived and worked for the last few years of his life.

Academia on the riverbank

From the charming Place de Fürstenburg, the streets to the Seine are awash with antique shops and art galleries, and the narrow Rue Visconti, where Racine died, is worth going down. This will take you to Paris's finest art school, the **Ecole Nationale Supérieure des Beaux-Arts ⓯** (open daily; closed weekends; free), which includes two *hôtels* fronting on to the Quai Malaquais. From 1608, the school was a monastery until the Revolution, when it was used to store pillaged works of art. In 1816, the School of Fine Arts moved in and, today, holds public exhibitions of students' work.

Close by, and a dictionary's throw from the river, squats the imposing and majestic **Institut de France** , incorporating the **Académie Française** (*see page 197*). The illustrious academy, created in 1635, concentrates on safeguarding the French language and compiling *the* French Dictionary. From here you can cross the Seine safely to the Louvre (*see pages 117–20, 134–35*) by way of the pedestrian-only **Pont des Arts**.

Next door is the 16th-century **Hôtel des Monnaies** . When Louis XV installed the royal mint here, he commissioned the architect Jacques Antoine to build the workshops, completed in 1775. Antoine so liked his creation that he lived there until his death in 1801. It now houses the **Musée de la Monnaie** (open daily, Wed till 9pm; closed Tues morning and Mon; entrance fee), a museum of money and medallions and not for the easily bored.

Along the Seine towards St-Michel is the **Quai des Grands-Augustins**. The oldest on the river, its facade is filled with ancient bookshops and antique dealers. Picasso lived for 20 years on Rue des Grands-Augustins, branching off it.

From art to business in Montparnasse

The once rural area around the Tour Montparnasse, southwest of the Jardin du Luxembourg, was christened Mount Parnassus (after the classical home of Apollo and his muses) by a local Dead Poets' Society in the 17th century, which gathered on quarry mounds to recite verse. Around the time of the Revolution, the district, then on the outskirts of Paris, became a pleasure ground as cafés, bars and dance halls sprang up everywhere. In the early 1900s, when the Bohemians decamped from Montmartre, young writers and artists such as Chagall and Léger set up studios in Montparnasse and were soon joined by Picasso.

Between the wars, the world was here – Lenin, Trotsky, Stravinsky, Man Ray,

Map, pages 184/5

TIP

Around the Ecole des Beaux-Arts – Picasso's old stamping ground – there is a notable concentration of art galleries, especially in the Rue de Seine, Rue des Beaux-Arts and the Rue Jacob.

BELOW LEFT: Tour Montparnasse – built for business. **BELOW:** view from the top of the tower.

La Closerie des Lilas, at 171 Boulevard du Montparnasse, was a favourite haunt of Jean-Paul Sartre (above). The mad 19th-century poet Gérard de Nerval used to walk his pet lobster on a lead at La Rotonde (No 105).

BELOW: busking in Rue Mouffetard.

Cocteau and the Americans including, Gertrude Stein, F. Scott Fitzgerald and Hemingway – and Montparnasse became known simply as the Quarter. You did not have to live here to belong to it, as Hemingway's character Jake Barnes explains in *The Sun Also Rises* (1926), "Perfectly good Quarterites live outside the actual boundaries of Montparnasse. They can live anywhere, as long as they come to the Quarter to think." In fact, Hemingway wrote this novel at the **Closerie des Lilas** 🔞, one of the many fashionable bars along Boulevard Montparnasse. The tables are inscribed with the names of its illustrious clients, including Lenin, Modigliani and Surrealist poet André Breton. Fittingly, Hemingway's plaque rests on the bar.

The Spanish Civil War (1936–39) brought this artistic era to an end as those with high socialist ideals went off to fight. After World War II, the philosophers such as Jean-Paul Sartre and Simone de Beauvoir moved in, fraternising the same cafés clustered around the lively Carrefour Vavin, now Place Pablo Picasso, which still throbs with life well into the early hours. Close by, Rodin's dramatic **Statue de Balzac**, once despised, is now adored. Magnificent studios still exist along Boulevard Raspail (peek in at Studio Raspail at No 216) and Boulevard Montparnasse (pass through to the second courtyard at No 126).

The district is dominated by the **Tour Montparnasse** 🔟 (open daily; entrance fee), 59 storeys high, inaugurated in 1973 as part of a new business complex. The tower has one asset: from its top floor you cannot see the Tour Montparnasse. You can, however, get a wonderful view of the city. Just below, before the **Place du 18 Juin 1940** – the date of General Charles de Gaulle's famous BBC speech, urging the Resistance to keep fighting against the German occupation – is the **Centre Commercial** on eight levels, six of which are below ground

THE PARIS CATACOMBS

Several million skeletons line the miles of passageways of the Catacombs ㉑ (open 2pm–4pm daily, also 9am–11am weekends; closed Mon and pub. hols; entrance fee) under Place Denfert-Rochereau. The Roman quarries became ossuaries in 1785, when, over 15 months, cartloads of skeletons and corpses were removed from the overflowing cemeteries at Place des Innocents (*see page 150*) and other areas. Take a torch, and someone to hold your hand, as the inscription on the door reads "Stop. Here begins the empire of the dead". However, not everyone has felt squeamish about fraternising with the dead. Wild parties used to be thrown here before the Revolution, and during World War II, the catacombs were the headquarters of the French Resistance.

Map, pages 184/5

with a shopping mall in the top three. Behind the tower is the modernised Gare Montparnasse from where thousands of Bretons emerged, fleeing rural poverty and famine in Brittany, during the mid-19th century. Consequently, Montparnasse is *the* place for crêpes, cider and wild bagpipe dances.

Heading east for a short way, stop for a drink at Le Café d'Edgar, a family-run, old-style café-theatre in **Rue de la Gaîté**, which, since the 18th century, has been lined with theatres and dance halls living up to its name. Further on is the densely populated, star-studded **Cimetière Montparnasse** ⓴ (open daily; free) which includes, among many others, the 19th-century novelist Guy de Maupassant (1893), the composer Saint-Saëns (1921), and the Irish playwright Samuel Beckett (1989).

Eastwards to Rue Mouffetard market

The area around Rue Mouffetard is one of the most ancient and colourful in France. Go via the beautifully restored square of **Place de la Contrescarpe** (Métro Monge, or a few minutes from Place du Panthéon eastwards along Rue de l'Estrapade). In the corner house (No 1) François Rabelais (1494–1553) composed risqué rhymes, as did Villon, the century before (*see page 183*).

Just off the square, Ernest Hemingway moved into his first Parisian residence at 74 Rue du Cardinal Lemoine in early 1922 and he tells of the experience in his novel *A Moveable Feast* (1964). He idealised the area as a place of danger and excitement and although, now, it has lost some of its edge, it has a refined charm.

Rue Mouffetard (*see pages 78–79*) is an intriguing blend of ethnic fast food and medieval passages. Walk down its cobbles in the early morning to the most enjoyable street market in Paris, a riot of bright vegetables and North African

Singer and composer Serge Gainsbourg is buried in Cimetière Montparnasse with writers, poets, composers, artists, industrialists, such as 2CV king André Citroën, Hollywood actress Jean Seberg and US photographer Man Ray.

BELOW: Islamic Parisians.

Map, pages 184/5

In the 18th century, Parisians flocked to the cemetery of St-Médard, at the end of Rue Mouffetard, to the tomb of a young priest whose ghost was said to cure all ailments. Eventually, as more and more people came, Louis XV closed it with a notice: "On the King's orders, it is forbidden for God to perform miracles in this place."

dialects. On your stroll, note the ancient shop fronts and narrow passages. At No 122, towards the bottom of the hill, the well carved on to the facade dates from Henri IV.

An Arab mosque and Roman ruins

From St-Médard, the Rue Daubenton leads to the green and white elegance of the **Mosquée de Paris** ㉒ (open daily, closed noon–2pm; closed Fri and Muslim hols; entrance fee) about five minutes away. Built in 1922 in the Hispano-Moorish style by three French architects, the mosque is a subtle reminder of Parisian ties with the Arab world and commemorates North African participation in World War I. Incorporating the **Institut Musulman**, the complex of buildings includes a museum of Muslim art, a large patio inspired by the Alhambra in Granada and an impressive selection of carvings and tiles. There is also a library, a restaurant and a *salon de thé*. Next door is a *Hamman* (Turkish bath).

Not far from the northwest entrance of the Jardin de Plantes is the ancient gladiatorial arena, the **Arènes de Lutèce** ㉓. The 15,000-seat arena, which was destroyed by barbarians in AD 280, was unearthed when building Rue Monge in 1869 and Victor Hugo (*see page 159*) led a campaign to restore it. Today, where gladiator fights were once popular spectacles, the arena serves as a children's playground and echoes to the clink of *pétanque* balls on shady afternoons.

A walk through the Jardin des Plantes

A large verdant retreat from the bustle of the city, the **Jardin des Plantes** ㉔ (open daily; entrance fee), the city's botanical gardens, was opened in 1640 and was originally conceived as a medicinal herb farm for Louis XIII. Between 1739 to 1788, the park flourished under the curatorship of the Comte de Buffon, author of the 36-volume *Natural History*, who created a maze over a public waste tip.

Within the park is the **Musée National d'Histoire Naturelle** ㉕ (open daily; closed Tues and weekday pub. hols; entrance fee). Both the museum and its contents have been restored, which now present an impressive survey of evolutionary development, from a marine world to a large open space with stuffed animals exhibited in their natural habitats. Live animals can be seen in the **Ménagerie** which includes a Micro Zoo.

For a riverside stroll leave the park at Place Valhubert and head west to the **Musée de la Sculpture en Plein Air** ㉖ (open daily; free), a lively park-cum-modern sculpture exhibition which opened in 1980. Continue walking and you will see the **Institut du Monde Arabe** ㉗ (open daily; closed Mon; entrance fee) across Quai St-Bernard. One of François Mitterrand's numerous *grands projets*, the nine-storey palace of glass, aluminium and concrete was built by France in conjunction with 20 Arab countries. The museum is a fascinating voyage around the Muslim world. Finish your visit on the roof, where the restaurant's breathtaking view is accompanied by strangely non-Arab, Gallic dishes.

For traditional Michelin three-star cuisine, reserve a table at **La Tour d'Argent** (15 Quai de la Tournelle).

EXOTIC PLANTS

When the Jardin des Plantes was being created in the 17th century, Louis XIV's doctor, Fagon, and botanists such as Tournefort and the three Jussieu brothers travelled far and wide bringing back seeds from around the world. The wild and wonderful collection of flora that resulted includes a 2,000-year-old American sequoia along with a Ginkgo biloba and iron tree from Persia. A laricio pine was grown from a seed brought back from Corsica in 1774 and the pistachio tree is almost 300 years old.

The oldest Lebanese cedar in France, planted in 1734, was brought from Kew Gardens in England by the Jussieu brothers' nephew, Bernard de Jussieu. The story goes that after dropping and breaking the pot the young cedar plants were in, he nurtured the seedlings in his hat until he could return. The oldest tree in Paris, the false acacia or Robinia, brought back from America in 1635, is also here.

The Académie Française

Traditionally seated at dinner parties above government ministers and just below cardinals and princes are the 40 members of the Académie Française, popularly known as the "*Immortels*". These chosen few are the watchdogs of the French language, compiling the *Dictionary of the French Language*, protecting it from the insidious onslaught of English (franglais) words, such as jogging, marketing and camping, despite their common useage in France. To be admitted to their ranks is the ultimate honour to which all *hommes de lettres* aspire.

The Académie shows the importance the French attach to their language. Yet, paradoxically, it is almost impossible to define. Simply put, it is uncertain what its members actually do. Even the *Immortels* themselves are confused about their role. Poet Paul Valbey said once, "We are what we believe we are, and what others believe we are, and neither we nor anyone else can say exactly what that is."

The Académie was founded in 1635 by Louis XIII at the prompting of Cardinal Richelieu. Its members were set the task of composing a dictionary and charged "to work with all possible care and diligence to give strict rules to our language and to make it pure, eloquent and capable of dealing with the arts and sciences". Louis XIV generously donated 660 volumes from his personal library, 40 goose quills and a lesson in equality. When one of the members, a cardinal, protested that his rank entitled him to a more comfortable seat than the chairs provided, Louis sent 40 of the now famous *fauteuils* (armchairs).

In 1793, during the Revolution, the Académie was accused of being infected with "the incurable gangrene of aristocracy". Three members were guillotined, two committed suicide and three died in prison. Restored by Napoleon in 1803, it was re-established in the Institut de France (*see pages 192–93*).

A vacancy occurs only after a member's death. While eligibility is simple (candidates must be of French nationality), being elected is difficult. Voltaire was so desperate, he was driven to write obsequious verses praising Louis XV. He even denied the authorship of his freethinking *Lettres Philosophiques* and finally made it on his third try. Victor Hugo's campaign lasted seven years, until he was accepted on his fourth attempt in 1841.

Emile Zola was unsuccessful 24 times. The conservative *Immortels* disliked the realism of his novels and were wary of his courage in the Dreyfus Affair in 1898. Others who failed were the literary giants Diderot, Flaubert, Molière, Balzac, Proust and Baudelaire. Women have been admitted since 1980, French-American author Marguerite Yourcenar being the first. Now there are two.

Not all members are geniuses – one is the author of a history of women's undergarments. As minor 19th-century novelist and *Immortel* Ludovic Halévy once said: "Some Academicians are talented, others aren't. The latter are especially worthy of respect because they made it without talent."

RIGHT: immortalised in stone outside the Académie Française.

LEFT BANK IN THE 1950s

After World War II, artists, musicians, writers and philosophers converged on the quartier of St-Germain-des-Prés, making it the centre of the intellectual and artistic world.

In Paris, the freedom of the post-war period was characterised by an outpouring of literature and ideas. One of the most important to emerge was existentialism, which soon dominated French intellectual life. Developed by the writer Jean-Paul Sartre, this philosophy was based on the concept of a universe that was meaningless, or absurd, in which people were meant to find greater freedoms by assuming greater personal responsibilities. In attempting to change the world rather than simply examine it, existentialism represented a hope for the future. Its key figures included Sartre's life-long companion, Simone de Beauvoir, and the writer Albert Camus.

LEFT BANK CAFÉ SOCIETY

Existentialists lived in cheap hotels and gathered in local cafés, such as Les Deux Magots and the Flore. At times, the Café de Flore was like a classroom, with Sartre writing at one table and de Beauvoir at another. Even after the couple's popularity forced them to stop working in public, their followers, wearing the "existentialist uniform" of black sweaters and berets, continued to flock to the cafés to drink, gossip and argue over the latest literary offerings.

▷ WRITERS' CAFÉ
The Deux Magots, like its neighbour the Café de Flore, had a tradition of supporting artistic and intellectual social life. It took its name from the sign of a draper's shop that had occupied the site. Simone de Beauvoir (above) regularly came to drink coffee and write. Her favourite seat was the wall banquette next to the window.

▷ THE TROGLODYTES
Young Parisians packed the Left Bank's basement jazz clubs, to dance wild new dances such as the jitterbug and the mambo. The regulars were affectionately known as *les rats*.

THE CLUBS OF ST-GERMAIN

Juliette Gréco (above) was the beautiful "face" of St-Germain-des-Prés. She was a young singer who helped to run Le Tabou, the first and most notorious of the clubs that appeared in the late 1940s.

The club's dance floor had just enough room for 20 enthusiastic couples to dance to the latest jazz. Smoke-filled and sweaty, it became the place to be after midnight, but its popularity proved its downfall; bad press about its supposedly wanton and hedonistic "existentialist" clientele attracted tourists, who soon outnumbered the beboppers themselves.

The club lasted only about one year, but other haunts such as the Vieux-Colombier and the Club St-Germain quickly sprung up to take its place.

Perhaps not all existentialists fully understood the philosophy, but they all loved the music and dancing that was associated with it.

◁ **LE JAZZ HOT**

St-Germain-des-Prés was a jazz mecca. Its clubs attracted both top French musicians, such as Claude Luter, and American jazzmen including Miles Davis, Coleman Hawkins and James Moody (bottom right).

◁ **JEAN-PAUL SARTRE**
Sartre was the epitome of a French intellectual and a prolific writer, communicating his ideas through plays and novels, including *Being and Nothingness* and *Nausea*.

▷ **ALBERT CAMUS**
The "Humphrey Bogart of the Absurd", Camus dealt with existentialist ideas in novels such as *The Outsider* and *The Plague*.

Map,
page 204

THE EIFFEL TOWER AND LES INVALIDES

Enjoy a bird's-eye view from the top of the symbol of Paris and experience a rat's-eye view underground. In between, explore military splendour and the magnificent art of the Musée d'Orsay

The Tour Eiffel, or Eiffel Tower, stands in one of the most spectacular – and one of the quietest – areas of Paris. Commanding the palatial Faubourg St-Germain quarter, and most of the city, with its presence, the Eiffel Tower symbolises Paris. Used in James Bond and *Superman* films, among many others, the tower is a world superstar. Whereas many monuments prove disappointing, it continues to impress, even though it has long been overtaken as the world's tallest building. Like some prehistoric behemoth stopping to drink at the riverside, it is the most impassive inhabitant of Paris, impervious to the daily chaos at its feet. From here, traditionally designed parks and magnificent buildings spread out on a grand scale, reaching across the Seine to the modern Palais de Chaillot, which complements the Classical facade of the Ecole Militaire on the opposite bank. Wide avenues link up with the imposing Hôtel des Invalides and the Sun King's splendid, gilt-domed church, bordering an area peppered with sumptuous *hôtels* (mansions).

Now mostly dedicated to embassies and government ministries, the secret courtyards of Pierre Laclos's *Les Liaisons Dangereuses* (1782) are still home to the nobility of Paris. Glimpses through the shuttered security are rare, but occasional open doorways reveal fountains, statues and soaring stairways. Rue de Grenelle and Rue de Varenne still retain an accessible charm, reflected in the streets leading to the Seine and the old railway station that is now bursting with fine art.

PRECEDING PAGES AND LEFT: having fun at the foot of the Eiffel Tower. **BELOW:** the altar in the Dôme, backed by a window into the soldiers' chapel.

Palais de Chaillot – palace of museums

For the best view of the tower, start at Trocadéro across the river. From here, looking over the cascading fountains and gold statues of the **Jardins du Trocadéro ❶**, the tower is at its most magnificent.

Trocadéro was named in 1827, following the re-enactment on this spot of a French victory at Fort Trocadéro in Southern Spain. Earlier, Napoleon had started work here on a palace for his son, but the Battle of Waterloo (1815) had intervened. Today, against the backdrop of the Palais de Chaillot, the beautifully laid out terraces and grassy banks of the garden, created after the 1937 World Fair, now play host to the capital's most flamboyant skateboarders and roller-bladers. At night, when the ornamental pool's huge fountains are lit up, the sight is spectacular.

Away from African street merchants selling "authentic" Senegalese and Camerooni plastic necklaces, elephants and walking sticks, the **Palais de Chaillot ❷** stands firmly and Neo-Classically on the hill. Jacques Carlu's design for the 1937 World Fair, the curved

Eiffel Tower and Les Invalides

winged edifices, with a wide parvis between and a terrace in front, contain four museums and a 1,000-seat theatre.

In the west wing is the **Musée de la Marine** (open daily; closed Tues and 1 May; entrance fee) which charts French maritime history from wooden warships to today's mean machines in scale models, some of which are two centuries old. Among exhibits of underwater exploration, naval art, navigational instruments and mementoes of naval heroes is the windsurf board that crossed the Atlantic in 38 days in 1985.

The **Musée de l'Homme** (open daily; closed Tues and pub. hols; entrance fee), or Museum of Mankind, has mummies, shrunken heads and exquisite rock crystal skulls from African, Aztec and Mayan collections, along with 400 musical instruments from around the world.

In the east wing is the **Musée des National Monuments Français** (open daily; closed Tues; entrance fee), dedicated to French monumental art with reproductions of monuments from around France, due to expand in 1999.

For cinema addicts the **Musée du Cinéma Henri Langlois** (open daily; closed Mon, Tues; entrance fee) is also in the east wing and traces celluloid history with an exhibition of more than 5,000 objects, including several film sets. The **Cinémathèque** (film library) shows four films daily.

Although about 10 minutes away in the opposite direction, the small **Musée Guimet ❸** in Place d'Iéna, will be well worth a visit when it reopens after renovation in 1999 – it is also in the company of two other worthwhile museums. One of the world's finest Asian museums, Guimet contains a superb collection of oriental art and will please lovers of silk, porcelain and jade.

Back on the Avenue du Président Wilson to the east, the Palais de Tokyo

Map, page 204

ABOVE: a gendarme ready for business.
BELOW: Palais de Chaillot, a 20th-century palace.

TIP

Queues for the Eiffel Tower can be up to two hours long in the summer, so get there early. A double-decker lift from the second level is the only means of reaching the top.

contains the underrated **Musée d'Art Moderne de Paris** ❹ (open daily; closed Mon; entrance fee), which is host to celebrity attractions, such as Picasso, Matisse (*La Danse* – 1932), Modigliani and Soutine, and the world's largest painting, Raoul Dufy's *Fée de l'Eléctricité* (Fairy of Electricity), a celebration of energy created for the 1937 World Fair. In 1999, the museum is due to become the Palais du Cinema.

Opposite is the **Musée de la Mode et du Costume** ❺ (open daily; closed Mon; entrance fee) in the Renaissance-style Palais Galliera, which has 12,000 outfits and 60,000 accessories dating from the 18th century to today that are exhibited in rotation twice a year.

The Eiffel Tower – a mighty symbol of Paris

Back at Trocadéro, cross the Pont d'Iéna, built by Napoleon to celebrate another of his victories, to the **Eiffel Tower** ❻ (open daily till 11pm, Jul, Aug till midnight; entrance fee). When Gustave Eiffel's icon of pig iron girders was chosen as the centrepiece to the World Fair of 1889, he claimed enthusiastically, "France will be the only country with a 300-metre flagpole!" But agitation overwhelmed the artistic community of the time. The Opéra architect Charles Garnier and the novelist Guy de Maupassant were the most vocal opponents and Maupassant organised a protest picnic under the tower's four legs – "the only place out of sight of the wretched construction".

However, the public (always a better judge) loved Paris's new tower and a few years later it was being lauded by writers and artists such as Apollinaire, Jean Cocteau, Dufy and Utrillo. Surviving a proposal for its dismantlement in 1909, when the placing of a radio transmitter at the top saved the day, the tower

BELOW: legging it up the Eiffel Tower.

THE TOWER'S VITAL STATISTICS

At 320 metres (1,051 ft) high, including the masts, the Eiffel Tower was the tallest building in the world until the Empire State Building went up in New York in 1931. On hot days, the ironwork expands enabling it to grow as much as 15cm (6 in).

A masterpiece of engineering, this world symbol of Paris is held together with 2.5 million rivets and the 10,100 tonnes of iron exerts a pressure of 4kg per sq cm (57lb per sq inch), the equivalent of the weight of a man sitting on a chair. Even in the strongest of winds, the tower has never swayed more than 12 cm (4 in). Up to 40 tonnes of paint has to be used, when it is painted every seven years.

There are 360 steps to the first level, where there is an audio-visual presentation of the tower's history, and another 700 to the second. On the third level is Gustave Eiffel's sitting room.

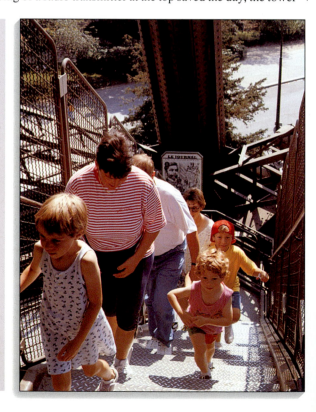

is now swarmed over by four million visitors a year. The first two floors are climbed by foot or by lift, and then another lift goes up to the top which, apart from being a meteorological station and aircraft navigation point, can hold 800 people at once. From here, the view is miraculous. At night, Paris appears as a horizontal Christmas tree of dancing illuminations stretching to the horizon, and the tower is transformed into a skeletal tableau, lit up by arc lights.

Ecole Militaire – military headquarters

From the Eiffel Tower, the gardens of the **Champ de Mars** spread down to the impressive **Ecole Militaire** (military school) ❼. Once the parade ground to the school where Napoleon practised triumphal marching in 1784, this park is now a haven of peace, love and picnics. The first balloon filled with hydrogen rather than hot air was launched from here in 1783 and the first anniversary of the storming of the Bastille was celebrated here in front of a miserable Louis XVI. At the far end is the imposing, 18th-century French military academy, still the centre of French military know-how, where Napoleon, having been admitted to the school on the recommendation that he would make a good sailor, graduated to lieutenant.

Behind this university of war is the foundation for reconciliation and understanding, the headquarters of UNESCO ❽ (open daily; closed 12.30pm–2.30pm and at weekends, pub. hols and conference sessions). The graceful Y-shaped building was designed by an alliance of American, French and Italian architects. Inside, 142 countries cooperate in educational, scientific and cultural projects. A temple of modern art, its decoration is equally cosmopolitan, including Joan Miró ceramics, Henry Moore sculptures, an Alexander Calder mobile and a huge

Map, page 204

As a cadet at the Ecole Militaire, Napoleon (above) was told that he would go far if circumstances allowed.

BELOW: a mural by Picasso in the UNESCO building.

Picasso mural. The Japanese garden displays a spine-chilling relic from our nuclear age – a stone angel found after the atomic bomb blast at Nagasaki in 1945.

Around the – very grand – houses

La Pagode was built by a Japanese devotee as a society ballroom in 1896. Almost bought by the Chinese as an embassy (until they found pictures of Japanese soldiers killing Chinese on the walls), it was saved from ruin by the film director Louis Malle.

Before tackling the vastness of Les Invalides and if you enjoy a good walk, it may be an idea to explore the top-class area around it first, going via Paris's most interesting cinema and tea house **La Pagode** ❾ in Rue de Babylone, about a 10-minute walk along Rue d'Estrées, where the tea is strong, the gardens tropical and the films up to date.

When Parisian nobility moved out of the Marais in the 18th century, and Versailles tumbled, the rich and famous built new town houses across the river from the Tuileries. Beautifully preserved, they are now mostly behind heavily secured gates, since only French ministries and foreign governments can afford the rent (along with the odd Greek arms dealer). About 15 minutes further on, across Boulevard Raspail (No 45), stands **Hôtel Lutétia** ❿, its extravagant statued facade fronting a deluxe four-star hotel where Charles de Gaulle enjoyed his first night of married life. When the hotel was requisitioned by the Gestapo in 1940, the owner bricked up the vintage wine cellar and, even though the hotel staff were interrogated to reveal the whereabouts of the finest wine collection in the capital, no one talked.

BELOW: the huge garden of Hôtel Biron, Rodin's home and museum.

About a five-minute walk along Boulevard Raspail towards the Seine, **Rue de Grenelle**, on the left, is bursting with beautiful buildings, including the Swiss and Dutch embassies, the Ministry of Education and the National Geographic Institute. Just into the street on the left is the **Hôtel Bouchardon** where the poet Alfred de Musset lived between 1824 and 1839, before going on an oriental voyage of discovery with George Sand. It is now the **Musée Maillol – Fondation Dina Vierney** ⓫ (open daily; closed Tues; entrance fee), where the works of Aristide Maillol, whose sculptures adorn the Jardin des Tuileries (*see pages 121–22*), are on show, along with art from his contemporaries such as Cezanne and Degas. Dina Vierny, owner of the private collection, was an art dealer and model for Maillol. Next door, the grandiose **Fontaine des Quatre Saisons** was a monumental response to a local complaint about lack of water.

Turning left up Rue du Bac, Rue de Varenne has a collection of fine old houses, the most famous being the residence of the French Prime Minister, **Hôtel Matignon** ⓬. It was here that the socialist leader Pierre Bérégovoy lived before his defeat in the elections in April 1993 and his subsequent suicide following the May Day celebrations.

Musée Rodin – a small man with a big talent

At the end of Rue de Varenne, next to Les Invalides, is the **Hôtel Biron**, housing the unmissable **Musée Rodin** ⓭ (open daily; closed Mon; entrance fee), containing the best of the sculptor's work. Auguste Rodin's first work of critical acclaim was *The Age of Bronze* in 1877, a naked youth caressing his hair, modelled by a Belgian soldier. The establishment was shocked, maintaining that the statue was too lifelike to be regarded as art. A card stuck to the work at the Paris *salon* read "Beware – moulded from the body of the model". Eventually, the French government bought the statue and Rodin's reputation was made.

Rodin came to live in the Hôtel Biron, owned by the state and ironically a former convent, in 1908 and stayed there until his death in 1917. He paid his rent with his best works, forming the basis of the museum, which overflows with

Map, page 204

ABOVE: a sculpture of the sculptor Rodin himself.
BELOW: the ornate doors of Hôtel Biron.

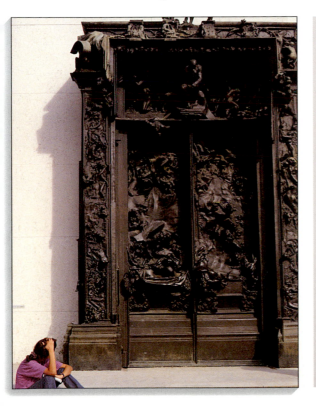

AUGUSTE RODIN – LOVER AND SCULPTOR

One of the world's smallest artists (at 1.65 metres/5 ft 4 in), Auguste Rodin was born in the Quartier Latin in 1840 and grew up wandering the markets of Rue Mouffetard (*see page 195*). Rejected by the Ecole des Beaux-Arts, he trained himself, visiting the zoo at the Jardin des Plantes and the horse markets on the Boulevard St-Michel for inspiration.

Further stimulus came from his incessant love affairs, which were interrupted only for a short while when the sculptor took holy orders. This was a reaction to the death of his sister in a convent, after she had been rejected in love by one of Rodin's close friends. Chastity did not suit him, however, and a year later he returned to his art. Some of his most famous works are *The Kiss*, *The Thinker*, *The Burghers of Calais*, *God's Hand* and the unfinished *Gates of Hell,* on which he worked from the 1880s until his death in 1917.

In the Dôme Church, Napoleon lies in six coffins, one inside the other. The first is white iron, then mahogany, two of lead, ebony and finally oak, on a base of green Vosges granite. When brought back to Paris after 19 years, his body was in perfect condition.

BELOW: the Hôtel des Invalides.

excellence. Here are *The Kiss* (removed from the Chicago World Fair of 1893 for being too shocking), *The Thinker* (reputedly Dante contemplating the *Inferno*), *The Burghers of Calais*, *The Hand of God* and other works. Recently restored to their white marble finish, the statues ripple with life, many being set outside in beautiful gardens of roses. Also included in the exhibition are works by Camille Claudel, the most famous of Rodin's countless mistresses.

Hôtel des Invalides

The **Hôtel des Invalides** ⓮ (open daily; closed pub. hols; free) is dramatic yet refined, as befits a one-time pensioners' retreat and mausoleum. Commissioned by war-loving Louis XIV as a retirement home for his soldiers in 1676, the buildings designed by Libéral Bruant once housed 4,000 men. It was here that revolutionaries seized 28,000 guns for the storming of the Bastille in 1789. The great courtyard, with its imposing arcades and array of captured cannons, now hosts the odd military parade and society wedding.

At the heart of Les Invalides lies the heart of an empire. The beautiful **Dôme Church**, the masterpiece of the Sun King Louis XIV's reign, contains the body of Napoleon. Returned to France in 1840, following much wrangling with the British, the little Emperor was given a state funeral during which a snowstorm enveloped the city. The interior of the Emperor's resting place is predictably over the top, with 12 damsels, symbolising his 12 military campaigns, guarding the polished oak coffin. High above the tomb, the dome, completed by Jules Hardouin-Mansart in 1706, is breathtaking, thanks in part to its new coat of gold leaf, regilded for the bicentennial celebrations in July 1989.

On the west side of the grounds is the **Musée de l'Ordre de la Libération**

(open daily; closed pub. hols; entrance fee) in memory of the Resistance fighters who received the Order of Liberation, France's highest honour created by Charles de Gaulle in 1940, during World War II.

On either side of the Cour d'Honneur, the **Musée de l'Armée** (open daily; closed pub. hols; entrance fee) offers an extensive glimpse of man's inhumanity and skill at warfare from the Stone Age to World War II with a terrifying selections of weapons, armour and poignant reminders of the two world wars, including the original copy of Adolf Hitler's *Mein Kampf*.

Stretching to the Seine, the beautiful **Esplanade des Invalides** is another symmetrically designed garden much loved by strollers and sports fanatics. Along the west side is a series of *boules* courts. Opposite is a small air terminal.

From here, you can either go west along the Seine to the Place de la Resistance and the sewers (*see page 212*) or east to the Musée d'Orsay. However, take into consideration that you will need some time at both. Heading east, you pass the colonnaded **Assemblée Nationale–Palais Bourbon** ⑮ (open Sat at 10am, 2pm, 3pm; closed during sessions; proof of identity required), which is the Lower House of the French Parliament. The extravagant columns were grafted on to an 18th-century facade by Napoleon to complement La Madeleine across the river and now shelter an armed guard, protecting the 491 *députés* (members of Parliament). Outside, the view from **Pont de la Concorde** is stunning.

Musée d'Orsay – a transformed railway station

No visit to Paris is complete without a pilgrimage to the **Musée d'Orsay** ⑯ (open daily, Thur till 9.45pm; closed Mon and some pub. hols; entrance fee). Considered by many as the most easy-to-use museum in the world, the former

Map, page 204

BELOW: preserved Gare d'Orsay is now a lavish museum.

Map,
page 204

TIP

Make a day of it at the Musée d'Orsay and take a break in the museum's restaurant or rooftop café.

railway station is spaciously arranged and sumptuously stuffed full of the most beautiful art from 1848 until World War I (which, by coincidence, is 95 percent French). The building, finished in two years in 1900, was almost torn down to make way for an immense hotel in 1970. Prompted by public outcry, government ministers fulfilled the prophesy of painter Edouard Detaille, at the opening ceremony in 1900, that the station would make a better museum. Its glass and iron construction was a triumph of modernity, rivalling Eiffel's tower, while the facade reflected the Palais du Louvre across the river. In the vast cavern of the interior, Orson Welles set his film of Kafka's *The Trial* (1962).

A tour of the Musée d'Orsay

It is difficult to get lost in this museum. Designed by an Italian, Gae Aulenti, and opened in 1986, the exhibitions are arranged on five levels, the central hall surrounded by terraces. As airy as the Louvre isn't, the museum's layout is deceptively approachable. How many have launched into an inclusive tour of its riches, only to be exhausted before even reaching the Impressionists on the Upper Level? Choose carefully, as this museum is a place to come back to.

The ground floor is dominated by the Academic School and its regimented style. In contrast, Edouard Manet's shameless nude – *Olympia* (1863), the first "modern" painting, stares insolently at her staid predecessors (the work was pronounced pornographic at the 1865 Paris *salon*). On the top floor is the museum's treasure trove. The Impressionists are bathed in soft light from the station's glass-vaulted roof, a setting they were painted for. Pass through galleries full of paintings by Monet, Manet, Renoir, Pissarro, Degas, Cézanne and Van Gogh. At the end is a small café under a large clock, from where an outside terrace runs high above the Seine, offering appetising views over Paris.

The central aisle makes a perfect setting for sculpture (David, Rodin, Maillol *et al*), while Art Nouveau overflows from the middle floor, including the two towers at the east end, which present a bird's-eye view of the museum. For more information on favourite works visit the documentation room upstairs, where computers give details and video reproductions on all exhibits.

Anyone interested in medals and military decorations should visit the next-door museum, **Musée Nationale de la Légion d'Honneur** ⓱ (open afternoons; closed Mon; entrance fee) tracing the history of France's most celebrated award, created by Napoleon I. The interior colonnaded courtyard is also a pleasant place to rest.

A trip round the city's underworld

For a surprisingly entertaining experience descend into the bowels of the capital at the Place de la Résistance, next to Pont l'Alma. The **Musée des Egouts de Paris** ⓲ (open daily, 11am–5pm, Oct–Apr till 4pm; closed Thurs and Fri and last three weeks of Jan; entrance fee) is more an excursion into the city's infinite sewer system. Described by novelist Victor Hugo in *Les Misérables* as the "other Paris", this network of tunnels follows the well-known streets above ground. Accompanied by a film and relevant odours, it is *the* alternative tour of Paris.

BELOW: down under in the Paris sewers.

Café life

The café is the Parisian's decompression chamber, easing the transition between *dodo-Métro-boulot* – sleeping, commuting and working. It provides a welcome pause in which to savour a *pet't noir* (espresso) or an apéritif, to empty the mind of troublesome thoughts and to watch the people go by. The café is also the place to meet friends, have a romantic tryst or even to do business in a relaxed atmosphere.

The first café ever to open was Le Procope in 1686 (*see pages 189 and 191*) and the literati soon started to congregate there, keen to discuss ideas with each other. More establishments quickly sprang up all over the country and it wasn't long before there was at least one café in every village and hamlet where people kept each other company. During the 18th century, the neighbourhood "zinc", named after its metal counter, became part of the fabric of French life.

In Paris, each café developed its own character, attracting different types of clientele, and with the widening of the boulevards in the 19th century, the tables spilled out on to the pavements. By 1910, there were 510,000 zincs in France, but now café life is in danger of extinction. The figures are alarming: 4,000 French cafés disappear each year. Paris alone has lost 1,000 in five years.

While the invasion of fast-food restaurants is partly to blame (a nearby McDonald's, "*McDo*", can slash a café's profits by 30 percent), changes in the French way of life are also culpable. When customers move out to spacious homes in the suburbs, they tend to "cocoon", staying in to watch television and the local café eventually has to close.

Then there are the ageing proprietors to consider. The café is traditionally a family business but, today, fewer sons and daughters are prepared to take on gruelling 16-hour days with sparse holidays and little reward.

Sadly, even the atmosphere of remaining cafés is not what it was. Now there is formica where once there was marble. Piped muzak and the electronic beep of video games have replaced the song of the accordionist and the furious volleys of the "Baby-foot" players. Only the Gauloise-induced haze (attitudes to the 1992 smoking ban are casual) and the hazards of the lavatories (some are literally a hole in the ground) are the same.

Yet all is not lost. Authentic "zincs" are still to be found in Paris and many are thriving. Try the stylish Café de l'Industrie on Rue St-Sabin, La Palette on Rue de Seine or the tiny but lovingly restored Le Cochon à l'Oreille on Rue Montorgueil. For literary atmosphere order a *verre* (glass of wine) at Les Deux Magots, which has been home to almost every Paris intellectual from Rimbaud to André Breton. At the nearby Café de Flore, Sartre and Simone de Beauvoir wrote by the stove. "My worst customer, Sartre," recalled the patron. "He spent the entire day scribbling away over one drink." (*See pages 198–199.*)

But go soon. For, if you have never ducked into a French café to make a quick phone call, met your lover for an apéritif on the *terrasse* or negotiated the contortionist's crouch of the *toilettes*, you cannot claim truly to know Paris.

RIGHT: a rare zinc-topped bar, which were once so numerous, cafés were nicknamed *les zincs*.

LA DÉFENSE – A MODERN METROPOLIS

Map, page 218

Dominated by the Grand Arche, La Défense is a concentrated business area where architects' futuristic imaginations have been allowed to run wild and avant-garde works of art are everywhere

Heading west, crossing the city boundary at Porte Maillot, the historic avenues of Paris suddenly vanish. There, on the horizon, rises a futuristic metropolis, a city of gigantic glass blocks marching to the gates of the capital. "America-on-the-Seine", as Parisians affectionately refer to **La Défense**, is the city's newest attraction, enticing a million visitors each year to experience "Europe's premier business centre", the capital of French industry and finance, and one of the world's most *avant-garde* architectural sites.

Once a desolate commuter land of office blocks, La Défense is rapidly becoming a bustling 21st-century community set around a vast concrete podium, with an enormous shopping complex, high-tech entertainment centres and, as its focus, the Grande Arche, the crowning glory of President Mitterrand's "progressive vision for the 1980s" (megalomania is another description offered by right-wing publications). The Grande Arche has given La Défense the symbol it needed and connects this modern upstart to the ancient heart of Paris, via the historic Triumphal Way, running east through the Arc de Triomphe to the Louvre.

PRECEDING PAGES: the Grande Arche in line with the Triumphal Way.
LEFT: art backs business in La Défense.
BELOW: an open-air modern art gallery.

The development of La Défense

Since 80 percent of Paris is protected by preservation orders, new developments have to move out of the city, adding successive layers to the core, like an onion. When, in 1958, it was decided that Paris needed a business centre, a small hill overlooking the Seine was selected for development. It was called La Défense, because this was where citizens defended the capital against the Prussian siege of 1870–71. The first phase of building by EPAD (Etablissement Public pour l'Aménagement de la Défense) was completed in the late 1960s – a complex of office towers, not exceeding 100 metres (330 ft) high, huddled above a pedestrian zone with roads passing underneath. The RER line was extended, placing the city centre five minutes away. Then recession hit and bankruptcy threatened.

It was not until the recovery of the 1980s that La Défense finally took permanent root. New towers soared to nearly twice the height of the old incumbents and the business world moved in. Today, teething troubles over, the continuous construction, thousands of serious-faced business people and almost as many tourists make the district one of the fastest growing and most adventurous in Paris. A "new spirituality" is being heralded in Paris's newest quarter.

It is not difficult to get to La Défense. Métro Line 1 cuts straight through the centre of Paris to end up beneath the Grande Arche, and the RER A line winds all

Avant-garde musician Jean-Michel Jarre gave a computerised concert extravaganza in La Défense on 14 July 1990 which was seen by two million people worldwide.

the way from Disneyland Paris (a journey of only 40 minutes) before branching out to the suburbs. In addition, 20 bus routes converge here, making this small district the most accessible in France and allowing 70 percent of the 110,000 workers to commute by public transport, 80 percent of whom spend less than an hour a day travelling.

La Défense, being a futuristic baby, loves statistics. There are 350,000 journeys to the district each workday, 66,000 parking spaces, 1,300 companies achieving an annual sales volume equivalent to France's national budget. Twelve of the top 20 French companies have headquarters at La Défense, such as Elf, Total and EDF, 13 of the world's top 50 companies are tenants – IBM, Apple, Hitachi, Unilever. In the residential sector, 30,000 people live in the great apartment complexes to the west.

The Grande Arche – symbol of success

On 14 July 1989, the day of the bicentennial celebrations of the storming of the Bastille, leaders of the seven richest nations paid a visit to La Défense for the inauguration of the **Grande Arche ❶** (open daily; Sat till 7pm; entrance fee). Previously, La Défense was a place to view from afar, with a certain traditionalist disdain. The spectacularly simple Grande Arche changed that, seducing public and politicians alike, and today the view from its lofty summit is as famous as that from the Eiffel Tower. The magician behind this dramatic transformation was unknown Danish architect Otto von Spreckelsen. It was his idea which most impressed President Mitterrand out of the 424 proposals for a building at the "head of the Défense".

The Grande Arche is the grandest of François Mitterrand's *grands projets* (*see*

page 95). Entitled "The Arch of Man's Triumph", von Spreckelsen's design completes the Triumphal Way without enclosing it and forms a window out on to the new developments in the west. As the architect, who died two years before the arch was completed, said, "This is an open cube, a window on the world. The arch will see far, in all directions."

Certainly, the view from the top is vast. Two glass bubbles whisk lines of visitors up to the roof at vertiginous speeds, through the symbolic "cloud", a canvas net suspended between the twin towers designed to cut down wind resistance. Funded by profits from rooftop tourists, the International Foundation for Human Rights, formed in 1989, has its headquarters in the top three stories across the arch, where it holds exhibitions and conferences. On the roof terrace, Raynaud's **Carte de Ciel** (Map of the Sky) resembles an enormous sundial. Housed in the huge flanks is the Ministry of Transport and Public Works, a conference centre and numerous offices. At weekends, the majestic sweep of steps down to the parvis is dotted with families, children and tour groups.

Some notable buildings

Right next to the arch, **La Colline de la Défense** ❷ (open afternoons, Sat till 10pm; entrance fee) is the district's most recent tourist attraction, created to cream off some of the coachloads of visitors heading for the arch. Wide steps lead past orange, blue and green cubes, designed by Piatr Kowalski to stimulate a "mental geometry". Inside is less intellectually demanding: to the left, the **Musée de l'Automobile** is a sparkling new display of the history of the car, exhibiting vehicles from pre-history to 1972, including the box-like hippomobile (horse-drawn), and the fantastical Rolls-Royce Phantom III. The museum is

Map, page 218

ABOVE AND BELOW: the Grande Arche was the grandest of President Mitterrand's *grands projets.*

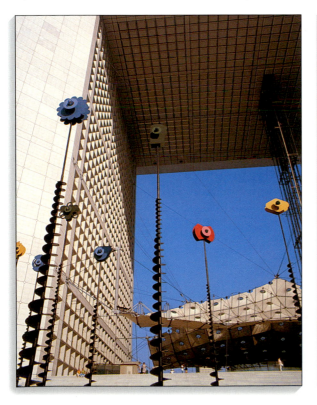

SIZING UP THE GRANDE ARCHE

From the Esplanade de la Défense at the entrance of the district, the great white arch seems two-dimensional. When viewed from the sides, the third dimension mysteriously appears, an illusion created by the arch's alignment six degrees off the axis of the Triumphal Way, or Royal Axis (a quirk shared by I.M. Peï's pyramid at the Louvre – *see page 118).*

The size of the arch is symbolic: measuring roughly 100 metres by 100 metres (330 ft by 330 ft), it has the same dimensions as the Cour Carrée at the Louvre. At 106 metres (348 ft) wide, the entire cathedral of Notre Dame could fit within the archway. The architect Otto von Spreckelsen's monumental vision also respects the historic pattern of Parisian arches. The Arc de Triomphe du Carrousel is 25 metres (82 ft) high, the Arc de Triomphe 50 metres (164 ft) high, so La Grande Arche is 100 metres (330 ft) high.

BELOW: the Palais de la Défense squats next to the Bull building (left).

surprisingly entertaining, even for automobile agnostics. Alongside the memories of yesterday, more up-to-date models are displayed in the **Espace Marques**, which is a unique car showroom that allows prospective buyers or just the simply curious to view and test-drive the latest offerings available from top car manufacturers.

Dominating the "colline" is the immense silver globe of the **Dôme IMAX ❸**, the world's largest hemispheric cinema. Designed by the IMAX Corporation of Canada, the screen is 1,000 sq. metres (10,700 sq. ft), and shows pictures 10 times the size of a normal cinema image at a viewing angle of 180 degrees, with seats tilted at 30 degrees. Reservations for each show are recommended, although the dome is less crowded than its rival La Géode over at the Parc de la Villette (*see page 229*).

Opposite is the district's oldest resident, the **Palais de la Défense ❹**, the CNIT business centre, which has recently been given a face-lift. This curvaceous structure was built in 1958 as the focus of La Défense, but now seems rather dated. Its lofty concave dome is supported by just three pillars, the roof seemingly hanging in mid-air. Inside, recent refurbishment has created a high-tech bowl of glass offices, tapering outwards from the roof to the floor, interspersed with hanging gardens of small trees and shrubs.

Within this deluxe greenhouse, the **World Trade Centre** is the heart of the Parisian business machine, where market dealers, business service consultants and researchers plug into the network of 237 trade centres around the world.

Since 1981, **Les Quatre Temps ❺** shopping centre across the Esplanade de la Défense has provided a social focus for the complex, as well as a place to buy everything that the time-squeezed business person of today needs. It contains

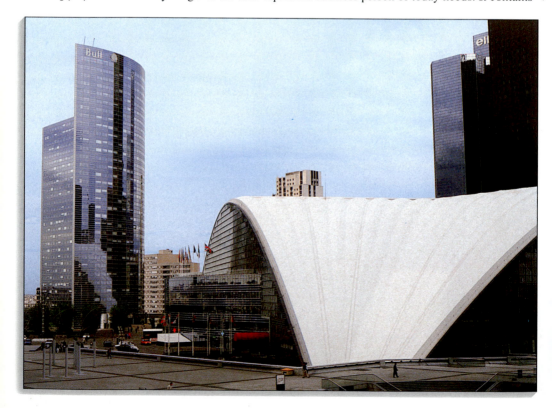

three hypermarkets, 260 shops, 26 restaurants and nine cinemas, and greets 50,000 customers a day. Rumour has it that this is the biggest shopping centre in Europe: at La Défense, superlatives have become a way of life.

Map, page 218

Exploring the skyscrapers

The Esplanade de la Défense stretches from the arch to the Seine, providing a new strolling arena which seems to double up as a high-tech soccer pitch for local children, while the major roads pass underneath, unseen and unheard. On either side of this marble plateau rise forests of towers, including some of the most adventurous architecture in Europe.

The newest developments in the district are growing up behind the Grande Arche and are beginning to make the central buildings look prehistoric in comparison. Here, the Japanese architect Kurokawa has conceived an oriental response to the classical rigidity of Spreckelsen's arch – his **Tour Pacific** is gracefully curved and set on a convex arch. Next door, the **Société Générale** headquarters is formed of two semi-circular edifices, both of which are seemingly on the verge of rotating. The Tour Fiat's windows are wider at the top to prevent one of the tallest buildings in the complex looking narrower as it rises.

Further down on the north side is the **Vision 80** tower built on stilts in the Place des Reflets, behind which loom the **Aurore** and **Manhattan** towers. **Les Miroirs**, set around a fountain decorated with mosaics, is further back. At the entrance to La Défense, dominating the Seine, the **Tour Roussel-Hoechst** was the first skyscraper to sprout – a mere 34 storeys built in 1967 in blue-green steel and glass. Just behind, Willerval's PFA tower is a triangular temple of sleek glass pointing towards Paris.

BELOW: the Takis pool, where 49 spiral rods sway and light up at night.

The Tour Fiat rises 45 storeys of tinted black glass above the Esplanade de la Défense. The Tour Elf behind matches it in height, its blue-tinted facades change intensity according to the colour of the sky.

BELOW: Catalan sculptor Joan Miró's *Two Figures.*

A cradle of art

In honour of the defenders of Paris against the Prussians in 1870, a bronze sculpture, **La Defense de Paris**, was made by Barrias following submissions by 100 artists, including Rodin. The monument still stands at the heart of the district and represents a young guardsman and girl symbolising the valour of the innocent civilian population confronting the Prussians. Above it, the quarter's most amusing attraction, the **Fontaine d'Agam**, designed by Yaacov Agam, erratically spurts water by way of a series of 66 fountains, each shooting up at different levels and at different times and cascading over a multicoloured mosaic, often to computerised music. The small white building to the left of the fountains, mysteriously named **Art Gallery 4**, is the office of the artistic wing of La Défense and provides a free guide to works of art on the site. Take the brochure, and sip a glass at **Le Bistro de Vins**, with a ringside view of Agam's fountains dancing and wriggling, as you decide what to see.

Modern sculpture park

With more than 50 modern sculptures, La Défense is one of Europe's most interesting open-air art museums. The works are consistently interactive, complementing and contrasting with surrounding buildings, demanding the participation of even the most preoccupied passer-by. A good one to start with is Miyawaki's **Utshori** ❻ sculpture, commissioned by Spreckelsen himself to sit alongside the Grande Arche – a series of pillars with nests of silver wires springing from them (the spectator is required to admire the space between the wires, according to Miyawaki).

At the entrance to the RER station, Rieti's 60-metre (200-ft) **mural** ❼ offers a teasing choice between a painted kiss, a flock of birds, or a running woman, depending on the perspective of the onlooker. Across the parvis, Joan Miró's **Two Figures** ❽ loom above the square, marking the entrance to the shopping centre. These surreal beasts leer happily at the rigid angles of surrounding buildings and are a favourite site for photographs with the prosaically white arch behind. Facing Miró's anarchic couple, **The Spider** ❾ by Alexander Calder is one of the American artist's "stabiles" and his last work, comprising huge steel structures, painted red-orange. Inside the shopping complex, Beatrice Casadesus has created **Charlie Chaplin** and **Brigitte Bardot** in bas reliefs.

Outside once more, in the shadow of the EDF and Aurore towers, Derbré's **The Earth** ❿ is a beautiful bronze of two figures suggesting the rotation of the globe. More dramatically, Guy-Rachel Grataloup has decorated the foot of the **Tour Total** with an 850-sq. metre (9,000 sq. ft) ceramic of tree-like branches swirling skywards into mists of colour.

Further to the east along the esplanade is the happiest sculpture in La Défense – Claude Torricini's **The Frog who Became as Big as an Ox** ⓫. This corpulent frog is a favourite with children and you can drink water from his mouth. In the centre of Place de l'Iris, Henri de Miller's **Sleepwalker** ⓬ is contrastingly graceful – a slender figure with arms outstretched, standing on a smooth sphere.

End a visit to La Défense at sunset by the huge pool which overlooks the Seine at the entrance. This mirror of water is inhabited by 49 spiralling, swaying rods, designed by the Greek artist Takis. Each rod is crowned by a coloured light which blinks lazily as twilight gathers and the Arc de Triomphe in the distance turns soft pink. Here, at the gateway to one of the most modern developments in the world, the future somehow doesn't feel quite so bad.

Map,
page 218

Parc André-Malraux, beyond La Défense to the west, has 24 hectares (59 acres) of rolling lawns, a lake, botanical gardens, an adventure sandpit and is home to the Paris Opera dance school.

BELOW: one of the many works of art to be found dotted around the complex.

PARKS ON THE PÉRIPHÉRIQUE

On both sides of the city's busy ring road lie havens of leisure, from the ancient and tranquil royal Bois de Boulogne to the new André Citroën and Villette parks offering futuristic horticulture and fun

Paris

I n 1759 Voltaire declared, "We must cultivate our garden," and Paris has not looked back since. Here is a city where parks and gardens are a matter of philosophy, a touchstone for the state of mind and health of the capital, a reflection of the sinuous course of the city's history. The French quality newspaper *Le Monde* once asserted that "when we argue in favour of our gardens, we are arguing for the whole city".

Now, more than ever, Parisians are looking to their green spaces as an escape from the increasing congestion of urban living. While the 1980s may be remembered as the decade of the *grands projets* and monumental building (*see page 95*), the 1990s have seen the city's parks and gardens flourish. Derelict industrial sites are flowering and blossoming into suburban parks, with a fervour not seen since Haussmann's day. Never before has Paris been so green.

The Bois de Bologne – a recreational paradise

Past the necklace of the Périphérique ring road to the west of Paris, the **Bois de Boulogne** (Métro Porte Maillot, Porte Dauphine, Porte d'Auteuil, Sablons) is one of the reasons that the 16th *arrondissement* alongside it is preferred by the wealthy as a place to live – Avenue Foch, perhaps the most expensive residential street in the capital, leads straight to park gates. Embraced by an elbow of the Seine, this 860-hectare (2,120-acre) expanse of woods and gardens has been the Sunday afternoon playground for generations of Parisian families. Historically, it has also had a reputation for love, as successive kings used to house their mistresses here and, after Louis XIV opened the woods to the public in the 17th century, it was noted that "marriages from the Bois de Boulogne do not get brought before the Right Reverend".

In 1852, Napoleon III had the surrounding wall of the royal hunting ground, built by Henri II, demolished and the park was remodelled on the Emperor's cherished Hyde Park in London. It now offers gardens, wild woods, horse racing at France's two famous racecourses, Longchamps and Auteuil, a sports stadium, boating, museums, restaurants, theatre and much more, making the park the main recreation area for Paris. However, it does have a reputation for being seedy at night.

A good place to start exploring the Bois de Boulogne is from the beautiful Art Nouveau Métro stop at Porte Dauphine (*see page 94*) and the best way is by bicycle, which can be rented (daily May–Sept; weekends Oct–Apr) near the **Pavillon Royal**, off the Route de Suresnes. A network of cycle paths and nature trails intersect the woods enabling easy access to the vast park and its scenic lakes and waterfall.

To the north is the **Jardin d'Acclimatation** (open

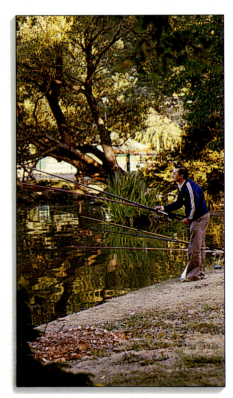

PRECEDING PAGES: the carefully laid out gardens of the Espace Albert Khan. **LEFT AND BELOW:** playing in the Bois de Boulogne.

Map, page 227

The great novelist Honoré de Balzac (1799–1850) lived at 47 Rue Raynouard, east of the Bois de Boulogne (above), from 1840–47 under a false name and wrote 16 hours a day to pay his creditors. Now Maison de Balzac is a museum (open daily; closed Mon and pub. hols; entrance fee).

BELOW: playing Shakespeare.

daily; entrance fee), an amusement park for children, with a hall of mirrors, zoo, go-kart racing, a wooden fort, theatre and puppet show. Here, the **Musée en Herbe** (open daily; closed Sat morning during school terms; entrance fee) organises art exhibits and workshops for future Picassos. Also here is the **Musée National des Arts et Traditions Populaires** (open daily; closed Tues and some pub. hols; entrance fee) which portrays life in France before industrialisation, incorporating local customs, crafts and folklore with an audio-visual show.

Westwards, the **Parc de Bagatelle** (open daily; entrance fee) surrounds a small château constructed by the Count of Artois, later Charles X, who bet Marie-Antoinette he could build a house in three months. The bet was won at great cost, hence the ironic name "bagatelle". The gardens are magnificent with 8,000 roses blooming from June to October, a walled iris garden flowering in May and a display of waterlilies in August. Art exhibitions are held in the Trianon and Orangery during the summer season.

In the centre of the Bois, the **Pré Catalan** is the most romantic spot in western Paris. In spring, narcissi, tulips and daffodils carpet the manicured lawns, bathing the foot of the colossal copper beech, well over 200 years old, whose branches span over half a kilometre (550 yds). Le Pré Catalan restaurant is a big attraction offering sumptuous fare in elegant *Belle Epoque* surroundings. Nearby, the intimate **Jardin Shakespeare** (mysteriously open only for guided tours daily 3–3.30pm, 4–4.30pm; entrance fee) is planted with flowers, trees and shrubs that star in Shakespeare's plays such as Macbeth's heather, Mediterranean herbs from *The Tempest* and Ophelia's stream. In summer, open-air productions are presented in the leafy theatre.

On the eastern border of the park, between the Place de la Porte de Passy and

ROYALTY IN THE BOIS

The Duke and Duchess of Windsor lived in a magnificent house at 4 Route du Champ d'Entrainement, in the Bois de Boulogne, from 1953 until their deaths in 1972 and 1986 respectively. The twice-divorced American, for whom Edward VIII gave up the British throne in 1936, ensured that her husband was able to live in the manner to which he was accustomed, decorating the house in a style "fit for a king". After the Duchess died, Harrods owner, Mohamed al-Fayed took over the house, buying their personal collection of 40,000 items. The royal memorabilia finally went under the hammer in New York in 1998 after it had been postponed the previous September following the deaths of al-Fayed's son and Diana, Princess of Wales.

Porte de la Muette, is the **Musée Marmottan** (2 Rue Louis Boilly; open daily; closed Mon; entrance fee), containing 65 paintings by Monet, donated by his son, Michel, in 1971, including his famous *Impression: Sunrise* (1872), which gave its name to the Impressionist movement. Once home to Paul Marmottan, art collector extraordinaire, this beautiful 19th-century mansion also exhibits works by Pissarro, Renoir and Gauguin.

Parc de la Villette – futuristic fun

To the northeast of Paris, nestling against the Périphérique, the **Parc de la Villette** (Métro Porte de Pantin, Porte de la Villette; open daily; closed Mon; entrance fee) is France's third most visited site after Disneyland Paris and the Centre Georges-Pompidou. Built on the site of a huge abattoir, which was rendered obsolete by improved refrigeration techniques and poor design (the cows could not even get up the steps), 55 hectares (136 acres) of futuristic gardens surround a colossal science museum – Cité des Sciences et de l'Industrie – as well as **La Géode** (open daily; closed Mon; entrance fee), a giant silver ball housing a huge wraparound cinema, **L'Argonaute** (included in the science museum's entrance fee), a retired naval submarine and **Cinaxe** (open daily; closed Mon; entrance fee), a flight-simulator-cum-cinema, which is definitely not for the queasy.

The **Cité des Sciences et de l'Industrie** (open daily; entrance fee) was designed by architect Adrien Fainsilber and built by the company that masterminded the moving of the temple of Abu Simbel in Egypt. This is not a museum for academics: the exhibits are interactive, with buttons, levers, keyboards and screens to keep mind and body alert. Begin at *L'Univers* with a spectacular

Map, page 227

TIPS

At La Villette, combined entrance tickets are available at the Cité des Sciences et de l'Industrie. Combinations include Cité-Géode, Cité-Cinaxe and Cité-Géode-Cinaxe.

For guided tours of the city's parks and gardens, phone 01 40 71 75 23.

BELOW: La Géode – Parc de la Villette's wraparound cinema.

planetarium and explanation of the inexplicable Big Bang. *La Vie* is an eclectic mix of medicine, agriculture and economics. A working meteorological station traces the day's weather in 240 cities across the world. *La Matière* reproduces a nuclear explosion and permits you to land an Airbus 320 and *La Communication* has displays of artificial intelligence, three-dimensional graphics and virtual reality.

Across the canal, the former cattle market now houses a cultural and conference centre in the immense 19th-century **Grande Halle**. Next door, the **Cité de la Musique** is an edifice of angles in two buildings designed by Christian de Portzamparc, holding the music and dance conservatory, concert hall and the **Musée de la Musique** (open afternoons, Thurs till 9.30pm, Sun all day; closed Mon; entrance fee) which contains over 4,500 musical instruments.

The gardens of the park are the biggest to be constructed in Paris since Haussmann. Designed by Bernard Tschumi and opened in 1993, they comprise several thematic areas such as the Jardin des Frayeurs Enfantines (Garden of Childhood Fears), with a huge dragon slide, Jardin des Brouillards (Garden of Mists), among sculptured streams, and the Jardin des Vents (Garden of Winds) growing multicoloured bamboo plants. Abstraction continues in the form of Tschumi's *folies*: red, angular tree houses minus the trees, each with a special function such as play area, workshop, daycare centre or café.

ABOVE AND BELOW: plenty for children to do at Parc de la Villette.

Parc des Buttes-Chaumont – a mountainous creation

To the south of La Villette and on the city side of the Périphérique, **Parc des Buttes-Chaumont** (Métro Botzaris, Buttes-Chaumont) was built by Haussmann in the 1860s on the site of a rubbish dump and gypsum quarry. The uneven ground provided a perfect setting for a wooded, rocky terrain and a lake has been created around an artificial 50-metre (150-ft) "mountain", capped by a Roman-style temple, with a waterfall and a cave containing artificial stalactites. Ice-skating, boating and donkey rides are also on offer and the puppet show or "Guignol" in the open-air theatre has been going for 150 years.

Map, page 227

The Bois de Vincennes – king of Parisian parks

On the southeast edge of Paris lies the **Bois de Vincennes**, (Métro Château de Vincennes, Porte de Charenton, Porte Dorée; RER Fontenay-sous-Bois, Joinville) which is renowned for its château, racecourse and zoo. Philippe-Auguste enclosed the forest in the 12th century with a 12-km (7-mile) wall to protect the royal hunting ground. In 1370, Charles V completed the **château** (open daily; entrance fee), which over the centuries has served as a prison, incarcerating among others the philosopher Diderot and Revolutionary Mirabeau, a porcelain factory and, under Napoleon I, an arsenal. Napoleon III started a restoration programme but the château was severely damaged by the Germans in 1944. Restoration is now complete and there is a museum in the 14th-century keep.

Just south of the château, **Le Parc Floral de Paris** (open daily; entrance fee) is a favourite with families who wander the Vallée des Fleurs, in bloom all year round, the pine wood and the water garden and take advantage of the adventure playground. Close by is **La Cartoucherie,** once an ancient arsenal, now a complex of theatres which resound to the sound of some of France's most *avantgarde* theatre companies, including the Théâtre du Soleil.

On the western side of the Bois is the **Parc Zoologique** (open daily; entrance fee). This zoo was all the rage when it opened in 1934, because the animals

When Henry V of England died of dysentery in the Château de Vincennes in 1422, staff boiled his body in the kitchen before shipping it back home for burial.

BELOW LEFT: the interactive Cité des Sciences.
BELOW: animal-friendly zoo at Bois de Vincennes.

Map,
page 227

*La Ruche, designed
by Gustave Eiffel as a
wine pavilion for the
1900 World
Exhibition , and
re-erected in 1902 as
artists' studios in
Passage Dantzig, just
west of Parc Georges
Brassens. Residents
included Fernand
Léger and Marc
Chagall. Now an
historical monument,
it still houses artists.*

BELOW: the site of
the old Citroën car
factory, now a park.
RIGHT: boating in the
Bois de Vincennes.

roamed free. Each enclosure is different, inspired by the animal's natural environment, and a giant artificial mound is home to monkeys, gazelles and goats.

At Porte Dorée, a few minutes walk away from the zoo, is the **Musée des Arts d'Afrique et d'Océanie** (open daily; closed 12–1.30pm weekdays, weekend mornings and pub. hols; entrance fee), one of the least known of Paris's museums that houses a fascinating collection of African and Australasian art. Picasso used to come here to wander round the displays of Nigerian death masks, Algerian jewels and South Pacific fertility symbols, seeking inspiration. The star attraction is an impressive tropical aquarium with a crocodile pit.

To the west of Vincennes lies **Parc Montsouris** (Métro Porte d'Orléans; RER Cité Universitaire), the second of Haussmann's 19th-century parks, comprising 16 hectares (40 acres) of gently undulating grass and trees, much loved by Cubist Georges Braque and the exiled Lenin, who both used to live close by. On the day the park opened, the lake suddenly and inexplicably drained dry, and its engineer committed suicide.

New-age parks and horticulture

The far-flung southwest of Paris is the capital's most populated district and home to two of its newest parks. **Parc Georges Brassens** on Rue des Morillons (Métro Convention) was opened in 1982 on the site of an old abbatoir and is now a child's paradise with playhouses, rock piles, rivers and mini-lakes. It includes a garden designed for the blind: close your eyes, follow the trickling of fountains and smell the fragrant foliage. Braille signs give relevant information on herbs and shrubs. Along Rue des Morillons grow 700 vines, producing the annual *Clos des Morillons* wine (full-bodied, fine bouquet). At weekends, the ancient slaughterhouses host a giant book market.

Further west on the banks of the Seine, dereliction became creation when the site of the Citroën car factory on Rue Balard was turned into the **Parc André-Citroën** (Métro Balard, Javel – André Citroën). Here industrial buildings have become floral palaces – two huge glasshouses shine forth over the esplanade where children leap in and out of spurting fountains. Behind the glass lie two gardens – "black" and "white", side-by side in botanical harmony. A series of six more colourful gardens completes the park – gold, silver, red, orange, green, and blue – with appropriately chromatic plants. Each garden is linked to a metal, a planet, a day of the week, and a sense: thus gold is linked to the sun, Sunday and the intangible sixth sense.

More traditional horticulture is found beyond the southeast of the Bois de Boulogne at the **Espace Albert Kahn** (14 Rue du Port, Métro Boulogne – Pont de St-Cloud) where the legacy of financier Albert Kahn takes the form of an extraordinary park, created between 1895 and 1910. Japanese, English and French gardens lie alongside an Alpine forest and North American prairie. The grass is cut at different levels, from "beatnik" style to "sailorboy". Kahn called the gardens "the vegetal expression of my thoughts concerning a reconciled world", an idea complemented by 72,000 photographs of world landscapes taken between 1910 and 1931 and exhibited on permanent rotation.

DISNEYLAND PARIS

Within easy reach of the city centre, this flamboyant slice of good, wholesome American entertainment provides fun for all, from a fairytale castle to the plunging delights of a runaway train

Map, page 237

Paris

With twice as many annual visitors as the Eiffel Tower or the Louvre, Disneyland Paris is the most popular tourist attraction in Europe. Located at Marne-la-Vallée, 32 km (20 miles) east of Paris on a 1,943-hectare (5,000-acre) site one-fifth the size of the city itself, the land "where dreams come true", as Walt Disney put it, has finally taken off after a rocky start in 1992 when bankruptcy threatened.

Although hordes of school buses are the resort's staple diet, many of Disneyland Paris's attractions may also stimulate more sophisticated imaginations. The park is worth the detour from Paris, if only to glimpse France's most incongruous, yet enjoyable tourist mecca at the end of RER line A (a regular TGV train service takes 15 minutes from Roissy-Charles de Gaulle airport and there's a shuttle bus service from Orly airport, *see page 266*).

Following the success of Tokyo Disneyland, opened in 1983, Europe was scoured for a suitable site for another non-American venture. The Disney empire eventually chose the land of Napoleon (the UK was discounted, thanks to lack of land and inconvenient geography, as was Spain, due to infrastructural inadequacies and the all-eclipsing 1992 Barcelona Olympics). France was somewhat of a homecoming, suggest Disney officials, since Walt's family originally came from Isigny-sur-Mer on the Normandy coast – d'Isigny (from Isigny) evolved to Disney once in America. Generous financial incentives from the French government might also have influenced the final decision.

Disney has enjoyed a love-hate relationship with its hosts since the opening of the park in April 1992. President Mitterrand turned down an official invitation to the inauguration, saying it was not his "cup of tea". Publications such as *Nouvel Observateur* and *Libération* tripped over each other in their race to condemn *"la folie Disney"*. Yet three and a half million visitors in the theme park's first year of operation were French.

Practicalities of Disneyland

With 40 attractions – 11 of them built since the opening – the whole site will not be fully developed, if present plans are maintained, until 2017, when there will be an MGM studio theme park, another new golf course and 13,000 more hotel rooms. But the resort is still impressive enough. Aside from the park itself, there is a complex of American theme bars, shops and restaurants known as Disney Village (*see page 241*), six hotels situated just outside the main turnstiles, a campsite and a 27-hole golf course.

Disneyland can be a daunting place, especially for mild-mannered Europeans unaccustomed to American-style fun. On popular days, the Magic Kingdom can receive more than 40,000 visitors (the park opens at

PRECEDING PAGES: The four-star Disneyland Hotel at the main entrance. **LEFT:** Sleeping Beauty's Castle – the centrepiece. **BELOW:** riverboat ride in Frontierland.

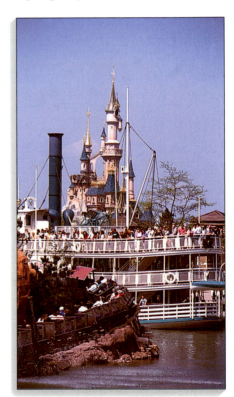

9am in the summer holidays and closes at 11pm). The best way to approach getting the most out of your time here is to decide on what you want to do in order of priority and get there early, as, by midday, lines of restless pilgrims at the most popular rides can be quite long. The longest wait can be up to 45 minutes, but the queues are well regulated and there is plenty to see while you gradually shift along. Heading round the park in an anti-clockwise direction avoids the bigger crowds, since the circular train chugs clockwise.

It does rain in Marne-La-Vallée, but most of the attractions have been built under cover and sheltered walkways lead from area to area, so the weather doesn't matter. Even the paint used is brighter than elsewhere in the Disney empire to counter grey skies. Eternally optimistic, Disney points out that rain leads to a stunning array of vegetation in the park, unrivalled by its developments in Florida and California.

The gardens are immaculate, as is the entire complex, with teams of roving cleaners ensuring nothing sullies the Disney brilliance. The code of cleanliness also extends to the employees across the board – from the managing director to the washer-up – who are not permitted facial hair, dangly earrings, tattoos or short skirts, causing intermittent disputes with French trade unions.

Getting your bearings

Disneyland Paris theme park is divided into five main areas, or "lands", each with attractions, restaurants and shops following a particular theme – a floor plan cloned from the other Disneylands in California, Florida and Tokyo. Designed by "Imagineers", the artistic and mechanical wizards who spend their lives thinking up weird and wonderful attractions, this is Disney's most technologically advanced park yet, benefiting from state-of-the-art robotics – the organisation's unique audio-animatronics, where life-size, lifelike figures speak, sing and dance with gusto.

Once through the Victorian turnstiles, already humming along to ubiquitous Disney music, you enter **Main Street USA**, the first of the five areas representing 19th-century, small-town America. City Hall, on the left, is the central information centre, a contact point for lost children and property. Here, too, is the Main Street Station, from where the Disneyland train circles the park. The station is often quite crowded, so it is often a good idea to get on it at one of the other stations en route, such as Frontierland.

The bandstand in Main Street square is the best place from which to view the parades (weekends, and daily during the summer season) which traverse the park, passing around the bandstand and out through the large green gates to the right, between Discovery Arcade and Ribbons and Bows Hat Shop. These are Mickey's 11.30am parade, the 4pm Grand Parade and the night-time Electrical Parade, with illuminated floats lit up by 700,000 light bulbs. The park takes on an even more mystical face at night, with thousands of miniature lights blinking like fireflies. At weekends, and each summer night, the bandstand is also the best spot from which to view the five-minute Fantasia in the Sky firework display.

DISNEYLAND MADE EASY

Different types of passes are available and prices are reduced during the low season during school term times.

The best option is a two- or three-day Passport, so you can spread out your visit. It does not have to be used on consecutive days, has no date limit and is more economical. You could combine a two-day Passport with a night in one of the resort hotels – during peak season, hotel guests are granted access to the park an hour before it opens. The Star Nights pass allows entrance after 5pm at a reduced rate in summer when it closes at 11pm.

Passports can be bought from the Disney Store and Virgin Megastore on the Champs-Elysées and from branches of FNAC, as well as at the gate. A Combi-ticket, combining a return RER ticket and passport, is available from main stations on RER line A in Paris. For details, including accommodation, phone 01 60 30 60 30 in France and 0990 030303 in the UK.

Frontierland – the Wild West

Many of the most popular attractions in the park are found in **Frontierland**, to the left of Main Street. Frontierland evokes dreams of the Wild West and its centrepiece, **Big Thunder Mountain**, is a towering triumph of red rock reminiscent of every Western movie you have seen. The surrounding small town of Thunder Mesa represents a pioneer settlement of the late 1800s, including Cavalry Fort and Lucky Nugget Saloon, where Miss Lil entertains on a vaudeville stage. Get to Big Thunder Mountain roller-coaster early to avoid a long wait and enjoy a bird's-eye view of the park before you hurtle spectacularly around an old gold mine on a runaway train. Even the waiting area is consistent with this theme – the queue moves through a mining shack, with the smell of oil and grease in the air, past the foreman's office and water pumping station.

Meticulous detail plays a part in all Disney's evocations – researchers scour the United States for period pieces such as iron mine pulleys from Montana and Minnesota light fittings. Such detail helps ease the wait and encourages visitors to enter into the spirit of the attraction before they embark. Anticipation is heightened by glimpses of the ride as you shuffle along to take your turn.

Phantom Manor, home to some of Disney's most spectacular audio-animatronics, provides a high-tech rollicking ride through a haunted house. If the house itself seems vaguely familiar, it may be because it is copied from Norman Bates's abode in Hitchcock's *Psycho*. The "dead" tree outside is not actually dead, but specially treated by Disney botanists so that it grows no leaves. Inside are singing cowboy skeletons and holographic ghosts.

The **Rivers of the Far West**, an artificial lake in the middle of Frontierland, can be enjoyed by Mississippi paddle steamer, keelboat or Indian canoe. The

Map, page 237

BELOW: riding high in the Orbitron in Discoveryland.

Indian canoe station, a quiet dead end, verdant and full of birdsong (taped, but it fools the real birds) is a tranquil contrast to the roller-coaster ride.

Adventureland – pirates and shipwreck

From Frontierland, paths lead almost imperceptibly into **Adventureland**. Sparse scrub gives way to lush bamboo and flowers, and the twang of Wild West guitar fades into the beat of African drums.

Here is another top attraction, the unforgettable **Pirates of the Caribbean** (queues move quickly as a rule). As you descend into the castle, the air cools, water drips and the darkness is punctuated only by flickering firelight. The water ride, through tropical swamp to the open sea, is orchestrated by jovially barbaric Disney workers. The boats pass the **Blue Lagoon Restaurant**, serving Caribbean fare in the heart of the attraction, under a starlit sky. For the six-minute journey you remain spellbound by animated pirates invading a treasure-rich port – here, a singing donkey, there, an inebriated pig that taps its trotters in time to the music.

Rival to Big Thunder Mountain, the first-ever 360° looping roller-coaster created by Disney is **Le Temple du Péril**, near Explorers' Club Restaurant. Hold on to your stomach as the ore-carts plunge through rain forest and turn upside down above a mock archaeological dig inspired by the *Indiana Jones* saga. As with other top rides, get here early. Elsewhere, Adventureland offers the ultimate treehouse, **La Cabane des Robinson**, home of the Swiss Family Robinson, an **Adventure Isle** based on Robert Louis Stevenson's *Treasure Island*, complete with rope bridge and Ben Gunn's cave, and **Captain Hook's Pirate Ship** which, along with Skull Rock, acts as a playground.

ABOVE: Big Thunder Mountain gives a screaming good ride.
BELOW: Tootling around on Main Street, USA.

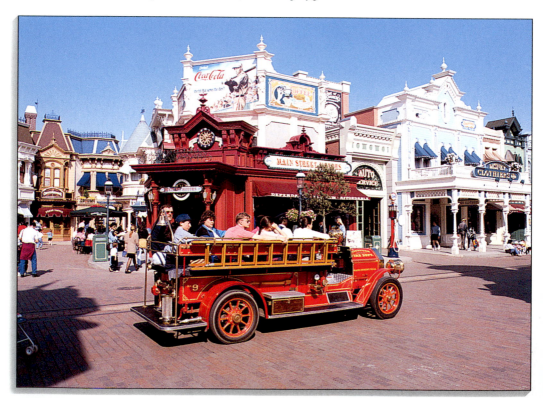

Fantasyland – favourite fairytales

The most popular land for younger children is **Fantasyland**, containing Disney's emblem **Le Château de la Belle au Bois Dormant** (Sleeping Beauty's Castle), the centrepiece of the park. Unlike in Florida, California or Tokyo, here you can enter into the French-style château, where Sleeping Beauty's tale is told through rich tapestries and stained-glass windows. Underneath, through Merlin's Workshop, lies *La Tanière du Dragon* (the Lair of the Dragon), hiding a breathtaking 27-metre (88-ft) long creature which roars, curls its claws and hisses smoke. Next door, **Blanche-Neige et les Sept Nains** (Snow White and the Seven Dwarfs) leads children through the classic fairytale in the mining cars from the dwarfs' mine and terrifies them with a holographic floating witch's head.

Not even Disney executives can account for the popularity of **Peter Pan's Flight**, which is another site to visit early in the day before the tour buses arrive, where you can take a pirate galleon into the skies above London, as far as Never-Never Land. Next door, **Toad Hall Restaurant** is Disney's impression of Ye Olde English Pub, which now even sells beer, since Disneyland Paris relaxed its ban on alcohol in order to increase profitability. Nearby, the **Fantasy Festival Stage** puts on glittering musical revues featuring favourite Disney characters. Whimsical madness is found in Alice's **Curious Labyrinth**, another mecca for small children, and the crazily spinning **Mad Hatter's Tea Cups**. You control how quickly you feel sick by regulating the speed at which the cups spin.

More sedate amusement is found in **It's a Small World**, where national stereotypes live in a cheerful puppet kingdom of singing children, first designed by Walt Disney for Pepsi's stand at the 1964 World Fair and sponsored by France Telecom. The other big attractions are similarly supported by multinational

Map, page 237

BELOW: in the drink in Fantasyland.

DISNEY VILLAGE

Open until the early hours, the complex between the park and the hotels buzzes with shops, restaurants, nightclubs and a massive cinema complex. Dramatic entertainment takes the form of Buffalo Bill's Legend, a 90-minute Wild West show with Indian chiefs, buffalo and carousing cowboys. For eating, the LA Bar and Grill offers a pizza terrace and Beach Boys' music, while Key West provides seafood at the sign of the life-size shark, a source of endless fun for children. Upstairs, you can sip a Cyclone Special under an alligator at the Hurricane Disco until 3am. Annette's Diner is the most reasonable and entertaining, and fills up early with families. A 1950s diner, it serves burgers and beer, brought by roller-skating waiters. The mood continues in Rock 'n' Roll America, a 1950s dance hall. Across the strip, Billy Bob's presents chicken and bluegrass. The area by the lake is more sedate and more expensive.

Map,
page 237

ABOVE: Michael
Jackson features in
a CinéMagique film.
BELOW: luxury hotel
outside the park.
RIGHT: Alice's
Curious Labyrinth.

companies, such as IBM, Coca-Cola and Renault, in collaboration with Disney,
and who receive advertising rights in exchange. It may be a small world – but
it's certainly lucrative.

Discoveryland – high-tech wizardry

The final stage of the journey, unless you've decided to go anti-clockwise, is
Discoveryland, providing an assortment of futuristic high-tech experiences.
Space Mountain is a roller-coaster ride into outer space inspired by Jules
Verne's novel *From the Earth to the Moon* and **Star Tours** offers a trip into space
with George Lucas's *Star Wars* characters. To get there, you walk past hard-
working robots complaining about the trials of life. Once at the ride itself, the
five minutes spent in the air force-designed flight simulator are riveting as the
spaceship crashes through meteors and engages in a laser battle with the enemy.

Next door's **CinéMagique** lets you sample Michael Jackson's feet in your
face, with a 3-D motion picture of Captain Eo and his merry band of dancers.
For a voyage through time in 10 minutes join the robotic timekeeper at the
Visionarium, where a 360° screen provides a panoramic view of Europe, from
the Swiss Alps to Gérard Depardieu's nose. The view of Paris 200 years from
now is the most interesting and disturbing feature of the show.

Beyond the rides – where to stay

The wider resort – **Disney Village** and the hotels (*see page 270*) – make up a celebration of "Americana", a direct response to Disney's vision of how Europeans
view America. Continuing the cinematic motif of the theme park, the six hotels
are Hollywoodesque in design. **Hotel Cheyenne** is the most imaginative – a

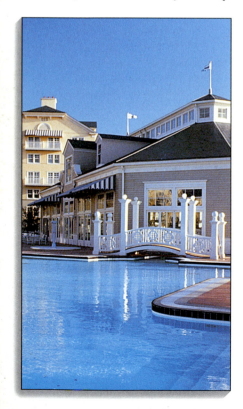

film-set Western town, complete with saloon, sheriff's
jail and wooden-planked stores. At the other "moder-
ately-priced" hotel, **Santa Fe**, Clint Eastwood grimaces
down from a mock drive-in movie screen above reception. Designed by Antoine Predock, the hotel is a series
of blocks recalling Mexican villages. Water runs in irri-
gation channels through desert landscapes, past a 1956
Cadillac buried in the sand.

The more expensive hotels, **Sequoia Lodge** and
Newport Bay Club, overlook Lake Disney. One recalls
Hitchcock's *North by North-West* in its pine surrounds,
and the other is a New England mansion straight from F.
Scott Fitzgerald's novel, *The Great Gatsby*. Across the
lake, **Hotel New York** offers luxury rooms in a Man-
hattan-style skyscape designed by Michael Graves.
Attached is the New York Coliseum Conference Centre, with capacity for 2,000 delegates.

But the jewel of the resort's hotels is, naturally, the
four-star **Disneyland Hotel** sprawling across the main
entrance. Its Victorian style whispers turn-of-the-century elegance and it is here that Michael Jackson comes
to stay when he jets in to enjoy the park after hours.

Five kilometres (3 miles) from the theme park (you
will need your own car) in natural forest is **Davy
Crockett Ranch**, with 97 camping places for tents and
caravans and 498 fully-equipped cabins in rustic logged
style. Set in a "pioneer" village, it provides sports facilities and bicycle hire.

TRIPS OUT OF TOWN

Visit Josephine's Malmaison or the royal Château de Fontainebleau, go cycling in an ancient forest or see the real waterlily pond that Monet painted – all within easy reach of Paris

Map, page 250

To visit many of the interesting places beyond the city limits, it is just a simple train ride, or you can hire a car (*see page 267*) to venture off the beaten track where your meanderings may lead to quaint old *auberges* serving hearty evening meals by the fire or lunch on a terrace overlooking a river. If time is limited, then a trip to Versailles is an obvious choice, but you could take a day or two to visit a town such as Rouen or Chartres further away, stopping at sights along the way. All of the noble forests of the Ile de France and surrounding regions are worth going to and are generously dotted with châteaux and monuments. SNCF trains are generally efficient and, on arrival at your destination, you will find the needs of visitors well catered for, with maps and information on tourist sights, hotels, restaurants and taxis. Some places can be reached by the speedy RER train (*see page 266*). In Compiègne and Fontainebleau, tour buses will take you into town or the countryside.

PRECEDING PAGES: solemnity in the Gothic Chartres cathedral; Monet's lily pond at Giverny. **LEFT:** formal Versailles in bloom. **BELOW:** home with the daily bread.

The shortest hops

Versailles ❶ (open daily; closed Mon and pub. hols; entrance fee; tel: 01 30 84 76 18), 23 km (14 miles) southwest of Paris, can be reached via RER line C5 which will drop you a short distance from the Sun King's magnificent château and gardens (*see pages 254–55*). You will have to pick and choose what to see as you will need much more than a day to take in everything. In the formal gardens on every Sunday from May to October, the fountains dance to music at 3.30pm.

Just half a day will suffice for a visit to **Sèvres** ❷ (Métro Pont de Sèvres), southwest of Paris. Situated on the left bank of the Seine, the suburb has been famous for its porcelain for more than 200 years and the ceramics workshops, set in a sloping, wooded park include the **Musée Nationale de la Céramique** (open daily; closed Tues; entrance fee; tel: 01 41 14 04 20).

Further westwards, en route to **St-Germain-en-Laye** ❸, is the **Château de Malmaison** (open daily; closed 12.30pm–1.30pm and Tues; entrance fee; tel: 01 41 29 05 55) in Rueil-Malmaison (RER line A to La Défense-Grande Arche then bus 258) which was the favourite home of Napoleon Bonaparte's first wife, Josephine, and where she lived after their divorce. Napoleon used to come here to wind down between battles. Now, along with the neighbouring Château de Bois-Préau, it is an important museum of the First Empire with rooms kitted out as they were originally. The rose garden has also been nurtured in keeping with Josephine's day.

The wealthy bourgeois Paris suburb of St-Germain-en-Laye, just five kilometres (3 miles) away (at the end of RER line 1), has perched above Paris since the 12th century and was once a royal retreat. The **château** (open

During the Revolution, the tombs in St-Denis (above) were vandalised and the royal bodies thrown into a pit. Fortunately, they were secretly rescued and finally returned to their original resting places in restored tombs by Louis XVIII in 1816.

daily; closed Tues; entrance fee; tel: 01 34 51 53 65), which still has a lovely Gothic chapel, was reconstructed under François I (his royal salamander and "F" can be seen in the courtyard) and again in the 19th century. Inside, you won't find any period furnishings or portraits, but rather a museum devoted to prehistoric and medieval times. The Gallo-Roman collection and the life-sized replica of the Lascaux cave drawings are favourite exhibits. The terrace gardens overlooking the Seine were designed by André Le Nôtre (*see page 122*) and later gave inspiration to the Impressionist painter Alfred Sisley (1839–99).

North of Paris, less than 4 km (3 miles) away, stands the basilica of **St-Denis** ❹ (Métro St-Denis – Basilique), the final resting place of France's kings and queens. Revered as an early masterpiece of Gothic architecture, the basilica (open daily; closed Sun morning; entrance fee; tel: 01 48 09 83 54) was mainly built by the charismatic Abbot Suger, close friend of Louis VII, in the 12th century on the site of an abbey church. According to legend, this is the spot reached by St Denis, first Bishop of Lutetia, when he walked out of Paris carrying his head, after having been beheaded in Montmartre (*see page 171*). Monarchs from as far back as Dagobert I (628–37) are buried here and the medieval and Renaissance sculptures, marking their tombs, are some of the finest in France.

North to Chantilly and Compiègne

Famous for horse racing, **Chantilly** ❺ – about 50 km (30 miles) away from Paris (SNCF from Gare du Nord) – offers a sumptuous palace, a magnificent park created by Le Nôtre and the splendid, 18th-century, palatial Grandes Ecuries, stables built by Prince Louis-Henri de Bourbon, who believed that he would be reincarnated as a horse. The château, nestling in a forest grove, is a real fairytale

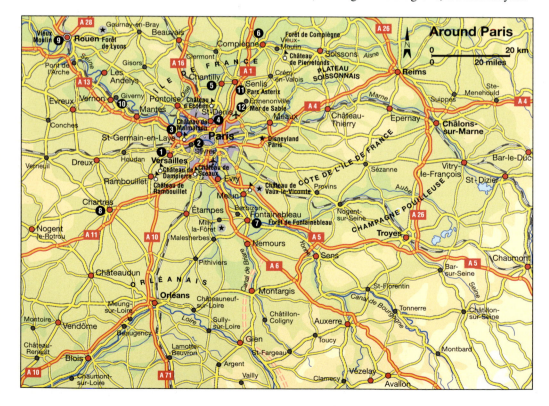

castle – white walls are topped by a blue-slate roof, and wild ducks bustle around its moat. Inside is the **Musée Condé** (open daily; closed Tues; entrance fee; tel: 03 44 62 62 62) with a comprehensive collection of works by Botticelli, Raphael, Giotto and Holbein.

You don't have to be a horse racing enthusiast to enjoy the **Musée Vivant du Cheval** (open daily, Wed – Mon afternoons; closed Tues; entrance fee; tel: 03 44 57 40 40) under the impressive dome of the Grandes Ecuries, with 30 horses of varying breeds on show and 31 exhibition rooms – these stables could once house 240 horses and 500 dogs. Riding displays are held on the first Sunday of each month. The Chantilly racecourse is the most fashionable in France and high society gathers here during June for the prestigious flat-racing trophies.

The town of **Compiègne** ❻ – 30 km (20 miles) northeast of Chantilly and 65 km (40 miles) northeast of Paris (SNCF from Gare du Nord) – sits between the Oise River and one of the largest forests in France. The town's Hôtel de Ville has the oldest bell in the country hanging in its clock tower and *picantins* (little figures) strike every hour. The **Château de Compiègne** (open daily; closed Tues; entrance fee; tel: 03 44 38 47 00) was once the favourite residence of Napoleon III and the Empress Eugénie and contains three museums including one for cars.

If you enjoy walking, make your way on foot to **Les Beaux Monts**, just outside the town, for a spectacular view of the château and the Oise. From here, a round walk, lasting between one and two hours, has been marked out, guiding you through the beautiful Forêt de Compiègne, an ancient royal hunting forest full of old oaks and beech trees. By car or SNCF bus from Compiègne station, you can visit the **Musée Wagon de l'Armistice** (open daily; closed Tues; entrance fee) in the Clairière de l'Armistice (Armistice Clearing), where the signing of the 1918 Armistice between France and Germany took place and where Hitler humiliated the French by making them surrender on 22 June 1940.

On the eastern edge of the forest is Napoleon III's unusual hunting palace, the **Château de Pierrefonds** (open daily; closed 11.45am – 2pm and Tues; entrance fee; tel: 03 44 42 72 72). Entirely reconstructed in the 19th century, in medieval military style by Viollet-le-Duc, with drawbridge, moat and towers, it is a remarkable architectural oddity, as inside the fanciful architect allowed his Romantic imagination a free rein.

Southeast to Fontainebleau

En route to **Fontainebleau** ❼, 40 km (25 miles) from Paris, is the luxurious 17th-century **Château de Vaux-le-Vicomte** (SNCF from Gare de Lyon to Melun; Feb – mid-Nov: open daily; entrance fee; tel: 01 64 14 41 90). Built by Louis XIV's powerful royal treasurer, Nicolas Fouquet, a devoted patron of the arts, the impeccable house along with a beautiful garden *à la française*, the first created by Le Nôtre, was his undoing. Jealous advisers whispered to the King that Fouquet had paid for it with treasury funds. After a grand housewarming party for the young monarch, Fouquet was imprisoned at Vincennes and the upstaged Louis set out to build something even more splendid – Versailles – using the very same architect and designers. The château, grounds and furnishings provide an intriguing visit. One room

Map, page 250

TIP

The SNCF runs a bike rental service (Train + Vélo) at many of its stations – when you buy your train ticket you can reserve a bike which will be waiting at your destination. This is the best way to visit Monet's house in Giverny or to explore the Forêt de Lyons. Or there is Train + Auto (*see page 267*).

BELOW: a royal stag in Fontainebleau.

*Forgotten by industry, spared by wars, the medieval, walled town of **Provins** (SNCF Gare de l'Est), 75 km (45 miles) east of Paris, seems to be under a spell. Once a Roman outpost perched above the Voulzie River, it grew to become the powerful seat of the medieval counts of Champagne and the third largest city in France. Every June, the town holds a crimson rose and medieval festival.*

BELOW: the apse in Chartres cathedral.

traces the history of its various owners, others are decorated in sumptuous period style, with coffered, painted ceilings and Gobelins tapestries, and the kitchen equipment is fascinating. The candlelit tour on Saturday evenings (May–mid-Oct) gives an added atmospheric dimension.

Melun sits on the edge of the **Forêt de Fontainebleau**, once a royal hunting ground and now, due to some giant rock formations, the haunt of cyclists, mushroom hunters, bird watchers, picnickers and rock climbers. The town of Fontainebleau (SNCF from Gare de Lyon) lies just 15 km (9 miles) away and is dominated by the first purpose-built royal **château** (open daily; closed 12.30pm–2pm and Tues; entrance fee; tel: 01 60 71 50 70), residence of French sovereigns from François I to Napoleon III. Each one has added something to the palace, creating a mixture of styles, but Napoleon I outdid them all by building an ornate throne room – his *grands appartements* are definitely worth seeing.

If you are driving, **Barbizon**, 7 km (4 miles) away on the eastern edge of the forest, is a village which has attracted landscape painters since the 1840s, when Théodore Rousseau (1812–67) and Jean-François Millet (1814–75) fled to the woods to escape the Industrial Revolution and rediscover nature. Rousseau's workshop is now a museum to the Ecole de Barbizon (open daily; closed Tues and 12.30pm – 2pm weekdays; entrance fee; tel: 01 60 66 22 38).

Southwest to medieval Chartres

A trip to **Chartres** ❽ – 89 km (55 miles) from Paris – in the Loire Valley can be taken slowly, stopping off at the **Châteaux de Dampierre** and **Rambouillet** (*see below*) on the way, or you can go straight there by train (SNCF from Gare Montparnasse). The two spires of the magnificent Gothic **cathedral** (open daily;

CHÂTEAUX AROUND PARIS

Ile de France is an area rich in châteaux, many built in the wake of the Sun King's extravagant palace at Versailles. The **Château de Sceaux** (tel: 01 46 61 06 71), 7 km (4 miles) south of Paris, was built in 1670 for Fouquet's successor, Colbert, with a beautiful park and gardens designed by Le Nôtre. Rebuilt in Louis XIII style in 1856, the château contains the Musée de l'île de France. More Le Nôtre gardens can be found at the **Château de Dampierre** (tel: 01 30 52 53 24), 35 km (22 miles) southwest of Paris, which has a touch of Versailles. The president's summer residence, **Château de Rambouillet** (tel: 01 34 83 00 25), 15 km (9 miles) further on, was once a feudal castle and is open when the president is away. In the **Château d'Ecouen** (01 34 38 38 50), 19 km (11 miles) north of Paris, is the Musée National de la Renaissance, with the finest tapestries in France and early mathematical instruments on display.

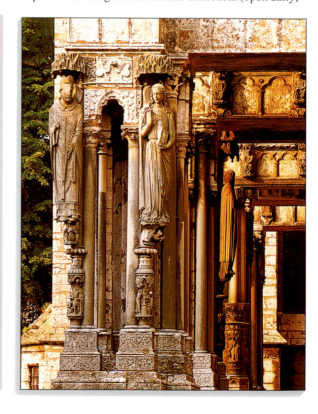

free) soar above the surrounding fields. Originally Romanesque, the cathedral dedicated to the Virgin Mary (Notre Dame) was destroyed by fire in 1194 but everyone from peasant to lord immediately contributed to the rebuilding, either with labour or finances. The famous rose windows fill the cathedral with changing colours along with 170 more of the finest original stained-glass windows. Behind the cathedral is the **Musée des Beaux-Arts** (open daily; closed Tues and some pub. hols; entrance fee; tel: 02 37 36 41 39) offering Renaissance paintings and fine tapestries. At the recently excavated Gallo-Roman city ruins nearby, a **Maison de l'Archaeologie** (14 Rue St-Pierre; Jul – Oct: open afternoons; Oct – May: open Wed and Sun only) has been opened, designed by the British architect Richard Rogers.

Part of a French urban conservation scheme, the town provides an authentic glimpse of life "in the provinces". Along the banks of the Eure, a path passes typical countryside *lavoirs* (wash houses) and steep staircases and quaint, cobbled streets take you past the medieval Benedictine abbey church of **St-Pierre** to the remains of the old city wall.

Westwards to Monet's Giverny

For a longer break from Paris, head for the industrial city of **Rouen** ❾ (SNCF from Gare St-Lazare) on the Seine – about 110 km (70 miles) along the N13 from Paris. This road passes through Saint-Germain-en-Laye (*see page 249*) and close to Giverny, home of the Impressionist painter Claude Monet (*see page 123*). Once the capital of Normandy and despite the damage it suffered during World War II, Rouen has a wealth of picturesque houses and narrow streets mostly centred around the impressive Gothic cathedral, much loved by Monet. Joan of Arc was burned at the stake here by a tribunal of clerics in cahoots with the English. They accused her of being a witch and a heretic, although her real "crimes" were courage and patriotism.

Giverny ❿ (SNCF from Gare St-Lazare to Vernon 6 km/3 miles away) is set on a hillside above the Seine and Monet lived and worked in the small village house for 43 years until his death, in 1926, at the age of 86. Now known as the **Fondation Claude Monet** (Apr – Oct: open daily; closed Mon; entrance fee; tel: 02 32 51 28 21), the house is a museum decorated in the colours that the painter loved. The gardens that the father of Impressionism designed and drew inspiration from are a living work of art – at their colourful best during May, June and July – with the Japanese bridge and the famous waterlilies on the pond. Only copies of his works are on display but, nearby, the modern **Musée d'Art Américain** (Apr–Oct: open daily; closed Mon; entrance fee; tel: 02 32 51 94 65) celebrates the original work of half a dozen American Impressionists, who worked in France during Monet's time, and provides a tea room.

Visitors who want to escape the tourist track should head for the **Forêt de Lyons** (SNCF from Rouen or Gare St-Lazare to Pont de l'Arche). The centennial beech trees, thin and tall, make a walk or cycle ride in this forest a particular pleasure, with fine views over Normandy-style villages full of half-timbered houses set off by potted geraniums in the windows.

Map, page 250

*Europe's most gut-wrenching roller-coaster ride can be experienced in **Parc Asterix** ⓫ (Apr–Aug: open daily, Sept–mid-Oct: open Wed and weekends; entrance fee) 45 km (28 miles) north of Paris. At Ermenonville, the **Mer de Sable** ⓬ theme park offers acres of sand and Wild West fun (mid-Apr–mid-Oct: open daily; entrance fee).*

BELOW: medieval streets in Rouen.

THE SPLENDOURS OF VERSAILLES

Paris was not always the capital of France. For a while the country was run from the sumptuous palace at Versailles to the southwest of the city

The Château of Versailles is the ultimate expression of the French monarchy's power and ostentation prior to the Revolution. Built in 1624 as Louis XIII's hunting lodge, the building and surrounding land were developed by Louis XIV, who employed the celebrated trio of definite articles – Le Vau, Le Nôtre and Le Brun – and the architect Mansart. Versailles became the capital of France and, by 1774, after alterations by Louis XV and XVI, the palace had 2,143 windows, 67 staircases and was home to 10,000 courtiers and servants. The gardens were designed by Le Nôtre on the same grand scale as the château itself, and adorned with statues and fountains. Their main theme was Louis's emblem of the Sun – he is pictured above dressed as the Sun for a ballet.

THE SOCIAL WORLD OF THE SUN KING

The name Versailles evokes not just a building but also the world of Louis XIV's court and the repetitive rituals which kept it turning around the king. Most famous were his *lever* and *coucher*, a ceremonial rising and going to bed. These normally private routines were performed in public and charged with symbolic meaning. Those present were deemed especially honoured; indeed, every act of the king was designed to establish differences of rank among his courtiers, and to distribute favours and evidence of his displeasure.

▽ **SATURN, OR THE FOUNTAIN OF WINTER**
Designed by Le Brun, this sculpture represents an old man (Saturn) surrounded by playful cupids.

▷ **MARBLE COURTYARD**
This courtyard is enclosed on three sides by the wings of Louis XIII's château. It is overlooked by Louis XIV's bedchamber, a first-floor room located at the exact centre of the palace. Steps leading up to the courtyard prevented anyone in a horse and carriage aproaching the royal apartments.

△ **FOUNTAINS**
Bronze statues, some representing the great rivers of France, surround the two large ornamental ponds in the *parterres d'eau* on the main terrace.

▽ **ROYAL CHAPEL**
A Baroque masterpiece, the magnificent two-storey chapel is adorned with carved white marble, gilding and murals. The royal family worshipped from the gallery.

PAVILIONS FOR THE MISTRESSES

▽ MARIE-ANTOINETTE

The daughter of the Empress of Austria married the future Louis XVI in the opera house at Versailles in 1770 when she was 14. She wanted to be surrounded by the latest fashions and was responsible for much redecoration. Her frivolity (she was nicknamed "Mme Déficit") contributed to the monarchy's downfall.

In 1668, Louis XIV built a pavilion where he could retire with his mistress, Madame de Montespan, and escape the demands of the court. Le Vau designed the charming Trianon de Porcelaine, which was decorated with Delft tiles throughout. It was soon outgrown by Louis and his entourage, and in 1688 it was replaced by the Marble Trianon (Grand Trianon), which had a beautiful white facade decorated with pink marble and balustrades.

Louis XV and XVI took little interest in the residence and during the Revolution furnishings were sold, but the building survived. Napoleon restored and refurnished it, and Louis-Philippe often stayed there with his family. Today, we see it in its 19th-century incarnation.

The Petit Trianon was built almost 100 years later by Jacques-Anges Gabriel for Louis XV and his mistress, Madame de Pompadour. However, this Classical Revival building is best known as the favourite residence of Marie-Antoinette, who transformed the gardens from a French to an English design. She also built the Hameau, a collection of rustic-style houses and the setting for her pretence of living the simple life.

It was in these gardens that, on 5 October 1789, the Queen heard that the mob was marching on Versailles. The days of Versailles as a royal palace were over.

△ QUEEN'S BEDCHAMBER

Nineteen royal offspring were born in this sumptuous room; the births took place in full public view, so that the legitimacy of the children could not be disputed.

▷ HALL OF MIRRORS

Le Brun decorated the ceiling of this stunning hall in 1686 with a gigantic painting, which depicts the glory of the reign of Louis XIV.

INSIGHT GUIDES

Travel Tips

Insight Guides portray destinations in depth, providing the complete picture and the top photography

Insight Pocket Guides focus on the best choices for places to see and things to do and include large fold-out maps

Insight Compact Guides' portability makes them the perfect books to carry with you for on-the-spot reference

Three types of guide for all types of travel

INSIGHT GUIDES Different people need different kinds of information. Some want *background information* to help them prepare for the trip. Others seek *personal recommendations* from someone who knows the destination well. And others look for *compactly presented data* for on-the-spot reference. With three carefully designed series, Insight Guides offer readers the perfect choice. Insight Guides will turn your visit into an experience.

The world's largest collection of visual travel guides

CONTENTS

Getting Acquainted

The Place

Situation 48°50N, 2°20W, on the same latitude as Mongolia, northern Newfoundland and the city of Montreal.

Population 2 million in the city of Paris, 11 million in the whole region of Ile de France.

Area 100sq km (40sq miles).

Language Everyone in France speaks French, but regional languages still exist in Brittany (Breton), Alsace (Alsatian), the western Pyrénées (Basque) and the eastern Pyrénées (Catalan).

Time zone France is one hour ahead of Greenwich Mean Time (GMT) and six hours ahead of Eastern Seaboard Time. Most French people use the 24-hour clock, so 1pm is 1300hrs on timetables and referred to as *treize heures*.

Currency French franc (FF). 8–10FF=£1 and 5–7FF=$1.

Electricity Generally 220/230 volts, but still 110 in a few areas, so pack the appropriate transformer or adapter. Round-pin plugs are used in France.

Weights & Measures Metric for all weights and measures, although old-fashioned terms such as *livre* (about 1lb or 500g) are still used by shopkeepers. For quick and easy conversion: 2.5cm is about 1in, 1metre is about a yard, 100g is just over 4oz and 1kg is just over 2lb. A kilometre is five-eighths of a mile, so 80km is 50 miles and 80kph is 50mph.

Direct Dialling 00 (international code) + 33 (France) + 1 (Paris) + an eight-figure number.

Climate

The French climate is varied and seasonal. France is the only European country that is both north European and Mediterranean, and it has an Atlantic coastline. In the north the climate is similar to that of southern England, while in the south summer temperatures can frequently rise to over 30°C (86°F). Springtime is often suggested as the best time to see Paris, and indeed the temperature then is ideal for sightseeing, but be prepared for showers. In the autumn, mornings can be quite sharp, but by midday the skies are usually clear and bright.

The Economy

France has the fourth largest economy in the OECD (Organisation for Economic Cooperation & Development) and is one of the most visited countries in the world. The Ile de France, which contains Paris, holds about a fifth of the French population and contributes 30 percent of France's gross domestic product. The Paris Stock Exchange is the fifth most active in the world.

Paris is France's largest consumer market and the focal point of all communications systems. Most of its industry is in the suburbs. Planning restraints downtown (the only building in the central zone over nine floors is the Tour Montparnasse), coupled with increasing demand for high-quality office space, led to the huge La Défense building project to the west of Paris.

Government

France became a Republic in 1792, after the abolition of the monarchy, and constitutional change created the Second, Third and Fourth Republics. The

Public Holidays

Banks and post offices close on the following dates:
- **1 January** *Jour de l'An*
- **Easter Monday** *Pâques*
- **1 May** *Fête du Travail*
- **8 May** *Victoire 1945*
- **Ascension Day** *Ascension*
- **Pentecost** *Pentecôte*
- **14 July** *Fête Nationale* (Bastille Day)
- **15 August** *Assomption*
- **1 November** *Toussaint*
- **11 November** *Armistice 1918*
- **25 December** *Noël*

For Parisians these days off are an opportunity to get out of the city. Banks and most shops close, but the Métro, cinemas, *tabacs* (tobacconists) and some restaurants and museums stay open.

Details of public holidays are normally posted outside banks and post offices a few days beforehand. A holiday that falls on Thursday or Tuesday is liable to cause a *pont* (bridge), where the day before or after is also taken as leave from work to make a long weekend.

Many small shops and restaurants close throughout August, when thousands of Parisians leave the city. If you can bear the heat, this is an excellent time to visit the capital as it is much quieter and calmer.

current Fifth Republic was created when General Charles de Gaulle became Prime Minister in 1958. The President holds a powerful office, is elected for a term of seven years and appoints the Prime Minister as head of government. Parliament has two houses: the National Assembly and the Senate. The most important political parties are the Partie Communiste Français (PCF) and the Partie Socialiste (PS) on the left, and the Rassemblement pour la République (RPR) and the Union pour la Démocratie Française (UDF) on the right. The Verts (Green Party) is gaining popularity and won several seats in the last election.

Since 1977 Paris has had an elected mayor, based in the Hôtel de Ville. The mayor is seconded by the members of the Conseil Municipal and the elected mayors of the 20 *arrondissements*. Each *arrondissement* has a town hall (*mairie*) and registers births, deaths and various legal documents; performs marriages (the civil ceremony is required by law and the religious ceremony optional); and hears complaints.

The suburban *départements* surrounding Paris each have a *préfecture* responsible for much of the local administration. Every French *département* has a number, which is convenient for administrative purposes: for example, the number forms the first two digits of the postcode in any address (Paris is 75) and the last two digits on vehicle licence plates.

The *départements* are numbered alphabetically as follows in the Paris region: Hauts-de-Seine 92, Seine-Saint-Denis 93 and Val-de-Marne 94.

Business Hours

Office workers normally start early (8.30am is not uncommon) and often stay at their desks until 6pm or later. This is partly to make up for the long lunch hours (two hours from noon or 12.30pm) that are traditional in shops and public offices. Many companies are changing to shorter lunchbreaks as employees appreciate the advantages of getting home earlier in the evening. Most banks in Paris open from Monday to Friday from about 9am to 4–5pm.

Planning the Trip

Clothing

Parisians are style-conscious and won't brave even the corner shop without displaying a fair amount of *élan*. To the Parisians, style is a way of life; it is innate and as natural as breathing. But don't worry – visitors may slob. Parisians are used to bizarrely dressed tourists and they won't turn a hair, but don't expect to catch a waiter's or shop assistant's eye quickly if you are wearing standard tourist garb. For more upmarket restaurants, you should dress up.

Bring warm clothes in winter and expect rain in spring and autumn. Comfortable walking shoes are essential.

Visas and Passports

All visitors to France require a valid passport. No visa is required by visitors from European Union (EU) member states, the US, Canada or Japan. Nationals of other countries need a visa. If in doubt, check with the French Consulate in your home country as the situation may change. To stay for more than 90 consecutive days everyone (including EU nationals) needs a *carte de séjour* from their French Consulate.

Money Matters

The French franc (FF) is divided into 100 centimes (c). Coins come in 5c, 10c, 20c and 50c and 1FF, 2FF, 5FF, 10FF and

20FF denominations. Notes come in 20FF, 50FF, 100FF, 200FF and 500FF denominations.

Credit cards Some credit cards are accepted, especially Visa, known as Carte Bleue or CB. Large shops and restaurants will take American Express (Amex), Diner's Club (DC) or Access/Mastercard, but check before buying.

Eurocheques can be cashed at any bank and are widely accepted by hotels and larger stores and supermarkets.

Bureaux de change Most banks have an exchange counter, or *change*, usually open Monday to Friday from 9am to 4.30pm. A few smaller branches close for lunch. You can draw cash from bank dispensing machines using a credit card or European bank cashpoint card, with your PIN number. Before leaving, check with your bank that your card is valid abroad.

Airport Orly Sud Exchange, on the departure level at gate H, is open seven days a week until 11pm. Airport Roissy Exchange, at terminals 2A, 2B and 2D, is also open seven days a week until 11pm.

The bureaux de change at train stations vary their hours according to high or low season but generally they are open five days a week from 7am to 7pm. Le Change de Paris at 2 Rue de L'Amiral de Coligny, 75001, is open every day from 10am to 7pm. Take your passport to cash traveller's cheques.

Tourist Information

For brochures on Paris contact the French Government Tourist Office in London, tel: 0891 244123 (calls cost 50p per minute). Operators can also answer most queries, from shop opening hours to details of where to stay and current shows.

Airports

The two international airports that serve Paris are:
- **Roissy/Charles de Gaulle** 23 km (15 miles) north of the city, tel: 01 48 62 12 12 and
- **Orly** 14 km (9 miles) south of Paris, tel: 01 49 75 15 15.

Health

If you are an EU national and you fall ill in France, you are entitled to emergency medical treatment from doctors, dentists and hospitals. You may have to pay part of the cost of this treatment, so you must fill in a form E111 and take this with you to claim a refund and keep it for any subsequent trips you take within the EC. The leaflet *Health Advice for Travellers* (from post offices or free on 0800 555777) outlines the reciprocal health arrangement the UK has with France and encloses a form E111.

As this reciprocal arrangement does not cover all medical expenses, such as the cost of bringing a sick person back to the UK, the Department of Health advises travellers to have holiday insurance as well as taking a form E111 with them. If you plan to drive in France, you should also check that your motor insurance covers you for accidents abroad.

In North America, contact the International Association for Medical Assistance to Travellers (IAMAT), 40 Regal Road, Guelph, Ontario N1K 1B5, Canada, tel: 519 836 0102. This is a non-profit-making organisation that offers members fixed rates for medical treatment from participating physicians. Members receive a passport-sized medical record completed by their doctor and a directory of English-speaking IAMAT doctors who are on call 24 hours a day. Membership is free, although a donation is requested.

Getting There

By Air

Most major airlines fly regularly to Paris. Air France is the main agent for flights to France from America and within Europe (tel: 0181-742 6600). It also handles bookings for smaller operators such as Air Vendée and Brit Air. For British travellers, the smaller operators offer select flights from British cities to provincial French airports.

Travellers from America and other countries can fly direct to Paris and larger cities such as Nice and Lyon on Air France and most US airlines. For long-haul passengers, a charter flight to London then onward to Paris may be cheaper. In Paris, Nouvelles Frontières and Forum offer competitive fares on scheduled and charter flights.

Students and young people can get discount charter flights through specialist travel agencies. In the UK, try Campus Travel, 52 Grosvenor Gardens, London SW1W 0AG, tel: 0171-730 3402. In the US, try USIT, New York Student Centre, 895 Amsterdam Avenue, New York, NY 10025, tel: 212 663 5435.

By Rail

Paris has six railway stations with lines radiating across France and Europe. Each connects with at least two Métro or RER lines and has left-luggage facilities (*consigne*) and coin-operated lockers (*consigne automatique*).

SNCF's much-publicised *Train à Grande Vitesse* (TGV) offers a rapid and comfortable service from Paris to Bordeaux, Brest, La Rochelle, Lille/Calais, Lyon and Marseille. It is not particularly cheap, so it pays to travel off-peak. Booking eight to 30 days in advance could get you a reduction of up to 55 percent on the Joker tariff. Information and reservations are available from Rail Europe, tel: 0990 300003.

Before boarding an SNCF train you must have your ticket date stamped or *composté*. Failure to do so is an offence and makes your ticket invalid. Simply insert it in the bright orange *compositeur* machine at the platform entrance.

Customs Regulations for EU Nationals

There are no official restrictions on the movement of goods within the European Union, provided the goods were purchased within the EU. It is no longer necessary for EU nationals to exit Customs through a red or green channel. **Duty-paid goods** If you buy goods in France for which you pay tax, there are no restrictions on the amounts you can take home. EU law has set "guidance levels", however, on the following:
- **Tobacco** 800 cigarettes, or 400 cigarillos, or 200 cigars or 1kg of tobacco.
- **Spirits** 10 litres
- **Fortified wine/wine** 90 litres
- **Beer** 110 litres

If you exceed these amounts you must be able to prove the goods are for personal use. **Duty-free goods** If you buy goods duty-free the following restrictions still apply:
- **Tobacco** 200 cigarettes, or 100 cigarillos, or 50 cigars, or 250g of tobacco.
- **Alcohol** 1 litre of spirits or liqueurs over 22 percent volume, or 2 litres of fortified, sparkling wine or other liqueurs.
- **Perfume** 60cc of perfume, plus 250cc of toilet water.

There are no restrictions on the amount of currency you can take into France.

Travelling with Children

In France, children are generally treated as people, not just nuisances, so you can take them into restaurants, even in the evening, without heads turning. French children, however, eat out from an early age and are well behaved in restaurants, so standards of conduct are high.

Many restaurants offer a children's menu. If not, they may split a *prix-fixe* menu between two children. With very young children, just request an extra plate and give them food from your own. French meals are generous so you won't go hungry yourself and *le patron* (or *la patronne*) won't mind. Alternatively, order a simple dish from the *à la carte* menu, such as an omelette or soup. With the bread that comes automatically to a French table, and ice-cream or fruit to follow, a small child is sure to be more than satisfied.

Weekly magazines like *l'Officiel des Spectacles* and *Pariscope* give details of plays, films, puppet shows and circuses and list babysitting services. Better hotels will arrange babysitters.

Most hotels have family rooms, so children are not separated from parents. A cot (*lit bébé*) can often be provided for a small supplement, but check if booking in advance.

● **Home Service** (babysitting service), tel: 01 42 82 05 04.
● **Marionettes du Luxembourg** tel: 01 43 26 46 47 or 01 43 29 50 97 for a recorded message (in French) about current children's shows.

Channel Tunnel The 50km (31-mile) Channel Tunnel enables fast, frequent rail services between London (Waterloo) or Ashford and Paris (Gare du Nord). Le Shuttle takes cars and passengers from Folkestone to Calais on a drive-on, drive-off service taking 35 minutes. Payment is at toll booths which accept cash, cheques or credit cards. You can book in advance or simply turn up and take the next available service. Le Shuttle runs 24 hours a day, all year, at least once an hour. For details, tel: 0990 353535 (UK) or 03 21 00 60 00 (France).

By Sea

Ferries from the UK, Ireland and the Channel Islands to the northern ports of France have reduced their prices since the Channel Tunnel opened. All carry cars and foot passengers. Hovercraft are faster but need better weather. The Seacat catamaran is the quickest service but, like the hovercraft, carries a limited number of cars. Boulogne, Calais and Le Havre have motorway links to Paris.

Hoverspeed, tel: 01304 240241, runs hovercraft and Seacat services from Dover to Calais or Boulogne.

P&O North Sea Ferries, tel: 01482 795141, runs from Hull to Zeebrugge, Belgium.

P&O European Ferries, tel: 0990 980980, sails from Dover to Calais and Portsmouth to Le Havre and Cherbourg.

Holyman Sally Line, tel: 01843 595522, sails from Ramsgate to Ostend.

Stena Line, tel: 01233 647047, runs from Dover to Calais.

Irish Ferries, tel: 003531 6610511, runs services from Rosslaire and Cork to Le Havre and Cherbourg.

By Bus

Eurolines is a consortium of almost 30 European coach companies. Its services run from London (Victoria) to Paris daily and are one of the cheapest ways to get there. Discounts are available for young people and senior citizens. The ticket includes the ferry crossing (via Dover) and National Express coaches from most major UK cities connect with the London departures.

Eurolines UK, 23 Crawley Road, Luton LU1 1PP, tel: 01582 404511; or Gare Routière Internationale, 2 Avenue Charles de Gaulle, 93541 Bagnolet Cedex, tel: 01 49 72 51 51.

Student Travel

Students and people under the age of 26 can get cut-price travel to Paris (see *Getting There*). For a prolonged stay, it may be worth finding out about an exchange visit or study holiday. These organisations provide information or arrange visits:

UK services The Central Bureau for Educational Visits & Exchanges, The British Council, 10 Spring Gardens, London SW1A 2BN (tel: 0171-389 4004), produces two books: *Working Holidays* (about all work, from conservation to fruit picking) and *Home from Home* (on staying with a French family).

Those who can speak French could approach a UK-based camping holiday operators. Many, such as Eurocamp Travel, Canute Court, Toft Road, Knutsford WA16 0NL (tel: 01565 625522), employ

Taking an Animal

● No animal under three months old can be taken into France.
● Pets must have a rabies vaccination certificate or a certificate showing your country has been rabies-free for three years.
● All animals coming into the UK from France will be kept in quarantine for six months.

students as site attendants in France during the summer.

US services American Council for International Studies Inc, 19 Bay State Road, Boston, Massachusetts 02215, tel: 617 236 2051.

The Council on International Educational Exchange (CIEE), 205 E. 42nd Street, New York, NY 10017, tel: 212 822 2600. Offers a wide range of services, including travel.

Youth for Understanding, 3501 Newark Street NW, Washington DC 20016, tel: 202 966 6800.

Study in France Several French tour operators can organise study tours and language courses (*also see page 280*). The Union National des Organisations de Séjours Linguistiques, 8 Rue César Franck, 75015, tel: 01 47 83 31 65, is a national association that quality-checks the 18 members of the organisation offering language courses. Write for a list of schools, or try the following:

Résidence OTU Bastille, 151 Avenue Ledru Rollin, 75011 (tel: 01 43 79 53 86). Offers French study programmes, inexpensive accommodation and tours for individuals or groups.

Centre des Echanges Internationeaux, 104 Rue de Vaugirard, 75006 (fax: 01 45 49 01 70). A non-profit-making group offering sporting and cultural holidays and educational tours for 15–30 year-olds.

Students will find a student identity card useful for discounts, including admission to museums, galleries, cinema, theatre, etc. If you don't have your card, your passport may prove your status.

The Centre d'Information et Documentation de Jeunesse (CIDJ), 101 Quai Branly, 75015 (tel: 01 44 49 12 00, fax: 01 40 65 02 61), is a national organisation that disseminates information on youth and student activities.

Useful Books

The following guides are useful for the disabled:
● **Access in Paris** A free booklet from the French Government Tourist Office, tel: 0891 244123 (calls 50p per minute).
● **Door-to-Door** is a Department of Transport guide to all types of travel abroad for the disabled, from Stationery Office Bookshops or mail order, tel: 0171-831 1326, fax: 0171-873 8200.
● **Michelin Red Guides** Both *France* and *Camping-Caravanning* note hotels that welcome disabled people.

Disabled Travellers

Less-able travellers should book accommodation in advance. Most official lists of hotels use a symbol to denote wheelchair access, but it is always advisable to check with the hotel what facilities are available.

Budget rooms Hotels in the budget Balladins chain have at least one room for disabled guests and all public areas are accessible. Contact Hotels Balladins, 20 Rue du Pont des Halles, 94656 Rungis Cedex (tel: 01 49 78 01 45, fax: 01 46 86 50 18).

Wheelchair users There is a French-language guide, *Où Ferons Nous Etape?*, that lists accommodation throughout France suitable for wheelchair users. If you have specific needs, double check when booking. It is available for FF40 from the Association des Paralysés de France, Service Information, 17 Boulevard August Blanqui, 75013 (tel: 01 40 78 69 00). This organisation may also answer specific enquiries and can provide addresses of its branches.

RADAR The Royal Association for Disability and Rehabilitation (RADAR), 250 City Road, London EC1V 8AF (tel: 0171-250 3222 or Minicom: 0171-250 4119), publishes a guide book, *Holidays and Travel Abroad*, which provides information about hotel chains and tour operators.

French organisations France's sister organisation to RADAR, the Comité National Français de Liaison pour la Réadaption des Handicapés (CNFLRH), 263 bis Rue Tolbiac (tel: 01 53 80 66 66), offers a good information service.

The Centre d'Information et de Documentation Jeunesse (CIDJ), 101 Quai Branly, 75740, Cedex 15, has information on services for young less-able travellers. It publishes *Vacances pour Personnes Handicapées* and annual leaflets on activity and sports holidays for young disabled people.

Parents may wish to contact the Union Nationale des Associations de Parents d'Enfants Inadaptés (UNAPEI), 15 Rue Coysevox, 75018, tel: 01 44 85 50 50.

The Comité de Liaison pour le Transport des Personnes Handicapées, Conseil National des Transports, 34 Avenue Marceau, 75009, publishes the booklet *Guide des Transport à l'Usage des Personnes à Mobilité Réduite*. This gives brief information on the accessibility and arrangements for less-able passengers on public transport and contacts for special transport schemes in France.

Some concessionary ferry fares are available for members of the following organisations:
The Disabled Drivers' Association tel: 01508 489449
Disabled Drivers' Motor Club tel: 01832 734724
Disabled Motorists' Federation tel: 01743 761181.

Practical Tips

Security

If you take sensible precautions with your personal possessions, you should be perfectly safe in Paris. At worst, tourists may be faced with pickpockets, especially in the Métro. But this can easily be avoided by carrying your money safely. Obvious centres of prostitution (such as Les Halles and parts of the Bois de Boulogne) are best avoided late at night.

Loss

If your personal documents, cash, belongings or traveller's cheques are lost or stolen, go to the Commissariat de Police nearest the scene of the crime as soon as possible – even before contacting the traveller's cheque service or your embassy or consulate.

If you lose your passport, report it to your consulate as soon as possible (a full list is in both *Pages Blanches* and *Pages Jaunes* phone books under *Ambassades et Consulats*).

If your credit card goes missing, numbers to ring are: American Express: 01 42 77 11 90. Diners Club: 01 49 06 17 25. Visa or Carte Bleue: 01 42 77 11 90. Access/Mastercard-Eurocard: 01 45 67 53 53.

To reclaim anything else you have lost, you could go (with ID) to the Service des Objets Trouvés, 36 Rue des Morillons, 75732 Cedex 15 (Métro Convention). It is open every weekday from 8.30am to 5pm, and Tuesday and Thursday until 8pm. You need to visit the office in person, as no information is given over the telephone.

Medical Services

In all emergencies **SOS Help** operates (tel: 01 47 23 80 80) an English helpline from 3pm to 11pm daily .

A doctor will pay a house call in an emergency if you dial **SOS Médecins** (tel: 01 47 07 77 77 or 01 43 37 77 77) and explain your situation in French. This is a 24-hour service.

You can reach English-speaking health services at the **American Hospital** (tel: 01 46 41 25 25) or the **British Hospital** (tel: 01 46 39 22 22). But neither of these hospitals has a casualty department.

The **SAMU** 24-hour ambulance service can be contacted by dialling 15. Otherwise, the *pompiers* (or fire brigade, who are trained paramedics) are extremely professional in any type of emergency (dial 18).

For urgent dental treatment contact **SOS Dentaire** (tel: 01

Hospitals

All state hospitals in Paris have casualty departments. The following are some of the larger ones:
● **Boucicaut**
78 Rue Convention, 75015, tel: 01 53 78 80 00.
● **Necker** (Children's Hospital) 149 Rue de Sèvres, 75015, tel: 01 44 49 40 00.
● **Bichat**
46 Rue Henri Huchard, 75018, tel: 01 40 25 80 80.
● **Hôtel-Dieu**
1 Place du Parvis-Notre-Dame, 75004, tel: 01 42 34 82 34.
● **Saint-Louis**
1 Avenue Claude Vellefaux, 75004, tel: 01 42 49 49 49.

43 37 51 00), which operates a 24-hour emergency service.

If you need to see a doctor, expect to pay at least FF100 per consultation, with prescription charges on top. The doctor will provide a statement of treatment (*feuille des soins*). With this EU citizens can reclaim around 75 percent of the cost. Check that the price stamp (*vignette*) from any prescribed medicine has been attached to the *feuille des soins* by the chemist so you can reclaim that cost too. When complete, the *feuille des soins* should be sent to the local *caisse primaire* (the doctor or chemist will have the address) for your refund, which will be sent on to your home.

If you have any difficulties, contact the **Service des Relations Internationales**, 173-5 Rue de Bercy, 75586 Cedex 12, tel: 01 43 46 12 53.
Pharmacies
Most pharmacies display flashing green neon crosses and are open from 9am to noon and 2–7pm. At night, they all post the address of the nearest pharmacy that is open in their window or doorway.

Pharmacie Dhéry, 84 Avenue des Champs-Elysées (Métro Georges V), tel: 01 45 62 02 41, is open all hours.

Religious Services

France is predominantly Roman Catholic and the many churches in Paris, including Notre Dame, are open to the public and display the hours of Mass.

For a list of all denominational churches, temples and synagogues, buy the small book *Plan de Paris par Arrondissement* from a kiosk or bookshop or the International Centre for Religious Information, 8 Rue de la Villa L'Eveque, 75008, tel: 01 49 24 11 44.

There are services in English around the capital, notably in the American church on Quai d'Orsay.

Media

Newspapers

The main national dailies are *Le Monde*, which has a rather dry and leftish slant on politics and economic news, and the more conservative *Le Figaro*, each of which sells about 400,000 copies. The paper representing the Communist Party is *L'Humanité* and not veering quite so heavily left is Jean-Paul Sartre's brainchild, *Libération*. The major weekly news publications are *Le Point* (right) and *L'Express* (left), which both also sell about 300,000–500,000 copies. British, American and other European dailies are available at city centre kiosks and shops displaying the sign *journaux* or *presse*.

The *International Herald Tribune*, published in Paris, has listings for the city. To find out what is going on in the capital try *L'Officiel des Spectacles* or *Pariscope* (both out on Wednesday), which give complete listings of museums, galleries, concerts, ballet, opera, theatre, cinema and nightlife in general.

Radio

France Inter (87.8 MHz) is the main national radio station, and it offers a bit of everything. Radio Classique (101.1 MHz) gives the listener uninterrupted lightweight classical music. If you're looking for something a bit more demanding, try France Musique (91.7 and 92.1 MHz). RTL (104.3 MHz) is the most popular station throughout France with the current charts, chat shows and so on.

Television

TF1, Antenne 2, FR3, M6 and Arte are the five television stations on offer. Most larger hotels receive cable as well. CNN is sometimes available.

Postal Services

The French post office is run by the PTT (Poste et Télécommunications). The main branches are open from 8am to 7pm on weekdays and 8am to noon on Saturday. The central post office at 52 Rue du Louvre, 75001, tel: 01 40 28 20 00, operates a 24-hour, seven-day service for international telegrams and telephone. Unless you arrive first thing in the morning or between 2.30pm and 3.30pm be prepared for a long wait in post offices.

To send a telegram in French, telephone 36 55. For telegrams in any other language, telephone 05 33 44 11.

Stamps are often available at *tabacs* (tobacconists) and other shops selling postcards or greetings cards. For postcards and letters weighing up to 20g, postage for within France and to most of the European Union costs FF3. Sending a letter airmail to Ireland, the US and Canada costs FF4.40, and airmail for Australia is FF5.20.

Telephones, telex, Minitel, fax and photocopying facilities are available in larger post offices and at the Centre Télégraphique Paris Bourse, 7 Rue Feydeau, 75001, tel: 01 42 47 12 12, open Monday to Saturday from 9am to 4.30pm.

Tipping

- **Restaurants** Most restaurant bills include a service charge. If in doubt ask, "*Le service, est-il compris*?" Even when this charge is included, it is common to leave a small additional tip for the waiter if the service has been very good. Remember to address waiters as *Monsieur* (never *Garçon*) and waitresses as *Mademoiselle* if they are young or *Madame* if older.
- **Taxis** A 2–5FF tip is regarded as polite.

Telecommunications

The French telephone system has recently been overhauled so that all telephone numbers have 10 digits. Paris and Ile de France

Useful Addresses and Numbers

- **Air France** 119 Champs Elysées, 75384, Paris Cedex 08, tel: 01 42 99 21 99. For reservations, tel: 01 44 08 22 22.
- **Automobile Club** 8 Place de la Concorde, 75008, tel: 01 43 12 43 12, fax: 01 47 20 88 98.
- **Customs Information** tel: 01 49 28 54 55
- **Information Service** General details about Paris in English, tel: 0836 68 41 14.
- **Paris Tourist Office** 127 Avenue des Champs Elysées, 75001, tel: 01 49 52 53 54, fax: 01 49 52 53 00. Open 9am–8pm daily except 1 January, 1 May and 25 December. Information, brochures, guidebooks and maps, plus hotel and train reservation services, theatre and concert ticket sales and a *bureau de change*. There are also subsidiary tourist offices at the Gare du Nord, Gare deLyon and Eiffel Tower railway stations, which are open from May to September.
- **RATP information** For Métro and bus details, tel: 08 36 68 77 14.
- **SNCF information** For information and reservations, tel: 08 36 35 35 35.
- **Traffic information** In English, mainly about *autoroutes*, tel: 01 47 05 90 01.

numbers begin with 01, while the rest of France is divided into four zones (North West 02, North East 03, South East and Corsica 04 and South West 05). Freephone numbers begin with 08 00; 08 36 numbers are charged at premium rates and 06 numbers are mobile phones.

There are two kinds of phone boxes in Paris from which you can make local and international calls: coin-operated phones, which are extremely difficult to find, and card-operated phones, which are replacing them. It may be difficult to find a telephone box that is working. Remember that you get 50 percent more call-time for your money if you ring 10.30pm–8am on weekdays and from 2pm at weekends.

Operator Services

- **Directory enquiries** 12
- **Operator** 12
- **Reverse charges**
You cannot reverse telephone charges within France but you can to other countries that accept such calls. Go through the operator and ask to make a PCV call.

A *télécarte* can be bought from kiosks, *tabacs* and post offices. Insert the card and follow the instructions on the screen: *Décrochez* (pick up the receiver); *Introduire votre carte* (insert your card); *Patientez* (wait); *Numérotez* (dial); *Raccrochez* (hang up).

You can also dial from all post offices, which have both coin- and card-operated phones. To call long distance ask at one of the counters and you will be assigned a booth – you pay when your call is over. Cafés and *tabacs* often have public phones next to the toilets. They use coins or *jetons*, coin-like discs bought at the bar.

To call other countries from France, first dial the

international access code (00), then the country code: Australia 61, UK 44, US and Canada 1. If using a US credit phone card, call the company's access number: Sprint, tel: 19 00 87; AT&T, tel: 19 00 11; MCI, tel: 19 00 19.

Doing Business

Business travel accounts for about a third of French tourism revenue. This important market has led to the creation of a special Conference and Incentive Department at the French Government Tourist Offices in London and New York. They deal with business travel enquiries, and will also help organise hotels, conference centres and incentive deals for groups of any size.

Conferences and exhibitions
Paris is a world leader for conferences, exhibitions and trade fairs. The building development at La Défense is the largest business district in Europe. For further information, call Info-Défense, tel: 01 47 74 84 24.

For a list of exhibitions and details about exhibiting, contact Promo Salons, The Colonnade, 82 Bishops Bridge Road, London W2 6BB, tel: 0171-221 3660, fax: 0171-792 3525.

Many *châteaux* offer luxurious accommodation for smaller gatherings, and you can even organise a congress at Disneyland Paris.

Organising a conference
For anyone wishing to put on a major business event in Paris, the first line of contact is the Bureau des Congrès de Paris, 5 Avenue de l'Opéra, 75001, tel: 01 47 03 16 16.

There are also several tour operators who specialise in conference organisation:
Convergences, 120 Avenue Gambetta, 75020, tel: 01 40 32 47 00, fax: 01 40 31 01 65.
SOCFI, 14 Rue Mandar,

75002, tel: 01 42 33 89 94, fax: 01 40 26 04 44.
Connexions Voyages Hamelin, 126 Avenue Georges Clémenceau, BP 805, 92008 Nanterre Cedex, tel: 01 46 69 64 64, fax: 01 46 69 64 53.
Wagonlit Travel Production, 50 Rue de Londres, 75008, tel: 01 44 90 33 10, fax: 01 44 90 33 15.

Chambers of Commerce
Another good source of business information about local companies, assistance with technicalities of export and import, interpretation and translation agencies and conference centres is the Chambres de Commerce et d'Industrie, 45 Avenue d'Iéna, 75016, tel: 01 40 69 37 00, fax: 01 47 20 61 28.

Most countries' Chambers of Commerce have conference facilities of some kind. There are French Chambers of Commerce in key cities around the world promoting business with France. In London, the Chambers are at 5th floor, Knightsbridge House, 197 Knightsbridge, London SW7 1RB, tel: 0171-304 4040, fax: 0171-304 7034.

Embassies

- **Australia**
4 Rue Jean Rey, 75015; tel: 01 40 59 33 00
- **Canada**
35 Avenue Montaigne, 75008; tel: 01 44 43 29 00
- **Ireland**
4 Rue Rude, 75016; tel: 01 44 17 67 00
- **New Zealand**
7 Rue Léonard de Vinci, 75016; tel: 01 45 00 24 11
- **United Kingdom**
35 Rue du Faubourg St Honoré, 75008; tel: 01 42 66 91 42
- **United States**
2 Rue St-Florentin, 75001; tel: 01 43 12 22 22.

Getting Around

From the Airports

From Roissy/Charles de Gaulle
Train The quickest and most reliable way to get to central Paris, RER trains go direct from terminal 2 (Air France flights), or you can take the free shuttle bus (*navette*) from terminal 1. Trains run every 15 minutes from 5am to 11.45pm to Métro Gare du Nord or Châtelet.
The average journey time is 45 minutes.
Bus The Roissy bus runs between the airport and Rue Scribe, near Place de l'Opéra from terminals 1 gate 30, 2A gate 10 and 2D gate 12. It runs every 15 minutes from 6am to 11pm and takes 45 minutes.

Alternatively, the Air France bus (to Métro Porte de Maillot or Charles-de-Gaulle Etoile) leaves from terminals 2A and 2B or terminal 1 arrival level gate 34. It runs every 12 minutes from 5.40am to 11pm.
Taxi This is by far the most expensive but unquestionably the easiest solution. It can take 30 minutes to over an hour, depending on traffic. The cost appears on the meter, but a supplement is charged for each large piece of luggage, pushchair and animal.

From Orly

Train Take the shuttle from gate H at Orly Sud or arrivals gate F at Orly Ouest to the Orly train station. The RER stops at Austerlitz, Pont St-Michel and the Quai d'Orsay. It runs every 15 minutes 5.50am–10.50pm

and takes about 30 minutes to Austerlitz.

The Orlybus (to Place Denfert-Rochereau) leaves from Orly Sud gate F or Orly Ouest arrivals gate D. It runs every 10–12 minutes from 6am to 11.30pm.

The Orlyval automatic train is a shuttle to Antony (the nearest RER to Orly). It runs every 5–8 minutes from 6.30am to 9.15pm Monday to Saturday and 7am–10.55pm on Sunday, and takes 30 minutes.

Air France buses (to Invalides and Gare Montparnasse) leave from Orly Sud, gate J or Orly Ouest arrivals gate E. They run every 20 minutes from 6am to 11pm and take 30 minutes. Tickets are available from the Air France terminus.
Taxi Takes 20–40 minutes.

Between Airports

An Air France bus links Roissy/Charles de Gaulle and Orly every 20 minutes from 6am to 11pm.

Public Transport

Métro and RER
Run by the Régie Autonome des Transports Parisiens (RATP), the Paris Métro is one of the world's oldest subway systems, and some of its stations are almost historic monuments. Despite that, it is quick and efficient.

The Métro operates from 5.30am, with the last train leaving end stations at 12.45am. Its comprehensive map (free at any Métro station) and signposting make it virtually impossible to get lost. The lines are identified by number and the names of their terminals, so Line 4 running north is shown as Porte de Clignancourt, while going south it is Porte d'Orléans. Follow orange *correspondance* signs to change lines.

The Métro runs in conjunction with the RER (suburban regional express trains), which operates four main lines, identified as A,

B, C and D. RER trains run daily every 12 minutes from 5.30am to midnight.

The Métro and the bus system use the same tickets (FF8 for a single fare). A book or *carnet* of 10 from bus or Métro stations and some *tabacs* (tobacconists) offers a considerable saving at just FF46.

Another option is the *Paris Visite* card, valid for three or five consecutive days on the Métro, bus and railway in the Paris/Ile de France region. The card entitles you to a discount at several tourist sites and can be bought from main Métro, RER and SNCF stations. It is only available to tourists. Fares start at FF105 for three zones over three days.

For shorter stays, buy the *Mobilis* card, which allows an unlimited number of trips for a day on the Métro, bus, suburban SNCF, RER and the night buses, extending as far as Disneyland Paris. It can be bought in all Métro stations. Fares range from FF30 for 1-2 zones up to FF70 for 1-5 zones.

A *Carte Orange* allows unlimited travel on the number of zones of your choice on any public transport system for a month. A *Carte Jaune* gives you unlimited travel from Monday to Monday. To buy either of these you need to take along a passport photograph to any Métro or SNCF station. Sign your card and copy its number on to your ticket – you will be fined by ticket inspectors if you fail to do this. For further information, contact RATP (see *Useful Addresses and Numbers*).

Buses

Taking the bus is a pleasant way to see the city but can be much slower than the Métro because of traffic. Tickets can be bought from the driver or from Métro stations as buses accept the same tickets as the Métro. Remember to punch your ticket, and not your travel card, in the *compositeur*.

Buses don't automatically stop, so when you want to get off push one of the request buttons (and the *arrêt demandé*, or stop requested, sign will light up). Each bus has a map of its route posted at the front and back and at every stop. Most buses run from 6.30am to 8.30pm, although some routes continue until 12.15am.

A night service leaves Place de Châtelet (Avenue Victoria or Rue St-Martin) at 1.30, 2.30, 3.30, 4.30 and 5.30am on 10 routes. Travel passes are valid on the bus and stops are marked by a special black and yellow owl logo.

Look out for the Balabus service at certain stops. It visits the main tourist sites every Sunday and on public holidays between 11 April and 26 September from 12.30 to 8pm. The tour lasts about 50 minutes.

Private Transport

Driving in Paris requires equal measures of insanity and desperation and acceptance of other drivers' madness.

Seat belts are obligatory in the front and back and the speed limit in town is 50kph (30mph). Do not drive in bus lanes at any time and give priority to vehicles approaching from the right. This applies to some roundabouts, where cars on the roundabout stop for those coming on to it. If in doubt, be cautious. Helmets are compulsory for motorbike riders and passengers.

Street parking is generally metered and the maximum stay is two hours. Car parks are mainly underground.

Petrol can be difficult to find in the city centre, so if you're almost empty you should head for a *porte* (exit) on the Périphérique (the multi-lane ring road). They have petrol stations

that are open 24 hours a day all year round.

Drivers are liable to heavy on-the-spot fines for speeding and drunk driving. The drink limit in France is 50mg/litre of alcohol in the blood (equivalent to about two glasses of wine) and is strictly enforced.

Car Hire

Hiring a car is expensive, partly because it incurs the highest rate of TVA tax at 33 percent. Some fly/drive packages are good value if you are on a short visit. SNCF offers a good deal on its combined train/car hire bookings (train + auto). Weekly rates often work out better than a daily rate, and it may be cheaper to hire from the UK or the US before leaving. The minimum age to hire a car is 23, or 21 if paying by credit card. The hirer must have held a full licence for at least a year.

The central reservation offices of the major car hire firms are:

Avis, tel: 01 49 06 68 68, fax: 01 47 78 98 98.

Budget/Milleville, tel: 01 46 86 65 65, fax: 01 46 86 22 17.

Europcar/National/InterRent, tel: 01 40 15 96 98, fax: 01 40 15 96 31.

Hertz, tel: 01 39 38 38 38.

Bicycles

If you know Paris well and have nerves of steel, a bicycle is an excellent way to explore the quieter areas. You can rent a bicycle from:

Paris-Vélo, 2 Rue du Fer à Moulin, 75005, tel: 01 43 37 59 22, fax: 01 47 07 67 45.

Paris à Vélo C'est Sympa, 37 Boulevard Bourdon, tel: 01 48 87 60 01.

Hitchhiking

With sensible precautions, hitchhiking can be an interesting and inexpensive way to get around France. Would-be

Taxis

Taxis are readily available at the airports and railway stations. In the city itself there are almost 500 taxi ranks, but be careful to hail only a genuine taxi (with a light on the roof). Other operators may charge exorbitant fares. The white light will be on if a cab is free, while a glowing orange light means that the taxi is engaged.

Taxi drivers in Paris operate on three rates:
● **Tariff A** 7am-7pm Monday to Saturday
● **Tariff B** 7pm-7am Monday to Saturday and all day Sunday
● **Tariff C** at night in the suburbs and during the day in the outlying districts of Hauts-de-Seine, Seine St-Denis and Val-de-Marne, when the taxi has no client for the return journey.

The following taxi companies take phone bookings 24 hours a day:
Alpha 01 45 85 85 85
Artaxi 01 42 41 50 50
G7 01 47 39 47 39
Taxis Bleus 01 49 36 10 10.

If you have a complaint about Paris taxis, it should be addressed to:
Services des Taxis, Préfecture de Police, 36 Rue des Morillons, 75015, tel: 01 55 76 20 00.

hitchhikers may be discouraged by the difficulty of getting a lift out of the channel ports, so take a bus or train for the first leg of your journey. Hitching is forbidden on the *autoroutes* (motorways), but you can wait on slip roads or at toll booths.

Allostop is a nationwide organisation that aims to connect hitchhikers with drivers. You simply pay a registration fee and a contribution towards the petrol. For more information, tel: 01 42 46 00 66.

Where to Stay

Paris is renowned for the diversity of its hotels, from the small, simple family-run hotel to the luxurious palace.

It is advisable to reserve accommodation in advance, either with the hotel or via the Paris Tourist Office (see *Useful Addresses and Numbers*) or one of its subsidiary offices, which will book your first night's accommodation if you apply in person. The tourist offices supply a free booklet listing all hotels (pensions and similar establishments) in Paris and neighbouring suburbs that have been awarded a classification by the Direction de l'Industrie Touristique.

The following organisations also offer reservation services:

Paris Séjour Réservations, tel: 01 53 89 10 50, fax: 01 53 89 10 59.

Prestotel, tel: 01 45 26 22 55, fax: 01 45 26 05 14.

Hotels

BUDGET

Albouy
4 Rue Lucien Sampaix, 75010, tel: 01 42 08 20 09, fax: 01 42 08 76 60. Well equipped but not central; close to Canal St-Martin; 34 rooms. Credit cards: Visa, Amex and Diners Club. **

Allies
20 Rue Berthollet, 75005, tel: 01 43 31 47 52, fax: 01 45 35 13 92. Few rooms have a bath/shower; 42 rooms. Credit cards: Visa. *

Andrea
3 Rue St-Bon, 75003, tel: 01 42 78 43 93, fax: 01 44 61 28 36.

Just off the Rue de Rivoli; 26 rooms. Credit cards: Visa. **

Castex
5 Rue Castex, 75004, tel: 01 42 72 31 52, fax: 01 42 72 57 91. Small well-run family hotel close to Bastille; book well in advance; 26 rooms. Credit cards: Visa. **

Des Argonautes
12 Rue de la Huchette, 75005, tel: 01 43 54 09 82, fax: 01 44 07 18 84. In a bustling part of town by the famous Théâtre de la Huchette; 25 rooms. Credit cards: Visa, Amex and DC. **

Marignan
13 Rue du Sommerard, 75005, tel: 01 43 25 31 03. Located in the Quartier Latin; 30 rooms. No credit cards. *

Pacific
77 Rue du Ruisseau, 75018, tel: 01 42 62 53 00, fax: 01 46 06 09 82. Couple of streets from the Périphérique; 44 rooms. Credit cards: Visa. *

Palais Bourbon
49 Rue Bourgogne 75007, tel: 01 47 05 29 26, fax: 01 45 55 20 21. Modern hotel in smart quiet area; book ahead for cheaper rooms; 33 rooms. Credit cards: Visa. **

Régence
3 Rue Laferrière, 75009, tel/fax: 01 48 78 29 96. Small comfortable hotel; will accept dogs; 18 rooms. Credit cards: Visa. **

Rouen
42 Rue Croix-des-Petits-Champs, 75001, tel/fax: 01 42 61 38 21. Small; excellent location by the Louvre; 22 rooms. Credit cards: Visa. *

Royal Montmartre
68 Boulevard de Clichy, 75018, tel: 01 42 64 15 26, fax: 01 46 06 35 03. All rooms have WC; dogs accepted; 48 rooms. Credit cards: Visa and Amex. **

Tiquetonne
6 Rue Tiquetonne, 75002, tel: 01 42 36 94 58. In an old part of Paris close to Les Halles; 47 rooms. Closed in August. No credit cards. *

INEXPENSIVE

Alexandre Montparnasse
71 Boulevard de Vaugirard, 75015, tel: 01 43 20 89 12, fax: 01 43 22 77 71. Handy for antique shops in the area; 31 rooms. Credit cards: Visa and Amex. **

Glasgow
3 Rue de la Félicité, 75017, tel: 01 42 27 93 95, fax: 01 40 53 92 52. Good facilities for the disabled; private parking; 38 rooms. Credit cards: Visa, Amex and DC. ***

Price Guide

Most of the hotels listed in this section are classified by the Direction de L'Industrie Touristique, whose price categories are as follows:
- **Budget** 200–300FF
- **Inexpensive** 300–500FF
- **Moderate** 500–1,000FF
- **Expensive** 1,000–2,000FF
- **Deluxe** 2,000+FF

Prices are per double room.

Grand Hotel de Lima
46 Boulevard St-Germain, 75005, tel: 01 46 34 02 12, fax: 01 43 25 47 73. At the quieter end of St-Germain; 39 rooms. Credit cards: Visa and Amex. **

Place des Vosges
12 rue Birague, 75004, tel: 01 42 72 60 46, fax: 01 42 72 02 64. Small but comfortable; 16 rooms. Credit cards: Visa, Amex and DC. **

Regyn's Montmartre
18 Place des Abbesses, 75018, tel: 01 42 54 45 21, fax: 01 42 23 76 69. Simple and quiet; 22 rooms. Credit cards: Visa. **

Saint-Thomas-d'Aquin
3 Rue Pré-aux-Clercs, 75007, tel: 01 42 61 01 22, fax: 01 42 61 41 43. Close to the Eiffel Tower and the Musée D'Orsay; 21 rooms. Credit cards: Visa, Amex and DC. **

Timhôtel
A chain with several Paris branches; all fairly modern. Central reservations, tel: 01 44 15 81 15, fax: 01 40 26 35 61. Credit cards: Visa, Amex and DC. **

Victoria Chatelet
17 Avenue Victoria, 75001, tel: 01 40 26 90 17. Small; bustling part of town; 24 rooms. Credit cards: Visa, Amex, DC. ***

Vivienne
40 Rue Vivienne, 75002, tel: 01 42 33 13 26, fax: 01 40 41 98 19. Close to the Bourse; 44 rooms. Credit cards: Visa. **

MODERATE

Angleterre
44 Rue Jacob, 75006, tel: 01 42 60 34 72, fax: 01 42 60 16 93. In a smart corner of the Left Bank; very comfortable; 29 rooms. Credit cards: Visa, Amex and DC. ***

Aramis
124 Rue de Rennes, 75006, tel: 01 45 48 03 75, fax: 01 45 44 99 29. Attractive rooms and well equipped bathrooms; 42 rooms. Credit cards: Visa, Amex, DC. ***

Banville
166 Boulevard Berthier, 75017, tel: 01 42 67 70 16, fax: 01 44 40 42 77. Marble bathrooms; 40 rooms. Credit cards: Visa and Amex. ***

Bac Saint-Germain
66 Rue du Bac, 75007,

tel: 01 42 22 20 03, fax: 01 45 48 52 30. Pleasant hotel; glassed-in terrace on 7th floor; 21 rooms. Credit cards: Visa, Amex and DC. ***

Berne
37 Rue de Berne, 75008, tel: 01 43 87 08 92, fax: 01 43 87 08 93. Comfortable; in quiet street; welcoming to young families; 136 rooms. Credit cards: Visa, Amex and DC. ***

Bradford
10 Rue St-Philippe-du-Roule, 75008, tel: 01 45 63 20 20, fax: 01 45 63 20 07. Large, light rooms by the Champs-Elysées; 48 rooms. Credit cards: Amex, DC, MC and Visa. ***

Brittanique
20 Avenue Victoria, 75001, tel: 01 42 33 74 59, fax: 01 42 33 82 65. Comfortable; central location; 40 rooms. Credit cards: Visa, Amex and DC. ***

Buci Latin
34 Rue de Buci, 75006, tel: 01 43 29 07 20, fax: 01 43 29 67 44. In the style of Philippe Starck; very fashionable area of St-Germain; 27 rooms. Credit cards: Visa, Amex and DC. ***

Deux-Iles
59 Rue St-Louis-en-l'Ile, 75004, tel: 01 43 26 13 35, fax: 01 43 29 60 25. Charming hotel in the heart of the Ile-St-Louis; 17 rooms. Credit cards: Visa. ***

Hôtel Lenox
9 Rue de l'Université, 75007, tel: 01 42 96 10 95, fax: 01 42 61 52 63. Trendy hotel

frequented by dress designers and artists; oil paintings in the lobby; spotless rooms. Credit cards: Amex, DC, MC and Visa. ***

Hôtel Place des Vosges
12 Rue de Birague, 75004, tel: 01 42 72 60, fax: 01 42 72 02 64. A former stables beautifully renovated; 16 rooms. Credit cards: DC, MC and Visa. ***

Timotel Invalides
35 Boulevard de Latour-Maubourg, 75007, tel: 01 45 56 10 78, fax: 401 7 05 65 08. Modern; well equipped; free sauna; 30 rooms. Credit cards: Visa, Amex and DC. ***

Louisiane
60 Rue de Seine, 75006, tel: 01 43 29 59 30, fax: 01 46 34 23 87. Overlooks the bustling Buci market in St-Germain; 80 rooms. Credit cards: Visa and DC. **

Saint-Germain
50 rue du Four, 75006, tel: 45 48 91 64, fax: 45 48 46 22. Excellent location on the Left Bank; 30 comfortable rooms. Credit cards: Visa, Amex, DC. **

Saint-Louis-Marals
1 Rue Charles V, 75004, tel: 01 48 87 87 04, fax: 01 48 87 33 26. Comfortable but small; 16 rooms. Credit cards: Visa. **

EXPENSIVE

Ambassador
16 Boulevard Haussmann, 75009, tel: 01 42 46 92 63, fax: 01 40 22 08 74. Pleasant; in the heart of the business

Hotel Star Ratings

* Hotels offer rooms with a bed, a minimum of furniture and (for at least 80 percent of the rooms) a shared bathroom. Many of these hotels are in the Marais or the Quartier Latin, and they can be pleasant if well run and kept clean. They are generally run by families, so there is often a curfew after which the front door is locked.

** Hotels have to equip 40 percent of their rooms with private bathrooms (shower or bath) and provide breakfast and telephones.

*** Eighty percent of the rooms must have private bathrooms and all rooms must have a telephone and television. Breakfast must be offered to all guests.

**** Hotels must have reception staff who speak several languages. All rooms should be equipped with private bathrooms, a telephone and a TV. Breakfast may be taken in the dining room or the bedroom and restaurant service must be available morning and evening. Four-star deluxe hotels have all conceivable amenities, top-quality service and very spacious rooms and bathrooms.

Price Guide

Most of the hotels listed in this section are classified by the Direction de L'Industrie Touristique, whose price categories are as follows:
● **Budget** FF200–300
● **Inexpensive** FF300–500
● **Moderate** FF500–1,000
● **Expensive** FF1,000–2,000
● **Deluxe** FF2,000+
Prices are per double room.

area; 298 rooms. Credit cards: Visa, Amex and DC.★★★★

Château Frontenac
54 Rue Pierre Charron, 75008, tel: 01 47 23 55 85, fax: 01 53 23 13 01. Modern, stylish and still intimate; 106 rooms. Credit cards: Visa and DC. ★★★★

Louvre
1 Place André Malraux, 75001, tel: 01 44 58 38 38, fax: 01 44 58 38 01. Comfortable and good location; 200 rooms, some over a busy junction. Credit cards: Visa, Amex and DC. ★★★★

Lutetia
45 Boulevard Raspail, 75006, tel: 01 49 54 46 46, fax: 01 49 54 46 00. Early Art Deco hotel; once frequented by writers Parker, Hemingway and Fitzgerald; 276 rooms. Credit cards: Visa, Amex and DC. ★★★★

La Montalembert
3 Rue de Montalembert, 75007, tel: 01 45 49 68 68, fax: 01 45 49 69 49. Ornate Beaux-Arts-style exterior; stylish rooms with antiques; the attic suite is Sir Terence Conran's *pied à terre*. Credit cards: Amex, DC, MC and Visa. ★★★★

Normandy
7 Rue de l'Echelle, 75001, tel: 01 42 60 30 21, fax: 01 42 60 45 81. Close to the Louvre; 138 rooms. Credit cards: Visa, Amex and DC. ★★★★

Pavillon de la Reine
28 Place des Vosges, 75003, tel: 01 42 77 96 40, fax: 01 42 77 63 06. The smartest hotel in the Marais; set in a popular

square; 55 rooms. Credit cards: Visa, Amex and DC. ★★★★

DELUXE
Bristol
112 Rue du Faubourg St-Honoré, 75008, tel: 01 42 66 91 45, fax: 01 42 66 68 68. 1920s hotel; period furniture in all 195 rooms. Lovely gardens. Credit cards: Visa, Amex and DC. ★★★★

Crillon
10 Place de la Concorde, 75008, tel: 01 44 71 15 00, fax: 01 44 71 15 02. By the Tuileries; 163 rooms. Credit cards: Visa, Amex and DC. ★★★★

George V
31 Avenue George V, 75008, tel: 01 47 23 54 00, fax: 01 47 20 40 00. Elegant; stylish. Credit cards: Visa, Amex and DC. ★★★★

Hilton International
18 Avenue de Suffren, 75015, tel: 01 44 38 56 00, fax: 01 44 38 56 10. Good quiet location on the Left Bank; view of the Eiffel Tower. Credit cards: Visa, Amex and DC. ★★★★

Meurice
228 Rue de Rivoli, 75001, tel: 01 44 58 10 10, fax: 01 44 58 10 15. Overlooks the Tuileries; 179 rooms. Credit cards: Visa, Amex and DC. ★★★★

Plaza-Athénée
25 Avenue Montaigne, 75008, tel: 01 47 23 78 33, fax: 01 47 20 20 70. More palace than hotel. Credit cards: Visa, Amex and DC. ★★★★

Ritz
15 Place Vendôme, 75001, tel: 01 42 60 38 30, fax: 01 42 60 23 71. Unashamed luxury in one of the most famous squares in the capital. Credit cards: Visa, Amex and DC. ★★★★

Royal Monceau
37 Avenue Hoche, 75008, tel: 01 42 99 88 00, fax: 01 42 99 89 90. Very central; tends to cater for business clientele. Credit cards: Visa, Amex, DC. ★★★★

Disneyland Paris Hotels
Local travel agents may offer better deals than Disney, especially for two or three-day stays. Reservations from Paris, tel: 01 60 30 60 30; from the UK, tel: 0990 0303 03. ★★★★

Disneyland Hotel
Luxury class; 500 rooms; expensive.★★★★

Hotel New York
Luxury convention-class; 574 rooms; expensive.★★★★

Newport Bay Club
First class; 1,098 rooms; moderately expensive.★★★★

Sequoia Lodge
First class; 1,011 rooms; moderately expensive.★★★★

Hotel Cheyenne
Moderate class; 1,000 rooms; moderately expensive.★★★★

Booking Hotels

Hotel prices in Paris are not subject to restrictions and can be changed without notice, so check before booking. The majority of hotels vary prices by season. State your arrival time if you book by phone or the hotelier will not keep your room after 7pm.

Hotel Santa Fe
Moderate class; 1,000 rooms, inexpensive.★★★★

Davy Crockett Campsite
3 miles from the resort; have to have own car; 181 pitches; 414 cabins for 4-6 people; inexpensive. ★★★★

Bed and Breakfast

The following organisations offer bed and breakfast and sometimes an evening meal in people's homes in and around Paris.
  France Lodge, 41 Rue Lafayette, 75009, tel: 01 53 20 02 54, fax: 01 53 20 01 25
  International Café Couette, 8 Rue d'Isly, 75008, tel: 01 42 94 92 00, fax: 01 42 94 93 12.

Holiday Flats

The following companies let apartments to tourists. These range from bedsits to five-bedroom flats.

France-Ermitage, 5 Rue Berryer, 75008, tel: 01 42 56 23 42, fax: 01 42 56 08 99.Flatotel Expo, 52 Rue d'Ouradour-sur-Glane, 75015, tel: 01 45 54 93 45, fax: 01 45 54 93 07.

ABM Rent-a-flat, 12 Rue Valentin Haüy, 75015, tel: 01 45 67 04 04, fax: 01 45 67 90 15.

At Home in Paris, 16 Rue Médéric, 75017, tel: 01 42 12 40 40, fax: 01 42 12 40 48.

Camping

The only campsite in central Paris is a four-star site at Bois de Boulogne:

Allée du Bord de l'Eau, tel: 01 45 24 30 00, fax: 01 42 24 42 95. Métro Porte Maillot, then 244 bus.

There are plenty of campsites within reach of Paris. Lists are available from The Caravan and Camping Service, 69 Westbourne Grove, London W2 4UJ, tel: 0171-792 1944 or from the Fédération Française de Camping Caravanning, 78 Rue de Rivoli, 75004, tel: 01 42 72 84 08, fax: 01 42 72 70 21.

Youth Hostels

Holders of accredited Youth Hostel Association cards may stay in French hostels for about FF60 per night. These are run by the following two organisations: Fédération Unie des Auberges de Jeunesse (FUAJ), 27 Rue Pajol, 75018, tel: 01 44 89 87 27, fax: 01 44 89 87 14, is affiliated to the International Youth Hostel Federation. Ligue Française pour les Auberges de Jeunesse (LFAJ), 38 Boulevard Raspail, 75007, tel: 01 45 48 69 84, fax: 01 45 44 57 47.

The British YHA publishes the *International Youth Hostel Handbook Vol I* (revised at the end of each year), which includes all the hostels in the Paris region. It is available by post (for £7 including p&p) from Youth Hostel Association, 8 St Stephen's Hill, St Albans AL1 2DY, tel: 01727 845047.

In the US, apply to American Youth Hostels Inc, PO Box 37613, Dept USA, Washington DC 20013/7613, tel: 202 783 6161.

The Office de Tourisme Universitaire (OTU) will also help find hostel accommodation, tel: 01 40 29 12 12, fax: 01 40 27 08 71.

Where to Eat

The restaurants below cover every level of dining in Paris. Fixed-price menus generally do not include wine: they are indicated by the word menu in this listing. A la carte estimates are for a full meal with a reasonably priced bottle of wine. For a fuller restaurant list, try the red *Michelin Guide to France*.

Tables should be reserved in most of the restaurants listed below. Those listed under the heading *The Chefs* have well-respected chefs, so make reservations up to several months in advance. Most restaurants in Paris close throughout August and some are closed both Saturday and Sunday night.

Restaurant Listings

BRASSERIES, BISTROS & WINE BARS
Allard
41 Rue St-André des Arts, 75006, tel: 01 43 26 48 23. Haute cuisine served in traditional bistro atmosphere near the Place St-Michel. Credit cards: Amex, DC, MC, Visa. **£££**
Astier
44 Rue Jean-Pierre Timbaud, 75011 , tel: 01 43 57 16 35. Closed weekends and public holidays, 24 April to 9 May and 31 July to 5 September. A modern bistro in the north of Paris. Home cooking with an inventive touch and a few classics, all for a modest price. Best reserve. Credit cards: Visa. **£** (menu only).

Au Fins Gourmets
213 Boulevard St-Germain, 75007, tel: 01 42 22 06 57. Classic French cuisine, with *cassoulet* (white bean and meat stew) a speciality. Great bistro atmosphere and a mature crowd. Good wine list. No credit cards. **££**

Au Sauvignon
80 Rue des Saints-Pères, 75007, tel: 01 45 48 49 02. Closed Sunday and public holidays, August and two weeks in February. A wine bar that does not serve hot food; Sancerre and a goat's cheese platter make an excellent lunch. Credit cards: MC and Visa. **£**

Aux Crus de Bourgogne
3 Rue Bachaumont, 75001, tel: 01 42 33 48 24. Quirky old bistro with tables spilling out on to the pedestrianised Rue Montorgueil market area in summer. Credit cards: Amex, MC and Visa. **£–££**

Benoît
20 Rue St-Martin, 75004, tel: 01 42 72 25 76. Closed weekends and August. The most expensive bistro in Paris but perhaps the best, with a chic clientele. The excellent *boeuf à la mode* (braised beef) merits every bit of applause and the wine list rivals restaurants in much more prestigious surroundings. Credit cards: Amex, MC, Visa. **££££**

Bofinger
5 Rue Bastille, 75004, tel: 01 42 72 87 82. Open daily. A classic brasserie that claims to be the oldest in the city. Excellent *fruits de mer* and one of the best Alsatian *choucroute*

(sauerkrauts) in Paris. The more creative dishes can be disappointing. Credit cards: Amex, DC and Visa. **££** (menu), **£££** (à la carte).

Brasserie de l'Isle St Louis
53 Quai de Bourbon, 75004, tel: 01 43 54 02 59. Lively Alsatian brasserie. Good prices. Closed August. Credit cards: MC and Visa. **££**

Café de la Mairie
8 Place St-Sulpice, 75006, tel: 01 43 26 67 82. Typical Left Bank eaterie undiscovered by most tourists. The decor leaves something to be desired, but a genuine piece of France, rubbing shoulders with aspiring writers. Open 7am–midnight Monday to Saturday. No credit cards. **£**

Chez Ribe
15 Avenue Suffren, 75007, tel: 01 45 66 53 79. Closed Saturday lunch and Sunday and 15–31 August. Near the Eiffel Tower and very good value. Traditional bistro fare with a sprinkling of southern dishes (fish soup, salt cod, etc). Credit cards: Visa, Amex and DC. **££** (menu only).

Chez Pierrot
18 Rue Etienne Marcel, 75002, tel: 01 45 08 05 48. A quiet, bistro near Les Halles, serving traditional French cuisine. Great selection of patés. Credit cards: Amex and Visa. **££**

L'Ange Vin
168 Rue Montmartre, 75002, tel: 01 42 36 20 20. Closed weekends and July. Dinner is served only on Tuesday and Thursday, lunch is served daily. The cooking is tasty, the cheeses superb and the wines good value. Usually filled with a noisy young crowd keeping the waitress busy. Best reserve. Credit cards: Visa. **££**

La Buddha Bar
8 Rue d'Anglas, 75008, tel: 01 53 05 90 00. Mecca for anyone who is anyone, including Isabelle Adjani and Naomi Campbell. Pacific Rim dishes overlooked by a giant buddha.

Open Monday to Friday 12.30–3pm, and 7.30pm–midnight. Balcony bar open 6pm–2am. Credit cards: Amex, MC and Visa. **£££**

La Closerie des Lilas
171 Boulevard du Montparnasse, 75006, tel: 01 40 51 34 50. The watering hole of numerous rich and famous, including Picasso and Hemingway. Classy with pianist in the evening. Open daily 11.30am–1am. Credit cards: Amex, DC, MC and Visa. **£££**

L'Ecluse
15 Place de la Madeleine, 75008, tel: 01 42 65 34 69. Open daily. The choicest of wine bars, serving Bordeaux only, L'Ecluse is a mini-chain offering famous growths by the glass and a small collection of elegant dishes: smoked salmon and green bean salad, beef in red wine, foie gras and so on. Very busy at lunch. Open until one in the morning. Other branches in Paris include: 64 Rue François 1er, 15 Quai des Grands-Augustins and 13 Rue de la Roquette. Credit cards: Visa. **££**

La Palette
43 Rue de Seine, 75006, tel:01 43 26 68 15. A favourite haunt for artists, art students and St-Germain art dealers. Closed August. Open Monday to Saturday 8am–2am. No credit cards. **£**

La Regalade
49 Avenue Jean-Moulin, 75014, tel: 01 45 45 68 58. Closed Saturday lunch, Monday and August. A much-praised newcomer to the Parisian scene. Classic bistro fare re-interpreted by a former chef of Le Crillon, one of the city's palatial hotel kitchens. Very popular, so reservations a must. Credit cards: Visa, Amex and DC. **££** (menu only).

Le Rubis
10 Rue du Marché St-Honoré, 75001, tel: 01 42 61 03 34. Closed Saturday dinner, Sunday, public holidays and two weeks in August. Wine bar/bistro. A favourite spot for a glass of Beaujolais and a slice of pâté. Several *plats du jour* are served, ranging from *boeuf bourguignon* to *petit salé aux lentilles* (lentils with salt pork). Very informal, crowded and very good. **££**

Le Temps des Cerises
31 Rue de la Cerisaie, 75004, tel: 01 42 72 08 63. Lunch only. Closed Saturday, Sunday and August. Extremely modest family restaurant in the Marais by the Bastille. Simple working man's food. Extremely good value. **£**

René
14 Boulevard St-Germain, 75005, tel: 01 43 54 30 23. Classic French bistro with elegant decor and service. Excellent wine list. The speciality is *trompette de la mort* mushrooms, when in season. Credit cards: Visa. **£££**

REGIONAL SPECIALITIES

Campagne et Provence
25 Quai de la Tournelle, 75005, tel: 01 43 54 05 17. Closed Saturday lunch and Sunday. A contemporary view of Provençal cooking. Excellent *salade niçoise* and a few specialities from the countryside beyond Provence. Reservations a must. Credit cards: Visa. **££**

L'Oulette
15 Place Lachambeaudie, 75012, tel: 01 40 02 02 12.

Closed Saturday lunch, Sunday and 1–15 August. Marcel Baudis's restaurant is difficult to class. It could have been listed with *Les Chefs* as he is equally at home with creative dishes and traditional fare. Dishes from his native Quercy in the southwest are exceptionally well done, the fixed-price menu (lunch and dinner) is particularly good value, and during the winter months the *grand menu* provides the best glimpse of Gascony cooking in the city today. Credit cards: Visa and Amex. **£** (menu), **££** (menu), **£££** (à la carte).

Moissonier
28 Rue Fossés St-Bernard, 75005, tel: 01 43 29 87 65. Closed Sunday evening, Monday, and 31 July to 7 September. A Parisian institution serving a mixture of specialities from the Jura and the Rhône. A magnificent *saladier lyonnais* (a trolley full of salads to sample) and *brési (*smoked beef) from the Franche-Comté. Credit cards: Visa. **££**

Pharamond
24 Rue de la Grande-Truanderie, 75001, tel: 01 42 33 06 72. Closed Sunday and Monday lunchtime. Once famous for dishes from Normandy, Pharamond is now noted mainly for its magnificent turn-of-the-century decor. Its most celebrated speciality, *tripes à la mode de Caen* (tripe as cooked in Caen, the most famous tripe dish in France) is worth a detour. It is served on a bed of hot coals

with a bottle of cider. Credit cards: Visa, Amex and DC. **£££**

THE CHEFS

Alain Ducasse
59 Avenue Raymond Poincaré, 75016, tel: 01 47 27 12 27. Closed weekends and July. Robouchon is the most admired chef in France. Modest and shy, he delights in juxtaposing ingredients to create unexpected and revealing taste combinations (like cauliflower and caviar) and turning humble dishes into culinary masterpieces (his mashed potatoes are as talked about as any foie gras dish). Reserve months in advance. Credit cards: Visa. **££££**

Arpège
84 Rue Varenne, 75007, tel: 01 45 51 47 33, fax: 01 47 05 09 06. Closed Sunday lunch and Saturday. Alain Passard is one of the rising stars of French cuisine. His small restaurant is generally crowded, and yet he still offers a fixed-price lunch menu that is one of the best in town. A rare chance to taste *haute cuisine* at a *bonne cuisine* price. Credit cards: Visa, Amex and DC. **£££** (menu, lunch only), **££££** (à la carte).

La Cagouille
10 Place Constantin Brancusi, 75014, tel: 01 43 22 09 01. Closed 1–10 May and 8–30 August. More a cook than a chef, Gérard Allemandou learned to love seafood on the Atlantic coast where he grew up. His restaurant could easily be transported to California, and his cooking has much in common with that of chefs in West-Coast USA. "The less you do to fish the better" is his creed. Grilled, roasted or fried, his seafood has an exquisite taste. Don't leave without trying one of the superb Cognacs culled from cellars in his native Charente. Credit cards: Visa and Amex. **££** (menu), **£££** (menu,

wine included), **££££** (à la carte).

La Timonerie
35 Quai de la Tournelle, 75005, tel: 01 43 25 44 42. Closed Sunday, Monday afternoon and 22–28 February. Chef De Givenchy is from Brittany and it shows. He loves fish but serves an extraordinary variety of meat dishes as well. Despite his rising popularity, he still offers a good-value fixed-price menu at lunch. Credit cards: Visa. **££** (menu, lunch only), **£££** (à la carte).

Le Bistro de L'Etoile
19 Rue Lauriston, 75016 (Métro Etoile), tel: 01 40 67 11 16. Closed Saturday lunch and Sunday. Not really a bistro but a fully fledged restaurant run by another of Paris's innovative chefs, Guy Savoy. Particularly good vegetables and fish. Reasonably priced wines. Credit cards: Amex. **£££**

Les Amongnes
243 Rue Faubourg St-Antoine, 75011 (Métro Faidherbe-Chaligny), tel: 01 43 72 73 05. Closed Sunday and Monday and 1–21 August. Once second to Alain Senderens (see *Lucas Carton* below), Thierry Coué is slowly making a name. His fixed-price menu is exceptionally good value. Credit cards: Visa. **££** (menu), **£££** (à la carte).

Lucas Carton
9 Place de la Madeleine, 75008 (Métro Madeleine), tel: 42 65 22 90, fax: 42 65 06 23. Closed Saturday lunch and Sunday, 31 July – 25 August and 23 December – 2 January. Alain Senderens is one of the most exciting chefs in France.

Gastronomic sparks fly amid the magnificent turn-of-the-century decor. A jolting culinary experience and a bill to match. Credit cards: Visa. **£££** (menu, lunch only), **££££** (menu) and **££££** (à la carte).

MIXED FARE
Au Pays du Sourire
32 Rue de Bièvre, 75005 (Métro Maubert-Mutualité), tel: 01 43 26 15 69. Closed Monday. Not the best known Chinese restaurant in town but on Sunday and Thursday the chef makes pork dumplings (*raviolis pékinois*) just as they are served in Beijing. An excellent and inexpensive meal. 50FF for 20

dumplings. Credit cards: Amex, MC and Visa. **£**

Chez Paul
13 Rue de Charonne, 75011, tel: 01 47 00 34 57. Neighbourhood restaurant serving traditional French cuisine at the corner of the popular Rue de Lappe. Informal atmosphere, but reservation recommended. Credit cards: Amex and Visa. **££**

Chez Henri
20 Rue des Fosses St-Bernard, 75005, tel: 01 43 54 99 37. Family-style French cooking, moderately priced, with a good wine list. Credit cards: MC and Visa. **££**

Davé
39 Rue St-Roch, 75001, tel: 01 42 61 49 48. Excellent Chinese, popular with the fashion world. Credit cards: Amex, DC,

Mastercard and Visa. **££**

Diep
22 Rue de Ponthien, 75008, tel: 01 42 56 23 96. Chinese cuisine, featuring *nem* (spring rolls). A small, quiet restaurant just off the Champs-Elysées. Credit cards: Amex, DC and Visa. **££**

Esther Street
6 Rue de Jarente, 75004 (Métro St-Paul), tel: 01 40 29 03 03. Closed Friday, Saturday lunch and August. *La nouvelle cuisine Yiddish* not far from the Jewish neighbourhood around Rue des Rosiers. The young chef prides herself on serving lightened versions of traditional Jewish fare. Delicious Gefilte Fish and a variety of starters that can be turned into a meal (chopped liver, marinated herring and so on). Credit cards: Visa. **££**

Fellini
47 Rue de L'Arbre Sec, 75001, tel: 01 42 60 90 66. Upmarket Italian restaurant, excellent wine list and service. Elegant, dedicated clientele. Credit cards: Amex, EC, MC and Visa. **£££**

Hawai
87 Avenue d'Ivry, 75013 (Métro Tolbiac), tel: 01 45 86 91 90. Closed Thursday. A Vietnamese soup kitchen on the edge of what Parisians call Chinatown. Inexpensive, authentic and popular. Credit cards: Visa. **£**

Isami
4 Quai d'Orléans, 75004, tel: 01 40 46 06 97. Popular Japanese with many Japanese diners.

Sushi is a work of art. Credit cards: MC and Visa. **£££**

Juvenile's
47 Rue de Richelieu, 75001 (Métro Palais Royal), tel: 01 42 97 46 49. Closed Sunday. Certainly one of the oddest combinations in Paris. British owners, French wines and *tapas* (tasters) of Spanish inspiration. Tim Johnston knows his wines (his selection of Rhône wines is exceptional) and the cooking can be quite good. Often crowded. Perfect post-cinema rendezvous. Credit cards: Visa. **££** (menu), **££** (à la carte).

Mansouria
11 Rue Faidherbe, 75011 (Métro Faidherbe-Chaligny), tel: 01 43 71 00 16. Closed Monday lunchtime and Sunday. Considered the best Moroccan restaurant in Paris, Mansouria serves excellent couscous and a collection of *tajines* (stews baked in a special utensil of the same name). Relaxed atmosphere. Credit cards: Visa. **££** (menu); **£££** (à la carte).

Mitsuko
8 Rue du Sabot, 75006, tel: 01 42 22 17 74. Bustling Japanese particularly popular at lunchtime. Quick and friendly service. Credit cards: Visa. **££**

Noura
21 Avenue Marceau, 75016 (Métro Alma-Marceau), tel: 01 47 20 33 33. Open daily. The finest Lebanese *mezze* in town and reasonably priced. A take-away shop run by the same owner faces the restaurant, and you can literally walk out with an entire feast in a plastic bag. Credit cards: Visa, Amex and DC. **£££** *(mezze* for four people); **££** (à la carte per person).

Attractions

Tours

By Boat
Cruises on the Seine last an hour with commentaries in several languages. In the high season, boats leave every half hour from 10am to 10pm.

Bâteaux Mouches depart Pont de l'Alma, tel: 01 42 25 96 10. **Bâteaux Parisiens** depart Quai Montebello, tel: 01 43 26 92 55. **Vedettes Paris Ile de France** depart Port de Suffren, tel: 01 47 05 71 29. **Vedettes du Pont Neuf** depart Pont Neuf, tel: 01 46 33 98 38.

There are interesting boat trips along the Canal St-Martin starting at the Port de l'Arsenal (Bastille) and continue almost to the Périphérique at the northeast of the city. Lasting three hours they are well worth the money, but take warm clothes as you spend a lot of time in shaded locks and under bridges. **Canauxrama**, 13 Quai de la Loire, 75019,tel:01 42 39 15 00. **Paris Canal**, 19/21 Quai de la Loire, 75019, tel: 01 42 40 96 97.

By Coach
Coach trips let you see Paris with minimum effort. Most companies provide a cassette commentary in several languages and will pass the major sights such as the Eiffel Tower and Notre Dame, but most do not stop along the way. **Cityrama** leaves from 4 Place des Pyramides, 75001, tel: 01 44 55 60 00. **Paris Vision** leaves from 214 Rue de Rivoli, 75001, tel: 01 42 60 31 25.

Parisbus runs double-decker buses that do stop at Trocadéro, Eiffel Tower, Louvre, Notre Dame, Musée D'Orsay, Opéra, Arc de Triomphe and the Grand Palais. You can hop off, sightsee, then catch a later bus. The trip takes 150 minutes. A commentary runs in English and French. Tel: 01 42 30 55 50.

Museums

Most state-owned museums charge a modest entrance fee. Sunday is half price, with reductions for children, senior citizens and students with a valid student card.

If you plan to visit several museums during your stay, buying a *Carte Musées* means you queue once to visit 65 museums or monuments in Paris or in the Ile de France region. A five-day ticket costs little more than three one-day tickets and can be bought from the tourist office, Métro or museum ticket office .

Most museums are open daily, though times vary on public holidays. As a general rule, national museums are closed on Tuesday and municipal museums on Monday. Major museums stay open through lunch, especially in summer, but the rest take a long lunch from noon or 12.30pm to about 2.30pm.

History Film

Paristoric screens an audiovisual history of Paris and its monuments over the past 2,000 years. Translated into 11 languages, performances are on the hour every hour 9am-9pm 1 April to 30 October and 9am-6pm 1 November-30 March. Details from Paristoric, 11 Bis Rue Scribe, 75009, tel: 01 42 66 62 06, fax 01 42 66 62 16.

Culture

Ticket Sales

The listings magazines *l'Officiel des Spectacles* and *Pariscope* appear every Wednesday with full details of cultural events and venues in the city.

The tourist office publishes a monthly listing, *Paris Selection*, and its information service is updated weekly, tel: 01 49 52 53 55 (French) or 01 49 52 53 56 (English).

Ticket agencies include:
Agence Spectaplus, Salle Pleyel, 252 Rue du Faubourg St-Honoré and 26 Avenue des Lernes, 75017 and branches.
FNAC Billeterie, at the FNAC stores, 135 Rue de Rennes, 75006, and 26 Avenue des Ternes, 75017.
Kiosque, 15 Place de la Madeleine, 75008, sells tickets on the day at half price. Open Tuesday to Friday 12.30–8pm; on Saturday from 12.30pm for matinées and from 2pm for

evening shows; on Sunday 12.30am-4pm.
CROUS (Centre Régional des Oeuvres Universitaires et Scolaires), 39 Avenue Georges-Bernanos, 75005, tel: 01 40 51 36 00. Reduced-price seats for students.

Theatre & Opera

There is a good choice of theatre, concerts, ballet and opera for all tastes. Some of the main venues are listed below:
Cité de la Musique, 223 Avenue Jean-Jaurès, 75019, tel: 01 44 84 45 00, fax: 01 44 84 45 01. Opened 1995, this complex at La Villette includes a concert hall, information service, museum and bookshop dedicated to music.
Comédie Française, 2 Rue Richelieu, 75001, tel: 01 44 58 15 15, fax: 01 44 58 15 00. Excellent classical productions.
Opéra Bastille, 2 bis Place de la Bastille, 75012, tel: 01 40 01 17 89, fax: 01 40 01 25 40. Booking tickets is time-consuming.
Opéra Garnier, 8 Rue Scribe, 75009, tel: 40 01 17 89, fax: 01 01 40 01 25 40. The 19th-century Paris opera house and home of the Paris Opera Ballet.
Théâtre du Châtelet, 1 Place du Châtelet, 75001, tel: 01 40

28 28 40, fax: 01 42 36 89 75. Opera and occasionally modern dance companies; also lunchtime concerts.
Théâtre du Vieux Colombier, 21 Rue du Vieux Colombier, 75006, tel: 01 44 39 87 00, fax: 01 44 39 87 19. Classical and modern drama from the Comédie Française troupe.

Cinema

Film programmes change every Wednesday. Films marked VO use the original soundtrack. On Wednesday, prices are 30 percent less than the rest of the week. These cinemas frequently show films in English:
Cinéma en Plein Air, Parc de la Villette, tel: 01 40 03 76 92. Sit back on a deckchair as dusk falls for open-air cinema.
Les Forums Cinemas Orient Express, Rue de l'Orient-Express, 75001, tel: 08 36 68 32 24.
Gaumont Champs-Elysées, 66 Avenue des Champs-Elysées, 75008, tel: 01 43 59 04 67.
Le Grand Rex, 1 Boulevard Poissonière, 75002, tel: 01 42 36 83 93. One screen, but it is the biggest in Paris.
La Pagode, 57 bis Rue de Babylone, 75007, tel: 01 45 55 48 48. The latest films in a Japanese setting. Good tea.

Paris Calendar

A listing of the major events in Paris is available from the tourist office (see *Useful Addresses and Numbers, page 264*). Ask for the *Saisons de Paris* brochure.

These are the main shows and festivals that run regularly every year:
● **January** Fashion shows
● **April** *Foire de Paris*
● **June** (first week) French Tennis open
● **June** Air Show
● **21 June** Paris celebrates the

longest day of the year with a huge musical festival (*Fête de la Musique*). Enjoy just about every type of music, from chamber to karaoke, in the streets. Everything is free.
● **Bastille Day** on 14 July celebrates the fall of the monarchy and the rise of the modern constitution. Celebrations begin the evening before. Only the brave and the mad take cars into Paris on 13 or 14 July. A military parade starts at

10am on the Champs-Elysées. It is splendid if you get there early and have a good vantage point.
● **September** The Autumn Festival, which runs right through to December, starts now.
● **October** is wine month as the Beaujolais Nouveau arrives. It also heralds the Montmartre Wine Harvest, Jazz Festival and Contemporary Art Fair.
● **December** Boat Show

Nightlife

Cabaret

Chez Michou
80 Rue des Martyrs, 75018, tel: 01 46 06 16 04, fax: 01 42 64 50 50. Drag shows every night.

The Crazy Horse
12 Avenue George V, 75008, tel: 01 47 23 32 32, fax: 01 47 23 48 26. Holds two or three shows every night.

Au Folies-Bergère
32 Rue Richer, 75009, tel: 01 44 79 98 98, fax: 01 47 70 98 28. Tourist prices, and you can hardly get near for the tour buses. Dine at 7pm, show at 9.30pm. Closed Monday.

Au Lapin Agile
22 Rue des Saules, 75018, tel: 01 46 06 85 87, fax: 01 42 54 63 04. Métro Lamarck-Caulaincourt. Old-fashioned mayhem in Picasso's old haunt. Get there early for a seat. You'll need to understand French.

Le Lido
116 Avenue des Champs-Elysées, 75008, tel: 01 40 76 56 10, fax: 01 45 61 19 41. Three shows daily. The slickest of Parisian cabarets.

Moulin Rouge
82 Boulevard de Clichy, 75011, tel: 01 46 06 00 19, fax: 01 42 23 02 00. Three shows a night. Tourist prices and surrounded by tour buses.

Paradis Latin
28 Rue Cardinal-Lemoine, 75005, tel: 01 43 25 28 28, fax: 01 43 29 63 63. Two shows a night Monday and Wednesday to Sunday.

Nightclubs and Discos

L'Elysée Montmartre
72 Boulevard Rochechouart, 75018, tel: 01 44 92 45 42. Fun for all ages, with theme evenings from rock 'n' roll to salsa (check listings magazines to find out what's coming). Open most Saturdays 11pm–5am.

Folies Pigalle
11 Place Pigalle, 75018, tel: 01 48 78 25 56. Very popular disco in an area that never sleeps. Open Thursday to Saturday 11pm–7am, Sunday 3–8pm.

La Java
105 Rue du Faubourg-du-Temple, 750011, tel: 01 42 02 20 52. Latin American music in a Belleville dance hall. Open Tuesday (salsa night) and Thursday to Saturday (Cuban band, then DJ).

La Locomotive
90 Boulevard de Clichy, 75009, tel: 01 53 41 88 88. Rough, ready, mainstream, enormous.

Le Balajo
9 Rue de Lappe, 75011, tel: 47 00 07 87. Popular venue attracting chic crowd to its hot Latin and rock-and-roll music. Open Monday and Thursday to Saturday 11pm–5am.

Le Moloko
26 Rue Fontaine, 75009, tel: 48 74 50 26. Chic, sharp and bedraggled – they're all here for cocktails, wine, or a boogie.

Les Bains
7 Rue du Bourg-l'Abbé, tel: 01 48 87 01 80. Ex-Turkish baths frequented by the smart set, there more for rubber necking than dancing. Open daily 11.30pm–6.30am.

Club Prices

Entrance to a club usually includes one drink, but take plenty of cash with you as food and drink are expensive. Most clubs accept credit cards for drinks only, not entry, and close in August.

Régine's
49–51 Rue de Ponthieu, 75007, tel: 01 43 59 21 13. The most famous Paris club, frequented by the rich and famous, and hard to get into unless you are a member. Open 11.30pm–dawn. There is a restaurant.

Sherezade
3 Rue de Liège, 75009, tel: 01 40 16 17 18. Spectacular Middle-Eastern decor with good dance music. Open Tuesday to Thursday 11pm–5am, Friday midnight–5am, and Saturday

Jazz Clubs

Caveau de la Huchette
5 Rue de la Huchette, 75006, tel: 01 43 26 65 05. Young clientele for jazz in a cellar. Open Monday to Friday from 9.30pm to 2.30am, and weekends 9.30pm–4am.

La Chapelle des Lombards
19 Rue de Lappe, 75011, tel: 01 43 57 24 24. 'Tropical' music in a popular club. Open Thursday 8pm–dawn, Friday and Saturday 10.30pm–dawn.

La Cigale
120 Boulevard de Rochechouart, 75018, tel: 01 42 23 15 15, fax: 01 42 23 67 04. Popular club. Telephone beforehand for details of concerts.

Le Montana
28 Rue St-Benoît, 75006, tel: 01 44 39 71 00. Different sets every night.

New Morning
7–9 Rue des Petites-Ecuries, 75010, tel: 01 45 23 51 41. For aficionados. Concerts start at 9.30pm.

Le Sunset
60 Rue des Lombards, 75001, tel: 01 40 26 46 60. Restaurant on the ground floor, jazz in the basement at 10.30pm. Closed on Sunday.

Shopping

Opening Hours

Food shops, especially bakers, tend to open early. Boutiques and department stores open about 9am, but sometimes not until 10am. Traditionally, most shops close noon–2.30pm or 3pm, but in Paris, main shops usually remain open until 7pm.

In the suburbs, hypermarkets usually stay open until 8–9pm. Most shops are closed on Monday morning, some all day Monday. If you want to buy a picnic lunch, get everything you need before midday.

To complain about a purchase, return it to the shop as soon as possible. In a serious dispute, contact the local Direction Départementale de la Concurrence et de la Consommation et de la Répression des Fraudes (see telephone directory for number).

Department Stores

Au Bon Marché
38 Rue de Sevres, 75007, tel: 01 44 39 80 00. The first department store in Paris. The Grande Epicurie sells every delicacy under the sun.

Printemps
64 Boulevard Haussmann, 75009, tel: 01 42 82 50 00. Good selection of new designers' collections, plus large china, kitchen and stationery departments.

BHV (Bazar de l'Hôtel de Ville)
52–64 Rue de Rivoli, 75004, tel: 01 42 74 90 00. All you ever wanted for DIY to your bathroom.

Bon Marché Rive Gauche
22 Rue de Sevres, 75007, tel: 01 44 39 80 00.

Galeries Lafayette
40 Boulevard Haussmann, 75009, tel: 01 42 82 34 56. An entire floor devoted to lingerie and the largest perfume department in the world are just some of the delights of this massive department store.

La Samaritaine
19 Rue de la Monnaie, 75001, tel: 01 40 41 20 20. An Art Nouveau building with fantastic views over the Seine from the rooftop bistro.

Clothes

Paris is the designer city of the world. Alongside France's chains such as Naf Naf and Kookaï, all the top name couturiers have boutiques. As Calvin Klein said when he opened his Avenue Montaigne store, "It's the most important city in Europe to show the world what you do." The top couture houses are in the Avenue Montaigne area and around Faubourg St-Honoré, with more individual boutiques clustering around the Marais and St-Germain-des-Près.

Agnès B
2–19 Rue du Jour, 75001, tel: 01 45 08 56 56 (women's clothes), tel: 01 42 33 04 13 (men's). The quintessential French designer.

Azzedine Alaïa
Silhouette-hugging dresses from 4,000F at 7 Rue de Moussy, 75004, tel: 01 42 72 19 19. Or last season's designs at a fraction of the price at 18 Rue de la Verrerie, tel: 01 42 72 19 19.

Calvin Klein
45 Avenue Montaigne, 75008, tel: 01 47 23 62 22.

Christian Lacroix
2–4 Place Saint-Sulpice, 75006, tel: 01 46 33 48 95; 73 Faubourg St-Honoré 75008

Comme des Garçons
40 Rue Etienne Marcel, tel: 01 42 33 05 21 (women) 42 Rue Etienne Marcel, tel: 01 42 36 91 54 (men).

Jil Sander
52 Avenue Montaigne, 75008, tel: 01 44 95 06 70. Trend-setting German fashion.

Kenzo
3 Place des Victoires, 75001, tel: 01 40 39 72 03. Flamboyant colours from the popular Japanese designer.

Kookaï
2 Rue Gustave-Courbet, 75016, tel: 01 47 55 18 00. Inexpensive fashion for the young. Other branches are at: Forum des Halles, Place St-Eustache, 75001, and 155 Rue de Rennes, 75006.

La Boutique de Floriane
17 Rue Tronchet, 75008, tel: 01 42 65 25 95. Top-quality children's clothes – plus Barbar.

Export Procedures

Most prices include TVA (a valued added tax). The base rate is currently 18.6 percent but can be as high as 33 percent on luxury items.

Foreign visitors can claim back TVA, and this is worth doing if you spend more than FF4,200 (FF2,000 for non-EU residents) in one place. Ask the store for a *bordereau* (export sales invoice). This must be completed and presented with the goods to customs officers on leaving France. Pack items separately for ease of access. The form is mailed back to the retailer, which refunds the TVA in a month or two. Certain goods (such as antiques) may need special clearance.

Sales

Traditionally the sales *(soldes)* have been held in July and just after Christmas but, with France struggling through a recession, many shops are offering mid-season reductions, so you may pick up bargains all year round.

L'Habilleur
44 Rue de Poitou, 75003, tel: 01 48 87 77 12. End-of-line and ex-catwalk clothes from some of the top designers.

Loft Design By
12 Rue du Faubourg St-Honoré, tel: 01 42 65 59 65. Gap French-style.

Patrick Cox
62 Rue Tiquetonne, 75002, tel: 01 40 26 65 55. The shoes to be seen in from British designer Patrick Cox.

Plein Sud
21 Rue de Sévigne, 75004, tel: 01 42 72 10 60.

Prada
10 Avenue Montaigne, 75008, tel: 01 53 23 99 40.

Sonia Rykiel
175 Boulevard Saint-Germain, 75006, tel: 01 49 54 60 60. Menswear is across the road. Also at 70 Rue du Faubourg St-Honoré.

Studio Lolita
2 bis Rue des Rosiers, 75004, tel: 01 48 87 09 67. Half-price items from Lolita Lempicka's previous seasons' collections.

Thierry Mügler
45 Rue du Bac, 75007, tel: 01 45 44 44 44.

Gifts

Androuet
6 Rue Arsène Houssaye, 75008, tel: 01 42 89 95 00. Excellent bakery with another branch at 83 Rue St-Dominique, 75007, tel: 01 42 89 95 00.

Bains Plus
51 Rue des Francs-Bourgeois, 75004, tel: 01 48 87 83 07.

Everything you could possibly imagine for the bathroom.

Beauvais
14 Rue du Bac, 75007, tel: 01 42 61 27 61. Designer stationery.

Caviar Kaspar
17 Place de la Madeleine, 75008, tel: 01 42 65 33 52. Delicacies including caviar, truffles, foie gras and salmon.

Conceptua
9 Rue de la Roquette, 75011, tel: 01 43 38 68 87. Candlesticks, vases, glassware and gifts.

The Conran Shop
117 Rue du Bac, 75007, tel: 01 42 84 10 01. Sir Terence Conran's emporium in a former Bon Marché warehouse designed by the architect Eiffel. All manner of designer gifts.

Debauve et Gallais
30 Rue des Saints-Pères, 75007, tel: 01 45 48 54 67. Chocolates.

Fromagerie Barthélémy
51 Rue de Grenelle, 75007, tel: 01 42 22 82 24. Cheeses.

Fauchon
26–8 Place de la Madeleine, 75008, tel: 01 47 42 60 11. Enormous luxury foodstore famous for its gourmets buffets,

English Shops

● **Virgin Megastore**
52 Avenue des Champs-Elysées, 75008, tel: 01 49 53 50 00.
● **Village Voice**
6 Rue Princesse, 75006, tel: 01 46 33 36 47. English books and films.
● **W.H. Smith**
248 Rue de Rivoli, tel: 01 44 77 88 99. Superior version of the British chain.
● **Marks & Spencer**
Branches are dotted round the city. The main two are at 88 Rue de Rivoli, 75004, tel: 01 44 61 08 00, and 37 Boulevard Haussmann, 75009, tel: 01 47 42 42 91.

excellent in-house brasserie and Italian trattoria.

Guerlain
68 Avenue des Champs-Elysées, 75008, tel: 01 45 62 52 57. The French perfumer.

Il Etait une Fois
1 Rue Cassette, 75006, tel: 01 45 48 21 10. Children's toys.

La Maison du Chocolat
52 Rue François 1er, 75008, tel: 01 47 23 38 25. Chocolate emporium.

La Maison Ivre
38 Rue Jacob, 75006, tel: 01 42 60 01 85. Pottery, table linen and many other gifts.

Pétrossian
18 Boulevard La Tour-Maubourg, 75007, tel: 01 44 11 32 22. Cheeses.

Markets

Ile de la Cité
Place Louis-Lépine, 75004. Flowers. Open daily 8am–7pm. Birds. Open Sun 9am–7pm.

Place de la Madeleine
Coté est de l'Eglise, 75008. Flowers. Open daily except Mon 8am–7.30pm.

Quai de la Mégisserie
75001. Birds, dogs, cats and fish. Open daily 10am–7pm.

Marché d'Aligre
Rue and Place d'Aligre. General. Open daily, mornings only.

Les Puces de St-Ouen
Between the Portes de St-Ouen and de Clignancourt, 75018. Flea market. Open Sat–Mon, 7.30am–7pm.

Les Puces de Vanves
Porte de Vanves–Porte Didot, Avenue Georges Lafenestre, Rue Marc Sangnier, 75014. Flea market. Open Sat–Sun, 7am–7.30pm.

Rue Mouffetard
75005. Produce. Open Tues, Thurs, Sat. 9am–1pm, 4–7pm.

Rue de Buci & Rue de Seine
75006. Off Boulevard St-Germain. Produce. Open Tues–Sun, 8am–1pm.

Sport

Participant

Parisians expend a lot of energy on lively exchanges of views, often from behind the wheel of a car or the butt of a cigarette. Nevertheless, Paris caters reasonably well for the sports enthusiast. You can find information on sporting events in *Le Figaro* each Wednesday or by phoning Allo-Sports, tel: 01 42 76 54 54. The latter can give you information about sporting facilities in Paris.

FITNESS CENTRES
Club Quartier Latin
19 Rue Pontoise, 75005, tel: 01 43 54 82 45. Health club with squash courts and pool.
Gymnase Club
17 Rue du Débarcadère, 75008, tel: 01 45 74 14 04. One of a chain of health clubs that offer step classes, weights, sauna and pool.

HORSE RIDING
Poney-Club de la Carthoucherie
Bois de Vincennes, tel: 01 43 74 61 25.
Societé d'Equitation de Paris
Rue de la Maette, Bois de Boulogne, 75116, tel: 01 45 01 20 06.
Ligue de Paris de la Féderation Equestre
69 Rue Langier, 75017, tel: 01 42 12 03 43.

SWIMMING
Piscine des Halles
Centre Suzanne-Berlioux, 10 Place de la Rotonde, 75001, tel: 01 42 36 98 44. Part of the

Forum des Halles. Has a 50-metre (55-yd) pool.
Piscine Georges Vallery
148 Avenue Gambetta, 75020, tel: 01 40 31 15 20. Built for the 1924 Olympic Games.
Aquaboulevard
4–6 Rue Louis Armand, 75015, tel: 01 53 78 10 27.

TENNIS
Centre du Tennis du Jardin du Luxembourg
tel: 01 43 25 79 18.
Centre Sportif d'Orléans
7–15 Avenue Paul Appell, 75014, tel: 45 40 55 88.
Courcelles
149 bis Rue Blomet, 75015, tel: 01 45 30 07 00.

Spectator

The huge Bercy sports stadium, built in 1984, offers a vast range of events including football, ice sports, motor sports and horse riding: Palais Omnisports de Bercy, 8 Boulevard de Bercy, 75012, tel: 01 44 68 44 68, fax: 01 40 02 61 15.

Major sporting events include the the Marathon in April, the French Tennis Open in June and the Paris Triathlon in September. For racing buffs, the Grand Prix de l'Arc de Triomphe takes place at Hippodrome de Longchamp in October.

Schools & Courses

Paris hosts many schools, ranging from language (*see also page 262*) and cookery to the famous Grandes Ecoles created by Napoleon with the sole purpose of training high-level technical specialists for the top posts in state adminis-tration. Today the Grandes Ecoles take in around 100,000 students.

Information sheets on education in France can be bought for a nominal sum from Le Centre d'Information et de Documentation Jeunesse (CIDJ),

101 Quai Branly, 75740 Paris Cedex 15, tel: 01 44 49 12 00.

Language and cookery
These schools will send you information and may help you with travel and accommodation:
Alliance Française
101 Boulevard Raspail, 75006, tel: 01 45 44 38 28.
Le Cordon Bleu
8 Rue Léon Delhomme, 75015, tel: 01 48 56 06 06, fax: 01 48 56 03 96. Courses are taught in French, English and Japanese.
Cours de Civilisation Française à la Sorbonne
47 Rue des Ecoles, 75005, tel: 01 40 46 22 11. Run at several levels throughout the year.
Ecole de Langue Française pour Etrangers (ELFE)
8 Villa Ballu, 75009, tel: 01 48 78 73 00. All levels in classes of four to six students.
Eurocentre
13 Passage Dauphine, 75006, tel: 01 40 46 72 00. Language and civilisation courses held at Paris, Amboise and La Rochelle.
France Langues
2 Rue de Sfax, 75116, tel: 01 45 00 40 15.

Language and civilisation
For courses in French or English:
Institut Parisien de Langue et de Civilisation Française
87 Boulevard de Grenelle, 75015, tel: 01 40 56 09 53, fax: 01 43 06 46 30.
Lenôtre
40 Rue Pierre Curie, BP 6, 78373 Plaisir Cedex, tel: 30 81 46 46, fax: 01 30 55 96 14.
Ritz Escoffier
15 Place Vendôme, 75001, tel: 01 43 16 31 43, fax: 01 43 16 31 50.
Union Nationale des Organisations de Séjours Linguistiques (UNOSEL)
19 Rue des Mathurins, 75009, tel: 01 49 24 03 61, fax: 01 42 65 39 38. Organises language-learning stays in regions of France. Tel: 01 42 46 00 66.

Language

French is the native language of more than 90 million people and the acquired language of 180 million. It is a Romance language descended from the Vulgar Latin spoken by the Roman conquerors of Gaul. It still carries the reputation of being the most cultured language in the world and, for what it's worth, the most beautiful. People often tell stories about the impatience of the French towards foreigners not blessed with fluency in their language. In general, however, if you attempt to communicate with them in French, they will be helpful.

Since much of the English vocabulary is related to French, thanks to the Norman Conquest of 1066, travellers will often recognise many helpful cognates: words such as *hôtel, café* and *bagages* hardly need to be translated.

You should be aware, however, of some misleading "false friends" (see panel on page 285).

The Alphabet

Learning the pronunciation of the French alphabet is a good idea. In particular, learn how to spell out your name.
a=ah, **b**=bay, **c**=say, **d**=day
e=er, **f**=ef, **g**=zhay, **h**=ash.
i=ee, **j**=zhee, **k**=ka, **l**=el,
m=em, **n** =en, **o**=oh, **p**=pay,
q=kew, **r**=ehr, **s**=ess, **t**=tay,
u=ew, **v**=vay, **w**=dooblah vay,
x-=eex, **y** ee grek, **z**=zed

Basic Rules

Even if you speak no French at all, it is worth trying to master a few simple phrases. The fact that you have made an effort is likely to get you a better response. More and more French people like practising their English on visitors, especially waiters in the cafés and restaurants and the younger generation. Pronunciation is the key; they really will not understand if you get it very wrong. Remember to **emphasise each syllable**, but not to pronounce the last consonant of a word as a rule (this includes the plural "s") and always to drop your "h"s. Whether to use "**vous**" or "**tu**" is a vexed question; increasingly the familiar form of "tu" is used by many people. However it is better to be too formal, and use "vous" if in doubt. It is very important to be polite; always address people as **Madame** or **Monsieur**, and address them by their surnames until you are confident first names are acceptable. When entering a shop always say, "Bonjour Monsieur/ Madame," and "Merci, au revoir," when leaving.

Words & Phrases

How much is it? *C'est combien?*
What is your name? *Comment vous appelez-vous?*
My name is… *Je m'appelle…*
Do you speak English? *Parlez-vous anglais?*
I am English/American *Je suis anglais/américain*
I don't understand *Je ne comprends pas*
Please speak more slowly? *Parlez plus lentement, s'il vous plaît?*
Can you help me? *Pouvez-vous m'aider?*
I'm looking for… *Je cherche*
Where is…? *Où est…?*
I'm sorry *Excusez-moi/Pardon*
I don't know *Je ne sais pas*
No problem *Pas de problème*
Have a good day! *Bonne journée!*
That's it *C'est ça*
Here it is *Voici*
There it is *Voilà*
Let's go *On y va. Allons-y*
See you tomorrow *A demain*
See you soon *A bientôt*
Show me the word in the book *Montrez-moi le mot dans le livre*
At what time? *A quelle heure?*
When? *Quand?*
What time is it? *Quelle heure est-il?*
● *Note. The French generally use the 24-hour clock.*

yes	*oui*
no	*non*
please	*s'il vous plaît*
thank you	*merci*
(very much)	*(beaucoup)*
you're welcome	*de rien*
excuse me	*excusez-moi*
hello	*bonjour*
OK	*d'accord*
goodbye	*au revoir*
good evening	*bonsoir*
here	*ici*
there	*là*
today	*aujourd'hui*
yesterday	*hier*
tomorrow	*demain*
now	*maintenant*
later	*plus tard*
right away	*tout de suite*
this morning	*ce matin*
this afternoon	*cet après-midi*
this evening	*ce soir*

On Arrival

I want to get off at…*Je voudrais descendre à…*
Is there a bus to the Louvre? *Est-ce qui'il ya un bus pour le Louvre?*
What street is this? *A quelle rue sommes-nous?*
Which line do I take for…? *Quelle ligne dois-je prendre pour…?*
How far is…*? A quelle distance se trouve…?*
Validate your ticket *Compostez votre billet*

Emergencies

Help! *Au secours!* **Stop!** *Arrêtez!*
Call a doctor *Appelez un médecin*
Call an ambulance *Appelez une ambulance*
Call the police *Appelez la police*
Call the fire brigade *Appelez les pompiers*
Where is the nearest telephone? *Où est le téléphone le plus proche?*
Where is the nearest hospital? *Où est l'hôpital le plus proche?*
I am sick *Je suis malade*
I have lost my passport/purse *J'ai perdu mon passeport/porte-monnaie*

airport	*l'aéroport*
train station	*la gare*
bus station	*la gare routière*
Métro stop	*la station de Métro*
bus	*l'autobus, le car*
bus stop	*l'arrêt*
platform	*le quai*
ticket	*le billet*
return ticket	*aller-retour*
hitchhiking	*l'autostop*
toilets	*les toilettes*

This is the hotel address *C'est l'adresse de l'hôtel*
I'd like a (single/double) room... *Je voudrais une chambre (pour une/deux personnes)* ...
...with shower *avec douche*
...with bath *avec salle de bain*
...with a view *avec vue*
Does that include breakfast? *Le prix comprend-il le petit déjeuner?*
May I see the room? *Je peux voir la chambre?*

washbasin	*le lavabo*
bed	*le lit*
key	*cléf*
elevator	*l'ascenseur*
air condition	*climatisé*

On the Telephone

How do I make an outside call? *Comment est-ce que je peux téléphoner à l'exterieur?*
I want to make an international (local) call *Je voudrais une communication pour l'étranger (une communication locale)*
What is the dialling code? *Quel est l'indicatif?*
I'd like an alarm call for 8 tomorrow morning. *Je voudrais être réveillé à huit heures demain martin*
Who's calling? *C'est qui à l'appareil?*
Hold on, please *Ne quittez pas s'il vous plaît*
The line is busy *La ligne est occupée*
I must have dialled the wrong number *J'ai dû faire un faux numéro*

On the Road

Where is the spare wheel? *Où est la roue de secours?*
Where is the nearest garage? *Où est le garage le plus proche?*
Our car has broken down *Notre voiture est en panne*
I want to have my car repaired *Je veux faire réparer ma voiture*
It's not your right of way *Vous n'avez pas la priorité*
I think I must have put diesel in the car by mistake *Je crois que j'ai mis le gazole dans la voiture par erreur*

the road to...	*la route pour...*
left	*gauche*
right	*droite*
straight on	*tout droit*
far	*loin*
near	*près d'ici*
opposite	*en face*
beside	*à côté de*
car park	*parking*
over there	*là-bas*
at the end	*au bout*
on foot	*à pied*

by car	*en voiture*
town map	*le plan*
road map	*la carte*
street	*la rue*
square	*la place*
give way	*céder le passage*
dead end	*impasse*
no parking	*stationnement interdit*
motorway	*l'autoroute*
toll	*le péage*
speed limit	*la limitation de vitesse*
petrol	*l'essence*
unleaded	*sans plomb*
diesel	*le gazole*
water/oil	*l'eau/l'huile*
puncture	*un pneu de crevé*
bulb	*l'ampoule*
wipers	*les essuies-glace*

Shopping

Where is the nearest bank (post office)? *Où est la banque Poste/PTT la plus proche?*
I'd like to buy *Je voudrais acheter*
How much is it? *C'est combien?*
Do you take credit cards? *Est-ce que vous acceptez les cartes de crédit?*
I'm just looking *Je regarde seulement*
Have you got? *Avez-vous...?*
I'll take it *Je le prends*
I'll take this one/that one *Je prends celui-ci/celui-là*
What size is it? *C'est de quelle taille?*
Anything else? *Avec ça?*

size (clothes)	*la taille*
size (shoes)	*la pointure*
cheap	*bon marché*
expensive	*cher*
enough	*assez*
too much	*trop*
a piece	*un morceau de*
each	*la piece (eg ananas, 15F la pièce)*
bill	*la note*
chemist	*la pharmacie*
bakery	*la boulangerie*
bookshop	*la librairie*
library	*la bibliothèque*
department store	*le grand magasin*

Market Shopping

In a market all goods have to be marked with the price by law. This will be written: 12F50 (centimes). Prices are usually by the kilo or by the *pièce*, that is, each item priced individually. Usually the stall holder (*marchand*) will select the goods for you. Sometimes there is a serve yourself system – observe everyone else! If you are choosing cheese, for example, you may be offered a taste to try first; *un goûter*.

tasting	*la dégustation*
organic	*la biologique*
flavour	*le parfum*
basket	*le panier*
bag	*le sac*

delicatessen	*la charcuterie/ le traiteur*
fishmonger's	*la poissonerie*
grocery	*l'alimentation/ l'épicerie*
tobacconist	*tabac (also sells stamps and newspapers)*
markets	*le marché*
supermarket	*le supermarché*
junk shop	*la brocante*

Sightseeing

town	*la ville*
old town	*la vieille ville*
abbey	*l'abbaye*
cathedral	*la cathédrale*
church	*l'église*
keep	*le donjon*
mansion	*l'hôtel*
hospital	*l'hôpital*
town hall	*l'hôtel de ville/ la mairie*
nave	*la nef*
stained glass	*le vitrail*
staircase	*l'escalier*
tower	*la tour (La Tour Eiffel)*
walk	*le tour*
country house/	
castle	*le château*
Gothic	*gothique*
Roman	*romain*

Romanesque	*roman*
museum	*la musée*
art gallery	*la galerie*
exhibition	*l'exposition*
tourist information office	*l'office du tourisme/ le syndicat d'initiative*
free	*gratuit*
open	*ouvert*
closed	*fermé*
every day	*tous les jours*
all year	*toute l'année*
all day	*toute la journée*
swimming pool	*la piscine*
to book	*réserver*

Dining Out

Table d'hôte (the "host's table") is one set menu served at a set price. **Prix fixe** is a fixed price menu. **A la carte** means dishes from the menu are charged separately.

breakfast	*le petit déjeuner*
lunch	*le déjeuner*
dinner	*le dîner*
meal	*le repas*
first course	*l'entrée/les hors d'oeuvre*
main course	*le plat principal*
made to order	*sur commande*
drink included	*boisson compris*
wine list	*la carte des vins*
the bill	*l'addition*
fork	*la forchette*
knife	*le couteau*
spoon	*la cuillère*
plate	*l'assiette*
glass	*le verre*
napkin	*la serviette*
ashtray	*le cendrier*

BREAKFAST AND SNACKS

baguette	long thin loaf
pain	bread
petits pains	rolls
beurre	butter
poivre	pepper
sel	salt
sucre	sugar
confiture	jam
miel	honey
oeufs	eggs
...à la coque	boiled eggs

...au bacon	bacon and eggs
...au jambon	ham and eggs
...sur le plat	fried eggs
...brouillés	scrambled eggs
tartine	bread with butter
yaourt	yoghurt
crêpe	pancake
croque-monsieur	ham and cheese toasted sandwich
croque-madame	...with a fried egg on top
galette	type of pancake
pan bagna	bread roll stuffed with salad Niçoise
quiche	tart of eggs and cream with various fillings
quiche lorraine	quiche with bacon

FIRST COURSE

An *amuse-bouche*, *amuse-gueule* or appetizer is something to "amuse the mouth", served before the first course

anchoiade	sauce of olive oil, anchovies and garlic, served with raw vegetables
assiette anglaise	cold meats
potage	soup
rillettes	rich fatty paste of shredded duck rabbit or pork
tapenade	spread of olives and anchovies
pissaladière	Provençal pizza with onions, olives and anchovies

Where to Eat

For the best places to dine out in Paris, see pages 271–74

MAIN COURSES

La Viande	**Meat**
bleu	rare
à point	medium
bien cuit	well done
grillé	grilled
agneau	lamb
andouille/ andouillette	tripe sausage

Non, Non, Garçon

Garçon is the word for waiter but is never used directly; say *Monsieur* or *Madame* to attract their attention.

bifteck	steak
boudin	sausage
boudin noir	black pudding
boudin blanc	white pudding (chicken or veal)
blanquette	stew of veal, lamb or chicken with creamy egg sauce
boeuf à la mode	beef in red wine with carrots, onions, mushroom and onions
á la bordelaise	beef with red wine and shallots
à la Bourguignonne	cooked in red wine, onions and mushrooms
brochette	kebab
caille	quail
canard	duck
carbonnade	casserole of beef, beer and onions
carré d'agneau	rack of lamb
cassoulet	stew of beans, sausages, pork and duck, from southwest France
cervelle	brains (food)
chateaubriand	thick steak
choucroute	Alsace dish of sauerkraut, bacon and sausages
confit	duck or goose preserved in its own fat
contre-filet	cut of sirloin steak
coq au vin	chicken in red wine
côte d'agneau	lamb chop
daube	beef stew with red wine, onions and tomatoes
dinde	turkey

entrecôte	beef rib steak
escargot	snail
faisan	pheasant
farci	stuffed
faux-filet	sirloin
feuilleté	puff pastry
foie	liver
foie de veau	calf's liver
foie gras	goose or duck liver pâté
gardiane	rich beef stew with olives and garlic, from the Camargue
cuisses de grenouille	frog's legs
grillade	grilled meat
hachis	minced meat
jambon	ham
langue	tongue
lapin	rabbit
lardon	small pieces of bacon, often added to salads
magret de canard	breast of duck
médaillon	round piece of meat
moelle	beef bone marrow
mouton navarin	stew of lamb with onions, carrots and turnips
oie	goose
perdrix	partridge
petit-gris	small snail
pieds de cochon	pig's trotters
pintade	guinea fowl
Pipérade	Basque dish of eggs, ham, peppers, onion
porc	pork
pot-au-feu	casserole of beef

	and vegetables
poulet	chicken
poussin	young chicken
rognons	kidneys
rôti	roast
sanglier	wild boar
saucisse	fresh sausage
saucisson	salami
veau	veal

Standard Fare

AOC, *Appellation d'Origine Contrôlée,* is a legal regulation for cheeses and poultry as well as wines, and it ensures the products conform to a particular standard

Poissons	**Fish**
Amoricaine	made with white wine, tomatoes, butter and cognac
anchois	anchovies
anguille	eel
bar (or *loup*)	sea bass
barbue	brill
belon	Brittany oyster
bigorneau	sea snail
Bercy	sauce of fish stock, butter, white wine and shallots
bouillabaisse	fish soup, served with grated cheese, garlic croutons and *rouille*, a spicy sauce
brandade	salt cod purée
cabillaud	cod
calmars	squid
colin	hake

Table Talk

I am a vegetarian *Je suis végétarien*
I am on a diet *Je suis au régime*
What do you recommend? *Que'est-ce que vous recommandez?*
Do you have local specialities? *Avez-vous des spécialités locales?*
I'd like to order *Je voudrais commander*
That is not what I ordered *Ce n'est pas ce que j'ai commandé*
Is service included? *Est-ce que le service est compris?*
May I have more wine? *Encore du vin, s'il vous plaît?*
Enjoy your meal *Bon appétit!*

False Friends

False friends are words that look like English words but mean something different.

le car coach car, also railway carriage
le conducteur bus driver
la monnaie change
l'argent money/silver
ça marche can sometimes mean walk, but is usually used to mean working (the TV, the car etc.) or going well
actuel "present time" (la situation actuelle the present situation)
rester to stay
location hiring/renting
personne person or nobody in different contexts.
le médecin doctor

coquillage	shellfish
coquilles Saint-Jacques	scallops
crevette	shrimp
daurade	sea bream
flétan	halibut
fruits de mer	seafood
hareng	herring
homard	lobster
huître	oyster
langoustine	large prawn
limande	lemon sole
lotte	monkfish
morue	salt cod
moule	mussel
moules marinières	mussels in white wine and onions
oursin	sea urchin
raie	skate
saumon	salmon
thon	tuna
truite	trout

Legumes	Vegetables
ail	garlic
artichaut	artichoke
asperge	asparagus
aubergine	eggplant
avocat	avocado
bolets	boletus mushrooms

céleri rémoulade	grated celery with mayonnaise
champignon	mushroom
cèpes	boletus mushroom
chanterelle	wild mushroom
cornichon	gherkin
courgette	zucchini
chips	potato crisps
chou	cabbage
chou-fleur	cauliflower
concombre	cucumber
cru	raw
crudités	raw vegetables
épinard	spinach
frites	chips, French fries
gratin dauphinois	sliced potatoes baked with cream
haricot	dried bean
haricots verts	green beans
lentilles	lentils
maïs	corn
mange-tout	snow pea
mesclun	mixed leaf salad
navet	turnip
noix	nut, walnut
noisette	hazelnut
oignon	onion
panais	parsnip
persil	parsley
pignon	pine nut
poireau	leek
pois	pea
poivron	bell pepper
pomme de terre	potato
pommes frites	chips, French fries
primeurs	early fruit and vegetables
radis	radis
roquette	arugula, rocket
ratatouille	Provençal vegetable stew of aubergines, courgettes, tomatoes, peppers and olive oil
riz	rice
salade Niçoise	egg, tuna, olives, onions and tomato salad
salade verte	green salad
truffe	truffle

Fruit	Fruit
ananas	pineapple
cavaillon	fragrant sweet melon from Cavaillon in Provence
cerise	cherry
citron	lemon
citron vert	lime
figue	fig
fraise	strawberry
framboise	raspberry
groseille	redcurrant
mangue	mango
mirabelle	yellow plum
pamplemousse	grapefruit
pêche	peach
poire	pear
pomme	apple
raisin	grape
prune	plum
pruneau	prune
Reine claude	greengage

Sauces	Sauces
aioli	garlic mayonnaise
bearnaise	sauce of egg, butter, wine and herbs
forestière	with mushrooms and bacon
hollandaise	egg, butter and lemon sauce
lyonnaise	with onions
meunière	fried fish with butter, lemon and parsley sauce
meurette	red wine sauce

Slang

metro, boulot, dodo nine-to-five syndrome
McDo McDonald's
branché trendy (literally "connected")
C'est du cinéma It's very unlikely.
une copine/ un copain friend/chum
un ami friend but **mon ami**, boyfriend; also **mon copain**.
un truc thing, "whatsit"
pas mal, not bad, good-looking
fantastic! fantastic! terrible!

Numbers

0 *zéro*	11 *onze*	30 *trente*	1000 *mille*
1 *un, une*	12 *douze*	40 *quarante*	1,000,000
2 *deux*	13 *treize*	50 *cinquante*	*un million*
3 *trois*	14 *quatorze*	60 *soixante*	
4 *quatre*	15 *quinze*	70 *soixante-*	● The number
5 *cinq*	16 *seize*	*dix*	1 is often
6 *six*	17 *dix-sept*	80 *quatre-*	written like an
7 *sept*	18 *dix-huit*	*vingt*	upside down
8 *huit*	19 *dix-neuf*	90 *quatre-*	V, and the
9 *neuf*	20 *vingt*	*vingt-dix*	number 7 is
10 *dix*	21 *vingt-et-un*	100 *cent*	crossed.

Mornay	sauce of cream, egg and cheese
Parmentier	served with potatoes
paysan	rustic style, ingredients depend on the region
pistou	Provençal sauce of basil, garlic and olive oil; vegetable soup with the sauce.
provençale	sauce of tomatoes, garlic and olive oil.
papillotte	cooked in paper
Pudding	**Dessert**
Belle Hélène	fruit with ice cream and chocolate sauce
clafoutis	baked pudding of batter and cherries
coulis	purée of fruit or vegetables
gâteau	cake
Ile flottante	whisked eggs whites in custard sauce
crème anglaise	custard
pêche melba	peaches with ice cream and raspberry sauce
tarte tatin	upside down tart of caramelised apples
crème caramel	caramelised egg custard
crème Chantilly	whipped cream
fromage	cheese
chèvre	goat's cheese

In the Café

If you sit at the bar (*le zinc*), drinks will be cheaper than at a table. Settle the bill when you leave; the waiter may leave a slip of paper on the table to keep track of the bill. The French enjoy bittersweet aperitifs, often diluted with ice and fizzy water.

drinks	*les boissons*
coffee	*café*
...with milk or cream	
	au lait or crème
...decaffeinated	*déca/décaféiné*
...black espresso	*express/noir*
...American filtered coffee	*filtre*
tea	*thé*
...herb infusion	*tisane*
...camomile	*verveine*
hot chocolate	*chocolat chaud*
milk	*lait*
mineral water	*eau minérale*
fizzy	*gazeux*
non-fizzy	*non-gazeux*
fizzy lemonade	*limonade*
fresh lemon juice served with	
sugar	*citron pressé*
fresh squeezed orange juice	
	orange pressé
full (eg full cream milk)	*entier*
fresh or cold	*frais, fraîche*
beer	*bière*
...bottled	*en bouteille*
...on tap	*à la pression*
pre-dinner drink	*apéritif*
white wine with cassis, black-	
currant liqueur	*kir*
***kir* with champagne**	*kir royale*
with ice	*avec des glaçons*
neat	*sec*
red	*rouge*

white	*blanc*
rose	*rosé*
dry	*brut*
sweet	*doux*
sparkling wine	*crémant*
house wine	*vin de maison*
local wine	*vin de pays*
Where is this wine from?	*De quelle région vient ce vin?*
pitcher	*carafe/ pichet*
...of water/wine	*d'eau/ de vin*
half litre	*demi-carafe*
quarter litre	*quart*
mixed	*panaché*
after dinner drink	*digestif*
brandy from Armagnac region of France	*Armagnac*
Normandy apple brandy	*calvados*
cheers!	*santé!*
hangover	*gueule de bois*

Days and Months

Days of the week, seasons and months are not capitalised in French.

● **Days of the week**

Monday *lundi*
Tuesday *mardi*
Wednesday *mercredi*
Thursday *jeudi*
Friday *vendredi*
Saturday *samedi*
Sunday *dimanche*

● **Seasons**

spring *le printemps*
summer *l'été*
autumn *l'automne*
winter *l'hiver*

● **Months**

January *janvier*
February *février*
March *mars*
April *avril*
May *mai*
June *juin*
July *juillet*
August *août*
September *septembre*
October *octobre*
November *novembre*
December *décembre*

● **Saying the date**

20th October 1999, *le vingt octobre, dix-neuf cent quatre-vingt-dix-neuf*

ART & PHOTO CREDITS

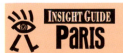

INSIGHT GUIDE
PARIS

Cover photograph
Pictures Colour Library
Maps **Polyglott Kartographie**
Berndtson & Berndtson Publications
Cartographic Editor **Zoë Goodwin**
Production **Mohammed Dar**
Design Consultants
Klaus Geisler, Graham Mitchener
Picture Research **Hilary Genin**

Index

n

The Insight Approach

The book you are holding is part of the world's largest range of guidebooks. Its purpose is to help you have the most valuable travel experience possible, and we try to achieve this by providing not only information about countries, regions and cities but also genuine insight into their history, culture, institutions and people.

Since the first Insight Guide – to Bali – was published in 1970, the series has been dedicated to the proposition that, with insight into a country's people and culture, visitors can both enhance their own experience and be accepted more easily by their hosts. Now, in a world where ethnic hostilities and nationalist conflicts are all too common, such attempts to increase understanding between peoples are more important than ever.

Insight Guides:
Essentials for understanding

Because a nation's past holds the key to its present, each Insight Guide kicks off with lively history chapters. These are followed by magazine-style essays on culture and daily life. This essential background information gives readers the necessary context for using the main Places section, with its comprehensive run-down on things worth seeing and doing.

Finally, a listings section contains all the information you'll need on travel, hotels, restaurants and opening times.

As far as possible, we rely on local writers and specialists to ensure that information is authoritative. The pictures, for which Insight Guides have become so celebrated, are just as important. Our photojournalistic approach aims not only to illustrate a destination but also to communicate visually and directly to readers life as it is lived by the locals. The series has grown to almost 200 titles.

Compact Guides:
The "great little guides"

As invaluable as such background information is, it isn't always fun to carry an Insight Guide through a crowded souk or up a church tower. Could we, readers asked, distil the key reference material into a slim volume for on-the-spot use?

Our response was to design Compact Guides as an entirely new series, with original text carefully cross-referenced to detailed maps and more than 200 photographs. In essence, they're miniature encyclopedias, concise and comprehensive, displaying reliable and up-to-date information in an accessible way. There are almost 100 titles.

Pocket Guides:
A local host in book form

However wide-ranging the information in a book, human beings still value the personal touch. Our editors are often asked the same questions. Where do *you* go to eat? What do *you* think is the best beach? What would *you* recommend if I have only three days? We invited our local correspondents to act as "substitute hosts" by revealing their preferred walks and trips, listing the restaurants they go to and structuring a visit into a series of timed itineraries.

The result: our Pocket Guides, complete with full-size fold-out maps. These 100-plus titles help readers plan a trip precisely, particularly if their time is short.

Exploring with Insight:
A valuable travel experience

In conjunction with co-publishers all over the world, we print in up to 10 languages, from German to Chinese, from Danish to Russian. But our aim remains simple: to enhance your travel experience by combining our expertise in guidebook publishing with the on-the-spot knowledge of our correspondents.

66 I was first drawn to the Insight Guides by the excellent "Nepal" volume. I can think of no book which so effectively captures the essence of a country. Out of these pages leaped the Nepal I know – the captivating charm of a people and their culture. I've since discovered and enjoyed the entire Insight Guide series. Each volume deals with a country in the same sensitive depth, which is nowhere more evident than in the superb photography. 99

Sir Edmund Hillary

The World of Insight Guides

400 books in three complementary series cover every major destination in every continent.

Insight Guides

Alaska
Alsace
Amazon Wildlife
American Southwest
Amsterdam
Argentina
Atlanta
Athens
Australia
Austria
Bahamas
Bali
Baltic States
Bangkok
Barbados
Barcelona
Bay of Naples
Beijing
Belgium
Belize
Berlin
Bermuda
Boston
Brazil
Brittany
Brussels
Budapest
Buenos Aires
Burgundy
Burma (Myanmar)
Cairo
Calcutta
California
Canada
Caribbean
Catalonia
Channel Islands
Chicago
Chile
China
Cologne
Continental Europe
Corsica
Costa Rica
Crete
Crossing America
Cuba
Cyprus
Czech & Slovak Republics
Delhi, Jaipur, Agra
Denmark
Dresden
Dublin
Düsseldorf
East African Wildlife
East Asia
Eastern Europe
Ecuador
Edinburgh
Egypt
Finland
Florence
Florida
France
Frankfurt
French Riviera
Gambia & Senegal
Germany
Glasgow

Gran Canaria
Great Barrier Reef
Great Britain
Greece
Greek Islands
Hamburg
Hawaii
Hong Kong
Hungary
Iceland
India
India's Western Himalaya
Indian Wildlife
Indonesia
Ireland
Israel
Istanbul
Italy
Jamaica
Japan
Java
Jerusalem
Jordan
Kathmandu
Kenya
Korea
Lisbon
Loire Valley
London
Los Angeles
Madeira
Madrid
Malaysia
Mallorca & Ibiza
Malta
Marine Life in the South
   China Sea
Melbourne
Mexico
Mexico City
Miami
Montreal
Morocco
Moscow
Munich
Namibia
Native America
Nepal
Netherlands
New England
New Orleans
New York City
New York State
New Zealand
Nile
Normandy
Northern California
Northern Spain
Norway
Oxford
Old South
Pacific Northwest
Pakistan
Paris
Peru
Philadelphia
Philippines
Poland
Portugal
Prague

Provence
Puerto Rico
Rajasthan
Rhine
Rio de Janeiro
Rockies
Rome
Russia
St Petersburg
San Francisco
Sardinia
Scotland
Seattle
Sicily
Singapore
South Africa
South America
South Asia
South India
South Tyrol
Southeast Asia
Southeast Asia Wildlife
Southern California
Southern Spain
Spain
Sri Lanka
Sweden
Switzerland
Sydney
Taiwan
Tenerife
Texas
Thailand
Tokyo
Trinidad & Tobago
Tunisia
Turkey
Turkish Coast
Tuscany
Umbria
US National Parks East
US National Parks West
Vancouver
Venezuela
Venice
Vienna
Vietnam
Wales
Washington DC
Waterways of Europe
Wild West
Yemen

Insight Pocket Guides

Aegean Islands★
Algarve★
Alsace
Amsterdam★
Athens★
Atlanta★
Bahamas★
Baja Peninsula★
Bali★
Bali *Bird Walks*
Bangkok★
Barbados★
Barcelona★
Bavaria★
Beijing★
Berlin★

Bermuda★
Bhutan★
Boston★
British Columbia★
Brittany★
Brussels★
Budapest &
   Surroundings★
Canton★
Chiang Mai★
Chicago★
Corsica★
Costa Blanca★
Costa Brava★
Costa del Sol/Marbella★
Costa Rica★
Côte d'Azur★
Crete★
Denmark★
Fiji★
Florence★
Florida★
Florida Keys★
Gran Canaria★
Hawaii★
Hong Kong★
Hungary
Ibiza★
Ireland★
Ireland's Southwest★
Israel★
Istanbul★
Jakarta★
Jamaica★
Kathmandu *Bikes &*
   Hikes★
Kenya
Kuala Lumpur★
Lisbon★
Loire Valley★
London★
Macau★
Madrid★
Malacca
Maldives
Mallorca★
Malta★
Mexico City★
Miami★
Milan★
Montreal★
Morocco★
Moscow
Munich★
Nepal★
New Delhi
New Orleans★
New York City★
New Zealand★
Northern California★
Oslo/Bergen★
Paris★
Penang★
Phuket★
Prague★
Provence★
Puerto Rico★
Quebec★
Rhodes★
Rome★
Sabah★

St Petersburg★
San Francisco★
Sardinia
Scotland★
Seville★
Seychelles★
Sicily★
Sikkim
Singapore★
Southeast England
Southern California★
Southern Spain★
Sri Lanka★
Sydney★
Tenerife★
Thailand★
Tibet★
Toronto★
Tunisia★
Turkish Coast★
Tuscany★
Venice★
Vienna★
Vietnam★
Yogyakarta
Yucatan Peninsula★

★ = Insight Pocket Guides
with Pull out Maps

Insight Compact Guides

Algarve
Amsterdam
Bahamas
Bali
Bangkok
Barbados
Barcelona
Beijing
Belgium
Berlin
Brittany
Brussels
Budapest
Burgundy
Copenhagen
Costa Brava
Costa Rica
Crete
Cyprus
Czech Republic
Denmark
Dominican Republic
Dublin
Egypt
Finland
Florence
Gran Canaria
Greece
Holland
Hong Kong
Ireland
Israel
Italian Lakes
Italian Riviera
Jamaica
Jerusalem
Lisbon
Madeira
Mallorca
Malta

Milan
Moscow
Munich
Normandy
Norway
Paris
Poland
Portugal
Prague
Provence
Rhodes
Rome
Salzburg
St Petersburg
Singapore
Switzerland
Sydney
Tenerife
Thailand
Turkey
Turkish Coast
Tuscany

UK regional titles:
   Bath & Surroundings
   Cambridge & East
   Anglia
   Cornwall
   Cotswolds
   Devon & Exmoor
   Edinburgh
   Lake District
   London
   New Forest
   North York Moors
   Northumbria
   Oxford
   Peak District
   Scotland
   Scottish Highlands
   Shakespeare Country
   Snowdonia
   South Downs
   York
   Yorkshire Dales
USA regional titles:
   Boston
   Cape Cod
   Chicago
   Florida
   Florida Keys
   Hawaii: Maui
   Hawaii: Oahu
   Las Vegas
   Los Angeles
   Martha's Vineyard &
   Nantucket
   New York
   San Francisco
   Washington D.C.
Venice
Vienna
West of Ireland